The
Christian's
Secret *of a*
Holy Life

The Unpublished Personal Writings of
Hannah Whitall Smith

Edited by Melvin E. Dieter

ZondervanPublishingHouse
Grand Rapids, Michigan

A Division of HarperCollins*Publishers*

THE CHRISTIAN'S SECRET OF A HOLY LIFE
Copyright © 1994 Melvin E. Dieter
Requests for information should be addressed to:
Zondervan Publishing House
Grand Rapids, MI 49530

Library of Congress Cataloging-in-Publication Data
Long, James, 1949–
        Why is God silent when we need him the most? / James Long.
                p. cm.
        ISBN 0-310-39621-3
        1. Hidden God. 2. Suffering—Religious aspects—Christianity. 3. Christian
life—1960– I. Title.
BT180.H54L66 1993
231.7—dc20   93-46443
                                                                                    CIP

Printed in the United States of America

94 95 96 97 98 99 00 01 02 03 / ❖ DH / 10 9 8 7 6 5 4 3 2 1

Preface

Hannah Whitall Smith was a remarkable Quaker woman, "a woman for all seasons," who after a long, tortuous spiritual journey discovered the secret of a "God for all seasons." She once described her experiential search and discovery mission in this way: "By the discovery of God . . . I do not mean anything mysterious, or mystical, or unattainable. I simply mean becoming acquainted with Him as one becomes acquainted with a human friend; that is, finding out what is His nature, and His character, and coming to understand His ways."*

These daily readings from previously unpublished sources allow readers of Hannah Whitall Smith's *The Christian's Secret of a Happy Life* and her other devotional writings to share in her spiritual pilgrimage "home to God" in a way never before possible. At times, she had felt that her "Diaries" should be burned and her letters destroyed; but in the main, they were not. As a result, hearts that are open to the Spirit and the human condition can know something of both the pain and the delight of discovery that she encountered as she set her own heart and will to know God at any cost.

I tasted some measure of this "delight of discovery" in 1982 at the kind urging of Dr. Steve Barabas of Wheaton College. Six weeks of research in the Smith family archives, then at the home of Mrs. Barbara Strachey Halpern in Oxford, England, opened up a gold mine of letters, pamphlets, photographs, books, and other memorabilia about one of the most remarkable couples and families in the history of evangelicalism. Mrs. Halpern, a great-granddaughter of Robert Pearsall and Hannah Whitall Smith through their daughter Mary, gave me free access to the collection and permission to publish the results of my research. Portions of the thousands of photocopies of Hannah's journals and letters that I carried back to Wilmore, Kentucky, made this volume possible. At the same time, she sold over 3,400 pieces from the collection itself to Asbury Theological Seminary at nominal cost for its B. L. Fisher Library's Wesleyan/Holiness Archival Collection.

Editorial notes have been kept to a minimum. Readers, I would hope, will sense for themselves the complexity of the often tedious and extended common-sense testing of truth and experience that brought her to the knowledge of God that she has shared with her readers over these past 125

---

* Hannah Whitall Smith, (New York: Fleming H. Revell Company, 1903), 14.

years. Editorial accommodations of the nineteenth-century language of the original documents to a more contemporary mode allow the reader to make better sense of the whole without altering the intent or diminishing the force of Hannah's style. Readers who have interests broader than devotional ones should consult the original documents for further use.

Melvin E. Dieter
Lyndhurst, Virginia
New Year's Eve 1992

Introduction

Hannah Whitall Smith was born on February 7, 1832. Her parents, John Mickle Whitall and Mary Tatum Whitall, were well-to-do Philadelphia Quakers. She might have been born with a silver spoon in her mouth except that the Society of Friends would have frowned on such displays of worldliness. Two young sisters, Sarah (Sally) Whitall Nicholson and Mary Whitall Thomas, and a younger brother, James Whitall, completed her family circle. In her spiritual autobiography, *The Unselfishness of God,* she said,

> My own experience has been something like this. My knowledge of God, beginning on a very low plane, and in the midst of greatest darkness and ignorance, advanced slowly through many stages, and with a vast amount of useless conflict and wrestling, to the place where I learned at last that Christ was the "express image" of God, and where I became therefore in measure acquainted with Him, and discovered to my amazement and delight His utter unselfishness, and saw it was safe to trust in Him. And from this time all my doubts and questioning have been slowly disappearing in the blaze of this magnificent knowledge.*

The often dreary, desperate journal entries of the first years, with which we join her on her pilgrimage home to God, contrast sharply with her own overwhelmingly enthusiastic accounts of her childhood happiness. When she reread these early entries later in life she concluded that, with the exception of those often doleful, religious reflections, her youth had been "one long jubilant song of happiness" and a "fairy scene of sunshine and flowers."† Her dire laments, she concluded, had been mainly for "diary" purposes, but they, nevertheless, mark the beginning of her long journey from traditional Quaker mysticism to an experience of God in which she found both justification and sanctification by faith in Jesus Christ and the fullness of the Holy Spirit. This "secret" of the happy Christian life came to her after a long and rough spiritual journey and at great personal cost to her because of her family's displeasure, especially her mother's.

---

* Hannah Whitall Smith,   (New York: Fleming H. Revell Company, 1903), 14.
†Smith, *The Unselfishness of God,* 18–19.

The Christian's Secret of a Holy Life

1. The Sunshine Years: The Beginning of the Pilgrimage

This afternoon, I took a lovely ride on Rollo with my brother. We went our favorite route, along the bank of the Wissahickon and home by the way of Germantown. It was a beautiful ride, the grass was so green, and the trees were just putting forth their leaves so beautifully. Oh, how numberless are my blessings! I have parents who gratify almost every wish, a noble father, a darling mother, and I am very proud of them; every one loves them and speaks highly of them, and my earnest hope is that I may one day be as good and as lovely. The English Friends [Quakers] are in the city, and I am so happy. I cannot help hoping they may prove to be messengers of mercy to my soul. I should be so happy to know for certain that this is no deception but really the voice of my heavenly Father calling me to follow Him. My heavenly Father! Who do I mean? God the Father, or His Son, the Lamb that was slain for the sins of the world? I cannot tell; my mind is very much confused on every subject connected with religion and especially on this. I cannot unite God and Our Redeemer in One Being, and I do not know to whom I ought to pray! I am very ignorant.

—Journal, April 13, 1849

2. The Prayer of a Seventeen-Year-Old Quaker Girl

Oh, my Father! stretch out your all-powerful arm in mercy and free me from the bonds of sin and death that hold me fast! You see that I am tired of trying to be good, that I don't really try to resist the temptations of the Evil One with all my might. And you know that my whole nature rebels against following you and serving you. But oh, Father! Strengthen my feeble knees, put a new and holy faith in my heart, and bring down my haughty nature to the very dust. You are my only refuge; therefore, listen, I pray you, to my prayer.

I am haughty and full of pride. I shrink from the suffering that I know is waiting for me. I look almost with disgust on the narrow, narrow path that I see lying out before me. I feel that I can never consent to become nothing for your name's sake. But you, oh Lord, are able to drive away all pride from every heart. Oh, won't you purify and wholly sanctify my heart and make me willing to become the very least of your servants that you may have all the glory and honor and praise for ever and ever world without end!

—Journal, 1849

3. Inside Out

I must clean up the inside of the cup and the platter before I begin to cleanse the outside. I think there is great danger that beginners in the work of salvation, and I in particular, might trust too much to what they do and what they profess, paying no attention to the essential work of inward purification, or at least leaving it only partially accomplished, while they forget that God never did nor ever can accept offerings He has not required, offerings made in our own will and way and time, proceeding from unsanctified and hardened hearts. John Barclay says, "Obedience is better than sacrifice: And it is not our simply doing what is good that pleases God, but the good that He wills us to do."

And the prayer of my heart is, "Oh, my Father, that you will keep me in the hollow of your holy hand, teaching me just what you want me to do; and giving me enough strength to do what you want me to. You know that it is hard for me to learn to wait until your time, for deliverance comes; therefore, don't withdraw from me until patience has had its perfect work and you see that all murmuring and rebellion are gone forever.

"Oh, if I could not trust in you, my Father, my soul would faint under the burden that presses on it. You are able to change every disposition of my heart and to conform me wholly to your blessed will. Oh, then, I humbly beseech you, lay your hands on me and save me for truly there is no help nor hope but in you!"

—Journal, 1849

4. Long-Faced Religion: A Young Quaker's View

Religion is in itself and in its effects so wonderful and so perfect that those who make it appear to be gloomy and harsh are sadly mistaken. And how easy it is to do this. Some look almost as if they think it is a sin to smile or speak a pleasant word. It appears to me that religion is supposed to make one happy, not miserable and disagreeable. It is full of intense and deeply pressing trials, I know, but the joys are so exquisite and the sense all the time of being loved by God and of doing His will are so rich in happiness, that, it seems to me, continual thanksgiving ought to fill our hearts and light up our faces.

But how difficult it often is. Instead of a cheerful voice there is a long, drawling, melancholy whisper or, as Whittier says, "length of face, and solemn tone," instead of love and concern for those who have not yet found the path of life. There is a cool standoffishness, a feeling of "I'm better than you"—that effectually closes off the slightest opening for good that may have been there before. Instead of a winning gentleness and loving-kindness to those around them, there is a kind of hidden snappishness and a continual comparing of oneself with them, followed by a disagreeable dictatorianism. And so, instead of the noble, beautiful, humble, liberal-minded, and happy religion I have so often pictured to myself, I see it as cross, gloomy, proud, bigoted, and narrow-minded. I do not mean always, for there are some just as lovely as I desire in everything; but so often that is not the way it is, especially among young Friends [Quakers] who become religious and could do immense good among their associates and friends.
—Journal, 1850

5. The Attractiveness of Love

The worst thing, I think, is the lack of love and charity for those who have not yet entered the narrow way, and the cross and gloomy representation that is given to them of religion. I think if we were told of the delight of it and the perfect joys of it and were shown that all the trials and sorrows were so far overbalanced by them, we would be more eager to attain it than we do now; but we are made afraid of it because we, too, might become cross and narrow-minded and may have a life of sorrow, without any joy at all. I know this ought not to have any influence on me, but still I know that it does. It is so hard to be religious when we can't expect any joy in it, and when now we are so happy and so free—can love everyone and be cheerful, and enjoy pleasant things, and can think that others are as good as we are.

There is such a great danger of going too far and placing too much stress on little unimportant actions. It requires such constant watchfulness not to imagine that things are required that are not really necessary and ridiculous that I know I never could become one, especially since I would always be imagining all sorts of dreadful and strange things. Young Friends, too, when they become religious, always become really disagreeable in their stiff, pious ways. Instead of continuing to love their old friends and trying to entice them by showing them the beautiful fruits of holiness, they turn from them entirely, in some instances, even refusing to speak to them, and love only the good ones who don't need any help. Christ didn't come to call "the righteous but sinners to repentance," and yet those who profess to follow Him in all things turn rigidly away and are often right cross.

—Journal, 1850

6. A Heedless, Wayward Child

One of my friends makes religion appear anything but desirable. It is so evident that she thinks that she is better than those around her, and she continually interferes with them and reproves them; and then she lays down her opinions with such an air of certainty as if a thing could not possibly be good after she had pronounced it bad; and she always seems so very unhappy and gloomy. I have heard her say that she would be glad if it were possible to be turned into a stone so that there would be an annihilation of her soul at once—and when writing or talking she says nothing of the peace or comforts but dwells entirely on the crosses to be taken up, the sufferings to be passed through, and the innumerable trials to be borne, until she has almost given me a horror of it all. I feel as if I could not willingly go into such a terribly gloomy and thorny path with only the uncertainty at the end of gaining a reward, and I shrink almost unknowingly from it.

If I think of religion as I see it in some others, I feel as if I loved it. But then, as soon as the remembrance of this friend comes, it makes me shudder with horror. I have struggled to get over this feeling, but it has been all in vain. I could not be good if I must be like her, losing, as she has said of herself, all my natural native affections. And so I continue to be what I am: a heedless, wayward child.

I long to love religion and to experience it, but I cannot bring myself to try as long as it looks so gloomy and disagreeable to me. And there is so little encouragement ever given us; we are never persuaded but rather turned away by talk of a fearful array of trials, and crosses, and tribulations without one consolation ever being shown us to balance them out. And all this, too, when I should think that one thought of loving and serving God and of being loved by Him, if dwelt upon, would be enough to lead us to give up much, if not all, to Him.

—Journal, 1850

7. Robert Pearsall Smith:
Agreeable as Common Young Men

I was right provoked not to be at home when Robert Smith called. I wanted to see him to talk over Newport, and besides, he was there after we left, and I wanted to hear about it. Hannah Folwell admires him very much, I believe, and I think he is about as agreeable as common young men—but alas! the nice ones are all old and settled in life!!

But I am not writing out of the fullness of my heart; I believe I am scarcely thinking of what I write—but all the time of the terrible trouble that is coming upon me. Today is Sunday, and on Tuesday the trouble begins. I am perfectly lost in a maze of bewilderment—I scarcely know what to do or what to think, and sometimes it seems to me I shall go crazy. If this state of suspense should last a month longer, I know I would. I long for the days to pass as quickly as possible, and yet as the time draws nearer I shrink in fear.

When I look in the glass and see the same face I have seen for years, I can scarcely believe that it is my face; I sometimes don't know if I am myself, as if there were one body and spirit, calling itself Hannah Whitall, that laughs and talks, and eats and sleeps, and cleans its teeth and goes to bed and gets up, and is happy but oh-so-very foolish and thoughtless—and another body and spirit, calling itself by the same name, that is going to teach school! And it seems to me that I am the first body that is so foolish, and the other body is someone else, and yet it is I, too, separated miles and miles from my other self.

Oh, how foolishly I am writing, and to think what is once written can never be recalled—only burnt or destroyed—but it is really a relief to me to write freely and unrestrainedly, and I can easily destroy it some day.
—Journal, 1851

In 1851, nineteen-year-old Hannah married Robert Pearsall Smith, son of John Jay and Rachel Pearsall Smith, prominent Philadelphia Quakers. The newlywed couple moved into a home near her parents in Germantown, Pennsylvania, just north of Philadelphia. Hannah and Robert became increasingly alienated from their traditional Quakerism by its apparent lack of spiritual life, due in large measure to the doctrinal strife that had been disturbing the fellowship for a generation. The surge of evangelical revivals that the Methodists, Baptists, and others were enjoying became more and more attractive to them.

13

8. Disciple in Word and in Deed

I long to follow and turn to Christ my Redeemer more fully than ever before—that I may let nothing stand in my way—no sacrifice cause me to hesitate. I pray that I may be entirely dedicated to the LORD—that the sacrifice may be a whole sacrifice. Today in the service I felt favored by God with feelings of faith in the merits of my Savior, and all day this text has been filling my mind: "The love of Christ constraineth us." The whole creed of a Christian is contained in this; it seems increasingly beautiful as I think of it.

How marvelously I am blessed outwardly and inwardly—outwardly I have nothing left to desire—inwardly how much more than I could dare to ask or think. I cannot express today's mercies. It is true that the "Kingdom of God cometh not with observation," so quietly does the blessed Redeemer enter into the heart to purify and change it. I believe I can write that tonight, my heart is full of love and gratitude toward Him—the Savior of the world—and my Savior; yet I know that I cannot yet fully appreciate all the riches of His "plenteous Redemption."

Oh, Blessed Savior, make me your disciple in word and in deed!
—Journal, 1851

9. Surprised by Love

I am surprised at the lowliness though happiness of religion. I can see now that my ideas of it were too gloomy, as if the Redeemer were a hard taskmaster and His servants became unwilling slaves, working only for the sake of the reward or because of the fear of the punishment. And now when I find such love, such joy, such beauty, it astonishes me. I trust I am grateful for it, but the remains of the old fears still cause me to be expecting the crosses and the unhappiness. Perhaps it is the way with many young Friends to look upon Christ's religion as one of austerity and gloom, but how different the truth is. His service is a service of love. His yoke is easy. His burden is indeed light—lightened and made easy even if hard and heavy, by the help of love.

I have read that the Shepherd first carries His sheep in His arms while they are weak and trembling—but afterward, when their strength increases, He sets them down to walk amid the thorns and rocks of the way. Surely He is carrying me in His arms now, weak, unworthy to be called one of

His lambs, yet trusting in Him. I am deeply and peacefully happy, believing that "he is my Shepherd, and I shall not want."

—Journal, 1851

10. The Confidence of Confession

I believe that I am learning to trust that my Savior's blood is all-sufficient and to look to Him alone for help and guidance. But I am very weak and trembling and at times almost despair of ever being able to walk along the straight and narrow way. Then at times God helps me to come unreservedly to Christ my Redeemer—to cast all my burdens at His feet. I say to Him, "Here I am, Lord, a poor, sinful, helpless person. Many times I have entered into a covenant to serve you, and as often as I have, I have rebelled and turned to other gods. But oh, my Lord, my heart longs to serve You and You alone. I have no burnt-offerings, no sacrifices to lay on your altar, for I have nothing. But you, oh, my Savior will give me a contrite spirit. For your mercy's sake, for the sake of your death on the cross, when you were lifted up on high that all who look to You may be saved. Oh, my only Savior, save me. 'Purge me with hyssop, and I shall be clean; wash me, and I shall be whiter than snow.'"

I want to constantly keep watching and praying that I may be in earnest about my soul's redemption from sin. I long to be rooted and built up in Christ and to grow daily more and more into the fullness of the stature of a perfect soldier in Him.

—Journal, January 16, 1852

11. How Can I Rebel?

I long to know what the apostle calls "living the life that is lived with Christ in God," but I have been doubting whether it is possible. So few, apparently, seem to do it. So often the first fervor of their spirits grows weaker as more progress is made. And if it were possible, could I attain it? No, not I, but Christ working in me both "to will and to do of His own good pleasure." He is able to make me a real Christian—a Christian whose life and conversation will be in heaven. And I can cast my cares upon Him in perfect confidence; He is—my Saviour and Redeemer—My Shepherd, Husband, Friend—My Prophet, Priest and King—My Lord, my Life, my Way, my End.

Through His merciful lovingkindness I believe I can say this in all sin-

15

cerity: He has redeemed me from the bondage of sin and death. He has crowned me with the blessings of His love and mercy. He has set my feet in the path that leads to His Kingdom. He has given me the glorious hope of a portion of His inheritance. Oh! My heart cannot recount His mercies and His love. Though my feet often wander from the narrow way, how gently He leads me back, how mercifully He reproves me, how lovingly He increases my strength! How can I rebel against Him?

Oh, Lord, you know the sinfulness of my heart, the pride, the impatience, the indolence, the rebellious thoughts that live there; therefore, I come to you for deliverance from them all.

—Journal, February 25, 1852

12. Submission Under Chastening

I believe I am deeply thankful for the cloud that has darkened the usual bright sunshine of my life, for it has taught me to cling more closely to my only sure refuge—Jesus my Savior and my Lord. That text "Whom the Lord loveth He chasteneth, and scourgeth every son whom He receiveth," is inexpressibly beautiful and comforting to me, and I think I can say in sincerity that I kiss the rod with which He has chastened me and pray that, until its work is fully accomplished, it may not be taken away. I think it is not presumption to say that I believe my Redeemer has chastened me to bring me to Himself, for with humility and trembling yet with exceeding great joy, I can call Him now my God in whom I trust.

At times, such a sense of His love and infinite mercy comes over me that I cannot believe it is possible that I, a weak miserable sinner, can indeed be a partaker of it. Yet I know that He came to save sinners, and that "whosoever believeth on Him shall not perish, but shall have everlasting life." It is not through any merit of ours, but simply because we believe on Him. I do, through His mercy, believe on Him as my only Redeemer and Mediator redeeming me from past sins through His blood shed on the cross and ready to redeem me from all future sins, from all sinful inclinations by the power of His Spirit and grace in my heart, if I will only submit myself wholly to Him.

—Journal, April 7, 1852

Anxiety about her marriage at too young an age, frustration at her lack of opportunity for further education, and the approaching birth of her first child frequently depressed Hannah. The year following her marriage a daughter—Nellie—was born and in 1854 a son—Frank.

13. Prayer of a Depressed Heart

"Satan hath desired to have you that he may sift you as wheat." This is true not only of the disciples to whom it was spoken but of everyone who intends to become Christ's servant. Satan is constantly desiring to have us that he may sift us as wheat.

But what if in the hour of temptation our faith fails, and we give ourselves up, willing victims, into his hands? I am afraid that lately my faith has been failing. I grew impatient with my continual unhappiness and looked for comfort in other places than under the shadow of His wing. I felt like murmuring as though it were not right that I should be chastened in this way. And, at last, heartsick and weary, I felt that I could not arouse myself to look to the Lord for help against all these rebellious thoughts. I sometimes fear that I have sunk down under my depression and shall never be able to shake it off.

Oh! that my faith may not fail. My Savior, grant this for your mercy's sake, and lead me back in humility of heart, to your feet. "Nothing in my hands I bring." I don't even have a contrite heart to offer you, but oh, for the sake of your precious blood shed for your people, receive me and from now on be my stay and my guide.

—Journal, May 1, 1852

14. The Year that Nellie Died—1856

God is a Father.
I a weary child.
He is beyond all thought or reach of mine,
But, if I come to Him, will lead me blind
And weak among the dangers—guiding on
I following through the strangest winding paths:
And He will lead me to His own belief
I trusting to Him.

—Journal, January 1, 1856

O God! where are you?
In this wild chaos of life

17

I reach out longing hands for your blessing
And it doesn't come.
I tremble with inward whirling—
I am blind, and deaf, and dumb.
I don't know where I am going—
or even where I am standing now.
O God, save me! Save us, oh God!
—Journal, January 2, 1856

15. Inside, Then Outside

The religious element in my nature is I think very strongly developed. I can scarcely remember a time when I have not been guided in my daily life by some religious principle, however imperfect. It is hard for me to be simply indifferent. If there is no religion in my heart, then there is outright rebellion. The question "What shall I do to be saved?" always is settling itself one way or the other; and that false rest that comes to the careless-hearted is never mine. To serve God or Mammon?—that is my choice, and always I am making it and remaking it.

But—why is it like this? I attributed it to a greater development of those faculties that are subject to religious influence—yet I have but little reverence and, naturally, I think am wanting in conscientiousness. And this forces me to attribute my religiousness simply to the effect of a very vivid imagination that is so vivid as to cause me to realize very forcibly the idea of endless misery or an eternity of joy. And this realization constantly of one or the other rules my life.

I remember the first real religious awakening I ever had was occasioned entirely by listening to an account of the potential glories of unknown worlds. And I thought if I were an angel, it would no longer be unknown to me. I question whether after all this religiousness is not a drawback to real conversion—whether there is not a danger of resting in it and coming short of a heartfelt change. For instance, because I am always raising the question of salvation in my own mind, do I not think myself safe compared to those who live in forgetfulness and thus lose the incentive to bring a speedy answer to my questioning?

For instance, the one subject of eternal life and death is constantly before me day and night—my last thought before sleeping is a prayer for light, and my first waking recollection is a weary sense of the struggle to attain it. Yet this is all I fear—I rest here, not because it is rest, but because of a hope-

18

less looking back to former efforts and failures, and also because of a little feeling of safety—as if God would never destroy a seeking soul. It seems strange to say I am naturally religious and am yet not conscientious—but they do not seem to me inseparable. Religion affects the principles of life—conscientiousness affects the life itself; and while religion is seeking to settle those principles, the life left without the restraining influence of conscientiousness may easily and will almost infallibly go widely wrong. The religious principle will first cleanse the inside of the cup—the conscientious principle attends first to the outside; and a man may be religious even when leading an outwardly wicked life. At least so it seems to me.

—Journal, August 11, 1856

16. Confession: The Beginning Point

"All his transgressions that he hath committed, they shall not be mentioned to him."

"O good God, heavenly Father, I have nothing to say; I am wrong; and yet I do not know how wrong I am; but You know. You see all my sins a thousand times more clearly than I do; and if I look black and sullied to myself, O God, how much more black and sullied must I look to You! I don't know. All I know is, that I am utterly wrong, and You are utterly right. I was formed in sin, conceived in iniquity.

"It is my heart that is wrong. Not merely this or that wrong thing that I have done; but it is my heart, my temper, that wants to have its own way, that cares for itself and not for you. I have nothing to plead, nothing to throw into the other side of the scale. If I have ever done anything right, it was You who did it in me and not I myself. Only my sins are my own doing; so the good in me is all yours. And the bad in me all my own, and in me dwells no good thing.

"And as for excusing myself by saying that I love you, I had better tell the truth since you know it already—I do not love you, O God; I love myself, my pitiful miserable self, well enough, and too well. My only comfort, my only hope is, that whether I love you or not, you love me and have sent your Son to seek and to save me. Help me now. Save me now out of my sin, and darkness, and self-deceit. Show your love to me by setting this wrong heart of mine right. Give me a clean heart, O God, and renew a right spirit within me.

"If I am wrong myself, how can I make myself right? No, you must do it. You must purge me or I shall never be clean; you must make me understand wisdom in the secret depth of my heart, or I shall never see my way. You must, for I cannot. Grant me, oh my God, the Holy Spirit!"

—Journal, September 14, 1856

Both Hannah and Robert were converted on the same day in 1858 under the influences of what is known as the "Layman's Revival" of the same year. Finally, in 1859, they left the Society of Friends and became involved with the Plymouth Brethren. "The Plymouths," as she often called them, eventually proved to be too rationalistic and legalistic in their scriptural understanding for these new "born-again" Quakers. The Smiths found the more ecumenical, experientially-centered stance of the Methodist Holiness Movement more to their liking. Robert eventually joined the Presbyterians. Hannah favored the Methodists, but never joined them. She finally rejoined the Quakers later in life.

17. God's Tender Teachings

It seems as if every day I discover new depths of depravity in my heart that were undreamed of before. The Lord is searching out my secret sins and bringing them to the light so that He may make me pure in my innermost being. I feel deeply thankful. Oh, how wise He is in His dealings with me and how inexpressibly tender! No words can express it. Yet I must thank Him.

He is teaching me more and more that my Christian journey is to be a warfare—a fight of faith—a constant battle. But thanks be unto His grace, also a constant victory—"for, greater is He that is in us, than he that is in the world." I am learning more and more that it can only be by a ceaseless, momentary looking to Jesus, and a continual dedication of my whole being to Him, that can preserve me. I dare not be off my guard one moment, or think of standing without Christ for even an instant. I am a poor sinner and nothing at all, but, thanks be unto God, "Jesus Christ is my all and all."

Indeed I feel that I have to thank to my dear Redeemer for all He has done for me. He is so tender and loving and leads me along so gently step by step. And He keeps me from falling, and is guiding me by His Spirit into the paths He has marked out for me. I feel this to be an inestimable privilege—to be consciously led by His Voice. Oh it is precious to walk in His path and I can say sometimes—"I delight to do thy will." Isn't it marvelous grace? And to one so unworthy!

—Journal, May 22, 1859

18. The Simplicity of Prayer

I want to realize the simplicity of prayer. I don't dare look at it as a religious exercise but rather as a child's going to a father to get what is needed in answer to prayer. And especially I must remember that my having access to God depends not upon my feelings but upon His—that He welcomes my ✓ approaches because of the ground upon which I draw near to Him and not because of the mere flow of emotion in my heart.

If my prayers were without one wandering thought and with most heavenly feelings, I would probably be tempted to congratulate myself and to say, "What a grand prayer!" But if, on the other hand, I am filled with many wandering thoughts and a lot of coldness, then I know that God can only hear me for Jesus' sake, and I shall say, "What a grand plea the Name of Jesus is!" It makes even my otherwise worthless prayer acceptable!

—Journal, July 4, 1859

When we love earthly friends we are not satisfied with only a few minutes together at a time, nor can we learn to know their real character, or appreciate the depths of their nature, if we only have a few passing words with them as we go about our daily routine, even if those passing words should occur every few minutes. Neither can we know God in this way.

How often we say about our earthly friends, "I really would like to have a good quiet settled talk with them so that I can really get to know them." And shouldn't we feel the same about our Heavenly Friend, that we may really get to know Him?

These thoughts have taught me the importance of the children of God taking time to commune daily with their Father, so that they may get to know His mind and to understand better what His will is. Oh dear Lord! keep me faithful in this, and enable me to feel this is a privilege and not merely a duty. My trust and my strength are all in you!

—Journal, July 6, 1859

19. Manifesting His Life in Me

In my reading today this verse has forcibly impressed itself on my mind: "I am crucified with Christ. Nevertheless I live, yet not I, but Christ lives in me, and the life which I now live in the flesh, I live by the faith of the Son of God, who loved me and gave Himself for me."

What a stupendous thought, "Christ lives in me!" I cannot express the feelings with which this verse has filled me! It seems as if I could never indulge in a sinful thought again; yet I am well aware of the power of the adversary. But, dear Lord, you have the power to keep me from falling. Oh, I come to you in faith to commit myself to your keeping. Since this is my high calling; oh, enable me to walk worthy of you! Solemnize my mind constantly with a realization of this truth and let me always remember that, it is Christ that lives in me and is manifesting His life through me.

—Journal, July 22, 1859

The revival of 1858–59 in which they had been converted was part of a rising tide of concern within the churches for Christian Holiness. The cardinal teaching of the Methodist Holiness Revival, sanctification by faith, was already beginning to find expression in the Calvinistic churches of America through the higher-life movement.

Hannah quickly became convinced that the early leaders of her own society of Friends had been preaching the same holiness of heart and life that she was hearing about from the Holiness advocates of her day. Her reading of the works of Methodist writers such as John Wesley and her contemporary, Phoebe Palmer, and the testimonies of friends and associates turned her to a long quest to love God out of a pure heart and enjoy victory over sin. She sought and struggled more than a decade to understand the truth and to finally experience it for herself. This understanding of a life completely yielded to the will of God she called "The Christian's Secret of a Happy Life."

20. Prayer for Holiness

"For God hath not called us unto uncleanness but unto holiness." "For this is the will of God even your sanctification."

These are two very special texts to me. They are a resting place for my faith in the darkest hour of temptation. Since my sanctification is indeed the "will of God," I know that He will perfectly accomplish it, if I give myself up wholly into His hands. And dearest Father, today I do give myself up to you without any reservation. Today, if never before, I dedicate myself— soul and body—to your service, for all that I know, and all that I do not know, perfectly certain that you, and you alone, are "able to keep me from falling." Oh, I pray, make me realize what the full extent of this entire dedication is. And grant me, dear Lord, a tender conscience, that I may know at once when I trespass against you. I feel that this tenderness of conscience is one of my greatest privileges, and yet I know how easily it may become scarred by willfully disregarding its admonitions; therefore I want to be made able to obey it at once.

Is it the child's privilege to know the will of the Father in every part of life? I believe that it is, and that the prayer of faith certainly will be answered by conscious guidance on any subject about which we may be in difficulty. And I need guidance now, on many points. Let me then come in faith to my Father for the wisdom I need to know His will and to do it.

—Journal, August 9, 1859

21. Only Because of Jesus

Twice yesterday I resisted a conviction of duty and brought a weary sense of condemnation on myself. But oh! How infinitely precious is the blood of Christ, which cleanseth from all sin. It brought me to realize what my ground of acceptance is before God, and to place my sanctification in its right position—as the consequence and not the cause of my justification. Jesus only is the cause of my justification. I realize that I do not have to lead a holy life in order to gain salvation but in order to please my Lord and Master. And how much stronger a motive is this.

It was wonderful to think of such a friend as Jesus is! To think that as I confessed my sin, and presented the infinite sacrifice of Jesus as my sin offering, it was taken away entirely and forever! Just as the old Israelite, bringing a lamb to the High Priest as a sacrifice, confessed his sin, and laying his hand on the lamb's head while it was being slain, was purified forever from that sin. And the Israelite knew that it was forever for he never brought a second sacrifice for the same sin. If he had, wouldn't the Priest have rebuked him for dishonoring the word of God who had declared that one sacrifice was sufficient?

Shouldn't we then who can present a sacrifice of so much more infinite value, know also that our sins are forgiven forever? Do we not dishonor the blood of Christ when we still keep the burden of them on our hearts? Oh, I feel that we do. I realized it last night, and that I should not dare to look to my past sins with any feeling but that of joy that they had been all washed away in this precious blood. How then? "Can I continue in sin that grace may abound? God forbid! How can I, who am dead to sin, live any longer therein?" Dear Lord, I cannot! I give myself to you, as wholly your servant. Do with me as you will, only I pray "count me worthy of this calling, and fulfil all the good pleasure of your goodness and the work of faith with

power:" "that the Name of our Lord Jesus Christ may be glorified in me, and I in Him according to the grace of our God and the Lord Jesus Christ."
—Journal, August 12, 1859

22. When We Do Not See Him

A strange sense of the vanity of all earthly things is growing upon me, and is making me deeply serious. I seem to hold everything with such a light grasp—to have my heart so increasingly set on unseen realities. In many ways my Father is answering my prayers for the destruction of self—ways which I cannot detail—by outward mortification and revelations of inward depravity and nothingness—until at last I have grown to look upon myself as almost a laughing stock and object of scorn to all my friends. Then too my perplexities are growing greater and greater every day. I see no way out of them. I know the Pilot is at the helm of my poor frail bark, but I do not see Him; and I seem to myself as a lovely boat tossed about on the wild ocean, blown by the winds, without rudder, or anchor, or pilot ready at any moment to be dashed to pieces on the treacherous rocks.

But thank the Lord, He preserves my faith in Him unshaken, and enables me to leave all the future entirely in His care, with a perfect confidence that He will, in His own time, make a plain path for my feet. I believe that He has given me a sincere desire above anything else to please Him and to do and to be just what He would have me to, and I return unto Him the thanksgiving of praise for this great blessing.
—Journal, September 14, 1859

The year 1859 was an especially difficult year for Hannah and her family. Their resignation from the Philadelphia Yearly Meeting of the Society of Friends created tensions with the parents she had always idolized. Hannah was still feeling the death of Nellie. She would experience the pain of such a loss two more times in her life. Of six children—Nellie, Frank, Mary, Alys, Logan, and Ray—only Mary, Alys and Logan survived into adulthood.

23. Trusting in the Hard Times

For the last week or two, a great stress of engagements has seemed to make it impossible for me to set any regular hour for communion alone with God, and the result is a great deadness and coldness of spirit. I awoke to the realization of it yesterday by finding myself indulging in some little questionable things without any rebuke from my conscience, which once would have caused me much regret. I am resolved now with or rather by the grace of God to be faithful in this one thing, since I see plainly that I cannot live or grow without it.

I long to have my soul filled with love to God—a personal realizing love that will be the root and spring of my whole life. I want to love Jesus as well as trust Him—to feel my affections engaged as well as my faith. My heart, as to earthly loves, often feels sad and lonely and unsatisfied. My daughter [Nellie] is dead, my own family disapproves of me, and only my husband and my son are left to me, and even with this I feel that the deepest part of my affection is not yet touched. None but Jesus can fill the place that often now is lonely and sad. And oh, that He may fill it!

That I may love Him with a soul satisfying love, and may find the desired rest for my poor torn affections in His loveliness.

I have no doubt that He has been teaching me my need of Him by causing me to pass through deep trials—trials in thoughts of my little daughter, and in the family trials that have so overwhelmed me. And having made me feel the need, I cannot doubt but that He will fill it. Oh how safe it is to trust our sanctification as well as our justification in His Hands!
—Journal, October 3, 1859

24. For Jesus' Sake

I could write a lot about the Lord's dealings with my soul for the last two weeks but time and words would fail me to tell of all His loving and wise ways. My heart often feels over-burdened with thanksgiving and praise, because I express it so inadequately. But the Lord knows, and soon I shall be where my only occupation will be to praise and magnify His holy and precious Name. Oh that that day would hasten!

Yet I do not want to be impatient, and I would love to do all I could for my Master before going to my rest. What if I have many trials, and am surrounded by many perplexities? He is sufficient for these things, and I feel and know Him to be so. And with all my heart I can adopt the language of the 91st Psalm—"I will say of the Lord, He is my refuge and my fortress: my God, in Him will I trust."

I have realized this week more than ever before that it is only for the sake of Jesus that my prayers are heard and not for the sake of their fervor, sincerity, or length, or of my goodness, or my sorrow for sin, or my good resolutions. And I see that even when Satan is besetting me with temptations during my prayers, when he is distracting my thoughts, trying to fill me with coldness or unbelief or in any other way assaulting me, so that my prayers are poor cold stammering utterances, still they are offered in the name of Jesus, and for His sake they are heard, because He is unchangeable and God looks upon Him and not upon me.

I see too, that even when my heart is fervently engaged in prayer and no distracting thoughts come in to disturb my devotions, still I am heard only in the name of and for the sake of Jesus. I know now what Paul meant when he wrote in Hebrews 10:19–22: "Having therefore, brethren, boldness to enter into the holiest by the blood of Jesus, let us draw near with a true heart in full assurance of faith."

—Journal, November 14, 1859

25. Resting in His Love

The Lord has been and is teaching us what a precious thing it is to trust our temporal affairs into His Hands. We have learned Mark 6:25–34 and Luke 12:22–32 are really true for us. It is wonderful that the Lord blesses His children like this, but He Himself has declared it, and His word stands sure.

And oh, it is infinitely precious to trust everything to Him. Even perplexities and trials that drive us to this entire dependence have something very sweet in them, and though often trying to the flesh—still I can thank and bless the Lord for such gracious dealings with me. I am His child—this comprises the whole breadth and extent of my faith. I know that I am "of more value than many sparrows."

Once it was as if I were walking along a certain pathway, upheld and guided it is true by the hand of God but still walking as we sometimes have seen pictures of children with their guardian angels. I felt that if God should let go of my hand, though I would certainly fall, still I would not fall far, nor be seriously injured.

But now I think far differently. I see God moving swiftly through the awful infinitudes of space and time. I see His arms outstretched over the fearful depths of infinity and eternity, and I see myself lying in those arms— a poor, weak, trembling, sin-defiled thing. I know that the depths are just beneath me and that nothing separates me from them but the arms of mercy in which I am lying; but my upturned face knows nothing but the tender Voice saying, "I will never leave thee nor forsake thee."

If those arms of mercy should grow weary of carrying me, then I should be lost indeed for I should sink down, down, down into the blackness of darkness forever. But as I lie in their strong embrace, I do not fear this. And the more I see of my own helplessness, and the more I know of my own vileness, the more closely I cling to those Arms of mercy and the more earnestly I gaze into that face of love. And I say to myself, "He knew all my unworthiness when He loved me and took me into His embrace, and though He continues to know it, He will not cease to love me or cast me off." I rest, oh, I rest in His Love!

—Journal, December 4, 1859

26. Grace, What a Word

It seems to me that I am but just beginning to see the vileness and utter depravity of my whole nature, and consequently, I am just beginning to understand what grace means. Oh what a word! It means that the infinitely holy God—the God who is of purer eyes than to behold iniquity, who is infinitely just to punish it, and infinitely powerful to wipe it and me out of existence—that this God, who can see in me nothing but depth below depth of iniquity, who cannot by searching find out in me one single particle of anything that He could love, who sees me worthy only of death and vengeance and that at once—it means that this pure, holy, just God loves me! Oh, as I write the words, my heart melts within me. He loves me! He loves me—loves me—loves even me! What shall I say, what can I do?

I can only turn from my needy self with a close clinging to that Love that is inconceivable, to that Love that is independent of anything in me, to that love that is the love of God. As when a child, lying in its mother's arms, sees a snake creeping along the floor and turns its eyes away, hiding in the loving mother's bosom, so I turn from my noisome loathsome self with a shudder of horror and hide myself in the bosom of that infinite, inconceivable, unspeakable love. Oh that I may lose myself in this love—that I may be filled with it, and may live in it and die in it.

Once I knew what it was to rest upon the rock of God's promises, and it was indeed a precious resting place, but now I rest in His grace, He is teaching me that the bosom of His love is a far sweeter resting-place than even the rock of His promises. Words and thoughts fail me, but oh my Saviour, do your work in me according to the good pleasure of your will, all that concerns me—and make me but clay in the hands of the potter; for thy own Name's sake!

—Journal, January 20, 1860

27. Giving Freely

Lately, my Father has revealed to me a depth of selfishness in myself that I never even so much as suspected. I find that all my kindness to others, my benevolence, and what seemed to be the most unselfish acts of my life—all have had their root in a deep and subtle form of self-love. My motto has for a long time been: "Freely ye have received, freely give," and I dreamed that in a certain sense I was living up to it not only as regards physical blessings but spiritual as well.

But I find now that I have never really given one thing freely in my life. I have always expected and demanded pay of some kind for every gift, and where the pay has failed to come, the gifts have invariably ceased to flow. If I gave love, I demanded love in return; if I gave kindness, I demanded gratitude as payment; if I gave counsel, I demanded obedience to it, or if not that, at least an increase of respect for my judgment on the part of the one counseled; if I gave the gospel, I demanded conversions or a reputation of zeal and holiness; if I gave consideration, I demanded consideration in return. In short, I sold everything, and gave nothing. I know nothing of the meaning of Christ's words, "Freely ye have received, freely give." But I did it ignorantly.

Now, however, the Lord has opened my eyes to see something of the nature and extent of this selfishness, and I believe He is also giving me grace to overcome it in a measure. I have been taking home to myself the lesson contained in Matthew 5:39–48. I desire to do everything now as to the Lord alone and to receive my pay only from Him. His grace must carry on this work in me for I am utterly powerless to do one thing toward it; but I feel assured that He will.

And I feel I have to thank Him for what He has already done. He has conquered a feeling of repugnance that was growing in me toward someone with whom I am brought into very close contact and enabled me to give freely, without even wanting any return. Oh how great He is in strength and wisdom!

—Journal, January 16, 1860

28. Unchangeably Faithful

Our prosperous nation has been plunged into a civil war, the horrors of which we are just beginning to feel. The state of money matters is distressing and Robert has suffered great losses, so that we have been obliged in every way to reduce our expenditures. We rented our Germantown house for the summer and moved to a place belonging to Robert's father. But as it was not healthy there, we have left it and are now entirely unsettled as regards our future. It does not distress me in the least for I know that the "Lord is my Shepherd" and therefore "I shall not want," and I am perfectly content to leave all my future in His care. I feel indeed that it is my greatest privilege that I may thus leave it with Him, for whom or what am I that He should care for my welfare?—a poor sinner saved by grace, this is what I am and what I love to be! And after all I well know it is not what I am, but what Christ is that is of any importance. For the safety and well-being of the flock depends not upon what they are but altogether upon what the Shepherd is. And the Lord is my shepherd! Well may I say, therefore, that "I shall not want!"

As to my spiritual life, I hardly know what to say. I am still just what I was a year ago and what I was two years ago—"a poor sinner and nothing at all and Jesus Christ is my all in all." What more could I say than that? Yet while I can write to His praise that my Savior has been unchangeably faithful to me during all this past year, I must confess to my bitter shame that oftentimes I have been very faithless to Him. Oh how could I, how can I! It is good for me that He is just the Saviour He is, or there would be no hope for me. No other one could have borne with me, no other could continue to love me! But He does! This is His blessedness! "He is the same yesterday today and forever," and in Him is no variableness nor even shadow of turning. He is just exactly the Saviour I need and is *all* I need! No words can even begin to tell what He is! Oh that I were a more faithful disciple!

—Journal, August 6, 1861

29. Resting in Love

My heart aches to think of my coldness and ingratitude and rebellion. Only yesterday I disregarded His loving voice of reproof and grieved Him. I do not serve Him as I should. I do not grow in grace as I ought to. I do not, it seems to me, walk worthy of the high calling wherewith I am called in any degree. Yet oh my God, I long to, and it is you who must work in me to will and to do of your own good pleasure. Oh, in your mercy and for Jesus' sake, sanctify me wholly!

Never did the love of Christ seem more real or more precious to me. It seems so astounding that He could love me, I am such an utterly vile and unworthy sinner, and yet in my heart of hearts I know that He does, and I revel in the thought. Often when I get into bed at night after praying, I feel as if I were just creeping into His dear arms, and going to sleep on His love! And no words can express the sweetness of the thought. Oh what wonderful infinite grace! My poor heart cannot compass the thought of it. I can only believe in it and rest in it. And this, in His grace, is all He asks me to do.

He knows I cannot even understand, much less adequately return love like His; and yet, this makes no difference in His love. He loves me first, for love's sake, not for the sake of anything in me, and therefore He will love me on to all eternity. I am sure of this. I never for a moment doubt my Jesus! But I don't love Him as I ought. Oh Jesus, let it be so no longer. Take my poor, foolish, ignorant, wayward heart, and fill it with love. Then I can hope to please you.

—Journal, August 6, 1861

1863 is the first year for which letters are available from the thousands which make up the Hannah Whitall Smith Collection. These letters to her family and to her special friends Anna Shipley, Abby Folwell, Priscilla Mounsey, her cousin Carrie Nicholson, and a whole circle of women who were part of the "Round Robin" circle who eventually read them give us one of the clearest pictures available to us today of the struggle of a Christian woman of the nineteenth century for spirituality and a place in the church as well as for improved status in the society in which she lived. Hannah and her friends were active in efforts to improve women's educational status, equality in marriage, the Prohibition Movement, supported the right of women to preach as Quakers always had done, and took part in the women's suffrage crusade.

30. Into Christ and Out of Self

I am enjoying a book by an old author—Romaine's *Life of Faith*. It is just the whole truth of the life of faith as we have apprehended it stated in the most forcible and beautiful way. I have never read anything that strengthened my faith so much. It does not turn your attention inward to yourselves at all, but all the time out and away to Christ. One favorite expression is to "live out of ourselves and in Christ"; it conveys a world of truth. I am learning the preciousness of Christ by being made to feel my utter need of Him more and more daily. I am so weak, and so ignorant, and so full of sin that nothing but Christ will do for me; and I must have Him every moment, or I am undone. There is a text which says, "Count it all joy when ye fall into divers temptations, knowing this, that the trying of your faith worketh patience. But let patience have her perfect work, that ye may be perfect and entire wanting nothing."

I take great comfort in this, for I am indeed surrounded by "divers temptations" and often sigh for deliverance from them. But if it is part of the refining work, I can try to endure, and may end perhaps in counting it all joy. I believe God is teaching me by means of them, lessons concerning the fullness of Christ that I could learn in no other way. Oh! to be lost & swallowed up in Him! I do not suppose others have such a monstrous self to get rid of as I have, so that I need more discipline. But the Lord Jesus is a glorious Saviour, His salvation is a full and complete salvation, this I know, and in this I rest & triumph!

—To a Friend, 1863

31. The Joy of Consecration

It seems to me that every day I experience more of the rest of faith, and I also realize the joy of consecration. It is really a blessing to feel that your will is consciously given up to God and that there is actually nothing, so far as you know, to hinder His grace from working in you. I love to feel just like a clay vessel in His hands which He is molding for His own purposes. It is not that my will may not rise up again soon in all its old force, but it seems to me that in this life of faith we speak only of present experiences.

I do long for more feeling, for more of the presence of Christ manifested in me, but I can wait on Him for this and there is a promise which says "They shall not be ashamed who wait for thee." The lesson from Joshua about hidden sin is very impressive, but we are safe are we not if we leave the discovering of any sinful thing to the Lord Jesus? The very thought of self examination seems so hopeless to me, but it is precious to have the Lord examine you.

—To Sally [1863]

32. No Resources of My Own

For myself I feel that the Lord must do the whole work of restoration for me, for I am powerless to do anything for myself. He must give me the desire even to be restored. I have been asking Him to do this, and I trust not in vain. Then He must also help me to view properly the earthly things for which I long, so that I will not grieve over their loss. And He must so satisfy me with Himself that all other joys will seem weak and poor in comparison. I have no doubt that this lesson of my own complete helplessness is what He has meant to teach me by allowing me to wander such distance from Himself. I am naturally so self-dependent, so conscious of possessing powers and capacities sufficient to carry me through all ordinary emergencies. But now I see that without the Lord to hold me up, I can't stand one moment.

I especially have needed this lesson in my work for the Lord. I have never known what it was to be utterly reliant on Him for this, but have always felt as though I had inward resources of my own to draw upon. (Except perhaps in one instance where I felt utterly empty and when the Lord filled me most). I believe this is why all my capacity for service seems to be taken from me. The vessel is being emptied and when the happy day comes again when I may work for Him, I believe it will be a work in which He will have all the glory, both in my own eyes, and in the eyes of others!

—Journal, June 1865

33. Self Has a Thousand Voices

It seems to me, in looking back, that the Master never used a more unfit and wretched instrument to do His work than when He used me. In fact I know He never did; and I don't wonder that He has laid me aside. If He needs me He will use me again someday, and meanwhile I trust He will fashion me into a vessel a little better fitted for His service. I cannot say that the fashioning process is pleasant. "No chastening seemeth for the present to be joyous but grievous" but, nevertheless do pray, dear Abby, that it may work in me the peaceable fruits of righteousness. Whenever I go to work again for my Master I want to do it without one remnant of my own strength and totally in the strength of His Spirit.

I feel, dear Abby, that we cannot follow the guidance of this blessed Spirit too clearly, nor lean too much on His power. And I fairly burn sometimes to go among the dead Christians and preach my convictions with regard to it. It is a glorious doctrine, but oh so little understood by the great bulk of those even who make it one of their principal articles of profession. How few among them for instance ever get out of self; how few realize that as to themselves they are dead, and it is only Christ who is alive, and they in Him! Yet until we are really out of self we cannot have any certain guidance.

Self has a thousand voices that assume the appearance of divine ones, and the heart that has any regard left for it is easily deceived. But let the soul lose absolutely all concern for self; let it be indifferent to its reputation; careless of its honor; inattentive to its ease; let it be really and practically to itself a stranger and what is there to hinder a clear discernment of the Spirit's voice? Oh, to be freed of every selfish interest in our own perfection, joy or consolation so that we may think only of the interests of God! To no longer ask anything for ourselves, but only that He may be glorified! This, dear Abby, would be self-abandonment in earnest, and why should not we seek after so blessed and happy a state?

Only I am so far, so far off from it! This makes me sigh and mourn. But God, the great Husbandman, is able to work greater wonders than even this.

—To Abby, Millville, N.J., August 20, 1865

34. Self-Abandonment

The soul where love reigns forgets herself wholly that she may think only upon her Well Beloved. She becomes divested of every selfish interest in her own Salvation, perfection, joy, or consolation, that she may only think of the interests of God. She no longer thinks of enjoying His embrace, but of suffering for Him. She no longer asks anything for herself, but only that He may be glorified. Madame Guyon Commentary on the Song of Solomon.

Is not this the true meaning of self-abandonment? Simplicity of spirit causes us to act in respect to God continually, without hesitation, straight forward, without reflections; and supremely, without complicated intentions, motives or designs with a single eye to the good pleasure of God. When simplicity is perfect, we even commonly act without a thought of it. To act with simplicity towards a neighbor, is to act with frankness, without affectation; with sincerity without disguise, and with liberty, without constraint. As an infant does in its mother's presence.

—Journal, Millville, N.J., August 27, 1865

35. Moment by Moment Guidance

I have been thinking a lot about the subject of guidance, and I am convinced more and more that it requires great simplicity of spirit to be able easily and clearly to discern the Voice that speaks so gently in our hearts. We must be in the hands of God, as Madame Guyon says, something "like a toy in the hands of a child" used or laid aside just as He pleases, brought out to be admired, or hidden away on the shelf, made to serve pleasant uses, or applied to disagreeable ends and, like a toy, careless of our own hopes of judgments, must desire nothing but to fulfil all the good pleasures of His will!

No doubt, if the toy were able to reason, it would often feel that it was used for very useless purposes, and would feel that it could arrange far better for itself, but the end of a toy is to give pleasure to its possessor and it is of no consequence how this end is attained. So our end, dear Abby, is to please our Lord and Master, and to bring glory to His Name, and we have no need to trouble ourselves as to how He brings this about. The realization of this will save us a lot of anxious questioning. Moment by moment we will hang upon His leading, never stopping to reason as to why we should do this or that, never troubled if it seems to produce results, not even anxious if it seems to have been a mistake—concerned still only for one thing, and that is to please our Lord now, in the present moment. And having pleased Him, we have nothing more to do with that act.

I do not believe that light is ever promised for a past step, nor for a future one; for God emphatically wants us to live in the present, moment by moment. And so, darling friend, let me beg you to rest quietly in your Saviour feeling your utter helplessness but His infinite strength!

—To Abby, Millville, N.J., September 6, 1865

36. With "Fear And Trembling"

Since being converted, I have done some work for my Master with some success, and in doing it, I believed I was under His direction and blessing, but I never felt, except in a very few instances, that sense of absolute and utter weakness and emptiness of which I have heard other Christians speak. I generally was conscious of a sort of reserve strength and capacity in myself which I felt would at least carry me through creditably even though God should not grant me His special blessing. This has always more or less troubled me, because it did not seem to fit with the scriptural thought of God's strength being made perfect in our weakness. But still what was I to do? The feeling of strength was there.

Now the question has suggested itself to me as to whether those who are consciously led of the Spirit of God are emptied of self by Him, and left with no consciousness of strength of their own whatever, in order that He may fill them with His fullness. I have thought perhaps this might be the meaning of that text "Work out your own salvation with fear and trembling, for it is God that worketh in you to will and to do of His good pleasure." "Working out," of course, does not mean "working for," but developing, as it were, the salvation already secured to us by the death of Christ, as one developed the resources of a mine. This part of the text never troubled me, but the "fear and trembling" did, because I could not see why a child of God needed to work in fear and trembling.

It seems to me, however, that the meaning dawns on me now. The connection "for it is God that worketh in you" seems to show that when God works in a soul, the soul itself always works in "fear and trembling," because He totally takes away from it that sense of its own strength and capacity which would prevent this feeling of fear and trembling. When we do a thing from our own idea that it would be a good thing to do, we do it with great confidence and a feeling of strength, but when we do that very same thing with the consciousness of His guidance we are filled with "fear and trembling."

—To Anna, September 17, 1866

During the Civil War period, Robert and Hannah moved to Millville, N.J. Robert became the general manager of the family's large glass factory there. Leaving her family and the culture of Philadelphia for a gritty manufacturing center was a difficult pill for Hannah to swallow. Nevertheless, it was here that her Methodist seamstress and the workers in Robert's factory began to witness to them more definitely about the blessing of entire sanctification or the Fullness of the Spirit.

Hannah and Robert both became convinced of the scriptural truth of the experience and sought it. Robert received the blessing at the great Methodist Holiness camp meeting at Vineland, N.J. in 1867 where ten thousand worshipers gathered for ten days to learn about the truth that one can be sanctified by faith just as one was saved by faith. They believed that God would free the believer from the power as well as the guilt of sin. When Christians offered themselves up completely to God by faith in Jesus Christ, God would cleanse their hearts of the fleshly nature of rebellion, which remained even in justified Christians and enabled them to love God and their neighbors with their whole heart. The Methodists often called this experience a personal Pentecost or the Baptism of the Holy Ghost, not however, accompanied by the sign of "speaking in tongues" as the later Pentecostal Movement taught.

The flood of emotion and the vivid awareness of God that accompanied Robert's "second blessing" created a problem for Hannah as did frequent similar experiences for many others who sought the "higher Christian life." Even after she too believed that God had sanctified her wholly, she struggled for years with the feeling that, in spite of her assurance that God had given her a pure heart and daily victory over sin, the experience had never brought to her the accompanying "manifested presence" or "demonstrated signs" of the spirit which Robert and many others testified to.

Her subsequent long search for a Baptism in the Spirit, as a distinct experience separate from the blessing of entire sanctification that she already enjoyed, led her and many others to seek a Baptism of the Holy Ghost as a third distinct crisis in Christian experience. She always had to test out to the utmost limits what the Bible taught. After years of seeking such an experience of more direct spiritual manifestations, she decided it was not for her. She believed that the full faith in God and his Word that she enjoyed, witnessed to by the assurance and fruits of the Spirit, was the highest knowledge of God that humankind could enjoy in this world. Further and seemingly more immediate experiences of the Spirit that anyone experienced must remain secondary to that or they were often prone to lead to all kinds of fanaticisms.

37. Cleansing

My prayer to have the hidden depth of my inward depravity revealed to me is being answered in a most humiliating way. I find myself actually full of sin, and utterly unable to get rid of a particle of it. I seem to be far off from God, and while longing to get nearer, still not really caring enough to make the necessary effort. In short I am just what Paul describes in Romans 7. When I would do good, evil is present with me; and the evil that I would not, that I do. I sorely need a deeper work of grace.

It is not knowledge that I am lacking, but inward power, and I have to believe that there is a work of cleansing or sanctification which is mine because of the death of Jesus, but which I have never yet experienced. It cannot be that Christ died only to purchase ultimate salvation for me, but to leave me during this life in a state of such bondage to sin. Surely when God tells me that Christ came to destroy the body of sin, that henceforth we might not serve sin, it meant something! Oh that I could but have it accomplished in me!

—Journal, June 29, 1866

38. Not By Works

And now, dear Carrie, for that subject that you wanted me to write to you about. There are not many direct texts upon it, but enough to establish the point fully, and a great deal of inferential teaching. First of all, why would there be any need of a new nature if the old one was able to please God? The very fact therefore of the new birth proves that the old birth had, as far as God is concerned, turned out a failure.

And now let us look at what is said of this old birth, or old nature. In the first place we are told that the natural man (that is the unconverted man) cannot even receive much less do the things of God's spirit for they are foolishness unto him. 1 Cor. 2:14. Again all the wisdom of the natural man cannot teach him anything about God. 1 Cor. 1:21. If then the natural man can neither know God by his own wisdom, nor can receive the teaching of God's spirit concerning Him, how can he possibly please Him? And the Scriptures declare that he cannot; they say "The carnal mind" (that is the mind that belongs to the unconverted man) is enmity against God for it is not subject to the law of God, neither indeed can be. "So then they that are in the flesh cannot please God." Rom. 8:7, 8. Words could not be fuller nor stronger than these. Still further we have the absolute declarations "Without faith it is impossible to please Him," Heb. 9:6, and "Whatsoever is not of faith is sin," Rom. 14:23.

Again also "unto them that are defiled and unbelieving is nothing pure; but even their mind and conscience is defiled." And how well the next verse describes the state of the "Christian man" as he is called who is unconverted. "They profess that they know God; but in works they deny Him, being abominable and disobedient and reprobate unto every good work," or, as the margin has it, "void of judgment." Titus 1:15, 16. Look also at the description given in Rom. 3:10–19 of God's opinion of the unconverted :"There is none righteous, no not one: there is none that understandeth, there is none that seeketh after God; they are all gone out of the way, they are together become unprofitable [sic]; there is none that doeth good, no not one," etc. Again in Prov. 21:27 we are told that "the sacrifice of the wicked (that is his religious service) is abomination" and in Prov. 15:8, 9 "The sacrifice of the wicked is an abomination to the Lord" and "The way of the wicked is an abomination unto the Lord" and "The thoughts of the wicked are an abomination unto the Lord" and "The ploughing of the wicked is sin" Prov. 21:4 and "He that turneth away his ear from hearing the law, even his prayer shall be abomination." Prov. 28:9.

In these passages we have the sacrifice, the way, the thought, the ploughing, and the prayer of the wicked man, that is of course the unconverted man, pronounced to be abomination unto the Lord. And to sum up all, our Lord Himself says to the Pharisees, that is the religious unconverted men of His day, "Ye are they which justify yourselves before men; but God knoweth your hearts, for that which is highly esteemed among men (their religious and moral life & profession doubtless) is an abomination in the sight of God." Luke 16:15.

I do not know that I can add any thing to these texts; no words could be stronger nor meaning plainer it seems to me. And it is indeed a very solemn thought for every unconverted soul to know that all their best deeds can ever amount to is "abomination in the sight of God!"

—To Carrie, Atlantic City, August 4, 1866

39. Christ Our Holiness

The Lord has been teaching me in many ways lately about my utter weakness in the presence of temptation. I have grown significantly in knowledge, but I have not grown in grace and feel that I actually don't have any more power over sin than when I was first converted. This hasn't made me to doubt that I am a child of God, justified and forgiven and a possessor of eternal life and an heir of a heavenly inheritance, but even while I have this assurance and never lose it, I have found that when my heart condemns me I cannot be happy. And lately I have been led to long for more holiness, for more power over sin, for more uninterrupted communion with God.

But how to get at it I could not tell. Resolutions have proved utterly useless. My own efforts have been worse than useless. My prayers have been in vain, and I have been ready to give up in despair and to conclude that it was not the will of God that I ever should have a complete victory over sin. And yet the Bible presents such a different picture of the Christian life— blameless—harmless—without rebuke—without reproof—with every temptation a way of escape—purified—conformed to the image of Christ—holy as He is holy!

There are some Christians who say that by receiving Christ by faith for our sanctification, just as we received Him by faith for our justification all this work is accomplished—that is, the way of accomplishing it is discovered. The soul sees that Jesus delivered from the power of sin as well as from its guilt, and learns to trust to Him this whole work of keeping from evil, and delivering from the power of temptation. We cease making resolutions or relying on our own efforts after holiness in the slightest degree and we give ourselves up unreservedly to Christ to be dealt with according to His will, believing that He is able and willing to keep us from falling.

And He will do it. Like a weak and helpless child we fall back exhausted into His arms and leave all our work and all our cares in His hands. Those who experience this say further that He really does cleanse their hearts from inbred sin, or at least that a work of grace is accomplished in their souls to such a degree that their Christian life thereafter is a triumphant and exalted one.

—Journal, October 18, 1866

40. Sanctification, the Will of God

I realize that Christ dwells in my heart by faith and that He is able and willing to subdue all things to Himself. And with a deep feeling of my own utter weakness and powerlessness to help myself, I give myself into His hands to be dealt with according to His will. If I am to be sanctified, if I am to be preserved blameless and harmless, it must be by the power of God for my own efforts have utterly failed. I believe that it is God's will that I should be sanctified in that way, and I know He never will cast out any who come to Him. Therefore I believe that He receives me, and that He is working in me now to will and to do of His good pleasure. I believe this simply because of His promises to do just what I am asking Him to do for me, and I know His promises never fail.

As for feeling, I don't have any. I see no signs of any work of God being wrought in me, but oh, I pray that I will not seek after a sign, but will simply take God at His word and will believe that He is doing what He has promised. Here I will wait and rest.

—Journal, October 22, 1866

41. A New Song

Moment by moment He keeps me trusting Him committing myself and all my cares, all my trials and especially my temptations to Him. And I find to my amazement and inexpressible joy that He does deliver me, that He does accept the trust I place in Him and does keep me continually. My heart burns to testify of this wonderful Saviour everywhere. Oh, why don't all Christians know about His willingness to save them to the very uttermost? And, why do they not trust Him? "Oh sing unto the Lord a new song, for He hath done wondrous things. His right hand & His holy arm hath gotten Him the victory!"

As Mary my sister often said, "I was nothing before, but I never knew it like I do now." Nor did I ever dream Christ would be so entirely my all and all. No one ever told me. I suppose no one could, for I feel as if my heart will burst from my inability to express the half of His wondrous goodness.

—To Sally, 1866

42. Power and Purity

It is very evident that the disciples had the Holy Spirit living in them long before they received that wonderful baptism on the day of Pentecost. And the question has come to me as to whether it isn't the privilege of Christians to receive the same Baptism now? The disciples were not endued with power until that was received, and in every instance where we read of any of the early Christians being baptized like that it is always connected with a record of increased power on their part—power for testimony and power over sin.

There is nothing in the Bible which suggests that this gift should cease, and yet as far as my experience goes it has ceased. But might this not be because we do not expect it or seek after it—because the church is not taught that it is her privilege and birthright? And isn't the lack of it the cause of the deadness and coldness in the children of God?

It seems to me that the early Friends must have known and experienced it, and that this accounts for their wonderful success. And isn't it the solution for all my difficulties and questions concerning the guidance of the Holy Spirit? At all events God cannot be displeased with me if I ask Him for it, and I believe this to be the very blessing of which the Methodists testify, calling it "entire sanctification," or "perfect love."

I feel my own ignorance and utter helplessness and inward depravity of heart far more than I ever did, and this leads me, even forces me, to throw myself headlong into the arms of Christ for Him to take me in hand and to create in me just the work that He sees I need. And here I have to wait; I cannot command the Baptism of the Holy Ghost—I cannot tell when He will be pleased to make my heart ready for it. But I believe He will do it and is doing it, and I abandon myself to Him.

Oh may He keep me in this abandonment! May He discover to me all the hidden depths of inward depravity that need His purging work and may He enable me to give my whole self unreservedly up into His hands!
—Journal, October 29, 1866

43. The Power of Confession

And now about Sally. I am convinced that she entered into this way of holiness seven years ago, but, because she didn't clearly understand what it was she had experienced, and didn't know it was different from the experience of others, she failed to continue to realize its blessings. All she has to do now is, not seek to experience anything new, or to enter into any new way, but simply to return to the old thing. She knows all about this life of faith moment by moment in Jesus. But she acknowledges having failed sadly in living it.

I am sure of one thing; she is suffering because she didn't confess it. Confession, it seems to me, is one of God's ways of strengthening us in our faith. In this, it is just like it is in justification: if we do not confess it, the sense of it becomes weakened in our own minds.

Let me testify of the real and actual deliverance I find daily and hourly in Jesus. My first impulse, of course, when temptation comes, is to turn at once to my old legalistic way of resisting it, but remembering that this is not the way to do it, I look to Jesus and commit the whole matter entirely into His hands, trusting Him to take all the care of it and turning my own thoughts away to something else. The result is a victory; but often brought about so quietly, that I can hardly believe there ever was any temptation at all. At other times I have to keep on committing it continually for a long time, and the temptation to resort to legalism is very strong; but in this case I also commit it to Jesus continually, and so far He has given me perfect victory. I am overwhelmed with astonishment at the results of trusting Jesus, and yet I shouldn't be, for I know He can not fail.

—To Mary, 1866/67

44. Buried with Christ

My sister has had a glorious experience during her recent illness. She has entered into this life of abiding in Jesus, and is finding that it is a blessed life. She says she has been baptized with the Holy Ghost—that she feels that she never before has known what it is to be buried with Christ and risen with Him to newness of life. She is just overflowing.

Yesterday I had a similar letter from Abby Folwell who has also entered upon the way of holiness. She says that always before this Jesus has been in Heaven and she on earth, and faith has built a bridge between her soul and Him. But now, He is with her, is dwelling in her and it is no more she that lives but Christ that lives in her.

And I, too, know what it is to abide in Christ and to have Him abiding in me! I never did before. I never dreamed there was such a life to be lived before. One with Jesus! Oh how perfectly wonderful it is! All His wisdom and His righteousness and His sanctification are mine now, just as before His redemption was. I have had no wonderful manifestations, such as others seem to have had, but I have Jesus! He is my all and in all, and I am satisfied that He lives in my very soul. I could write all day of Him, of His love, His mercy, His grace, His power. I trust Him & He does save me.

—To Sally, 1866

45. Christ Our Righteousness

This morning, in our family reading, we read the eighth chapter of Romans. It was so impressive that we were all struck by it in a way we had never been before. It seemed such a wonderful and precious combination in sequence with the seventh chapter. The Apostle describes the wearying and unsuccessful conflict with sin which so many of us have realized, showing how impossible it is for an individual, even the Christian individual, to obey God's law or attain to righteousness. But the chapter ends by declaring that in Christ we can find deliverance from this bondage to sin.

But then, in chapter eight, he enlarges upon this deliverance and triumphantly sets forth the blessed and glorious privileges stored up for us in Christ and the fullness of the deliverance purchased by His death. That not only did His death deliver us from the penalty of sin, but it also delivered us from sin itself, so that the righteousness of the law can be fulfilled in us who walk not after the flesh but after the Spirit.

It is unspeakably blessed to know that holiness is our privilege and is made possible for us by the death of our dear Redeemer, and that it is by faith we are to have access to it. Surely in view of this, we can really say, "We are more than conquerors through Him that loved us!"

—To an unknown correspondent, 1866

46. Rest in Christ

Richard [her son's tutor], I think, has been delivered from his Unitarian tendencies entirely by having realized the life of faith this summer at the Vineland Camp Meeting. He is greatly changed, and is really lovely. Oh! what a wonderful and what a perfect Saviour we have, who can so enter into our souls and take possession of them and really work in us to will and to do His own good pleasure! Making each of us, in spite of our utter unworthiness, vessels meet for the Master's use! Therefore, when I look at myself, knowing my own utter nothingness, I can give God thanks that His strength is made perfect in my weakness. Isn't it wonderful that we have such a Saviour? And isn't it far more wonderful that, knowing what we do of Him, we still are always afraid to trust Him to the uttermost and, therefore, stop short of perfect rest in Him because of our unbelief?

What a lesson as Hebrews 3 and 4 teach us of the sorry consequences of unbelief, and yet how often we lightly use the words "only unbelief" as though we might at our option credit or reject the word of the unchangeable God! I confess that I stand confounded before the discovery of the latent unbelief of my own heart. God's promises and His declarations are so wonderful, so amazing, that it seems as if I can not grasp them. And so, I continually come short of the glory of God. I do not mean of course with regard to salvation but with regard to the rest of faith, the abiding in Christ, and our absolute oneness with Him. "He that hath entered into rest hath ceased from his own works as God did from His." Oh, to know this as an actual and constantly realized experience! I thank God that I do know something of it, but my soul is thirsty for more and more of the fullness of rest!

Do read the 18th Psalm in connection with Hebrews 3 and 4 and tell me if it does not seem to you to mean the rest of faith, now in this present life?
—To Sister, 1867

47. The Simplicity of Faith

Your letter stirs me up to realize more and more of my privileges, and to enter more deeply into the spiritual life. I am so glad you are making spiritual progress and that the simplicity of the life of faith is opening out before you. Sometimes it seems to me that it is all so simple that there is nothing to be said about it, but that it is just to be lived, and that is it. Isn't it really wonderful that such a life is possible? That we all can enjoy rest and peace and child-like freedom from care with no responsibilities, no anxieties, no fears, no regrets—nothing to do but to trust and to obey! Let's pray for each other and stir each other up more and more to enter into this experience.

That is a great thought, "Even Christ pleased not Himself." How often I have read it, and yet it seems to me that I never saw it before! It has gotten hold of my heart, and I hope it will be blessed to me. But oh how deep it will probe, if I allow it to have its full effect!

I wish you would often write and tell me your thoughts about things. I have enjoyed so deeply some things you have sent me. That about darling Nellie, and giving her up as an Alabaster Box, has fed my soul and several thoughts, that I have not time to speak of. And after all, among all my religious friends, I have so little real communion. I must thank you again for the text "Even Christ pleased not Himself." How often I have read it, and yet it seems to me that I never saw it before!

—To Mary, June/July 1867

48. Deliverance in Jesus

There is a deliverance! Paul knew it, and answered—"I thank God, through Jesus Christ our Lord!" George Fox knew it, and said—"I clearly saw that all was done and to be done in and by Christ; and that He conquers and destroys this tempter the devil, and all his works, and is atop of him. My living faith was raised that I saw all was done by Christ the Life, and my belief was in Him." Thousands of Christians in all ages have known it, and have rejoiced to testify of its wondrous blessedness. For this deliverance is in Jesus.

His death purchased for us not only the forgiveness of our sins, but also victory over them, not only freedom from their guilt, but freedom from their power as well. And faith in Him will bring us much beside salvation from eternal condemnation. It is because we try to live our lives apart from Him that we fail so in the living. We realize that He gives us life in the first place, but we do not see that He also must live it for us. We trust Him for the forgiveness of our sins, but we trust ourselves for the daily conquering of them. It is true we pray for divine aid, and for the influences of the Holy Spirit, but still our thought is that they are to be given to us, and we are to fight and to conquer. This is the secret of our failures. For the truth is we are as completely helpless in the matter of sanctification as in the matter of justification. We are as thoroughly dependent upon Christ for the control of an irritable temper as for the pardon of all our sins. Christ must be all in all to us every moment. "Without me," He says, "ye can do nothing." This is the secret of peace and victory.

—Journal, from the first article she ever published in the *Friends Review*

49. The Secret at Last: Abandoned to Christ

"The just shall live by faith." We not only receive life by faith, but, in just the same way, we must live life by faith. We must cease from our own works in this matter of living, just as we did in the matter of getting life. Christ must be the one who does it all. He must work in us to will and to do of His good pleasure. It must be no longer we who live, but Christ who liveth in us. And what words can express the possibilities of a life where His abiding is known and realized? Surely here is the secret for which our souls have been seeking so long in vain. For if we are dead, and Christ alone is our life, then His wisdom, His power, and His righteousness are all ours, and we cannot possibly lack any good thing. If we will stop frustrating the grace of God by our strivings; if we will come to the end of self and all self's efforts immediately; if we will acknowledge our utter helplessness and will commit everything to the Lord Jesus Christ; if we will trust Him to fight our battles for us; if we will, in short, reckon ourselves to be dead, and take Him as our life,—then the work is done. He never refuses to take possession of the soul that truly abandons itself to Him. Let us then no longer hold on to our possession of ourselves; but abandoning ourselves, and confessing our utter and absolute helplessness and nothingness, let us commit the daily and hourly, and even the momentary keeping of our souls to Jesus. Let us come to Him saying: "Lord Jesus, I commit myself to you. I cannot help myself. I cannot save myself from sinning, nor make myself holy, but you can, and you will! I cast all the burden of it on you." We shall find that He will not fail us. I am happy in Jesus; my soul is filled with a quiet calm and peaceful rest that cannot be described. I find that He is a perfect, present Saviour. I have had no overwhelming revelations, but my soul is being filled drop by drop with Jesus, and I have even felt sometimes as if I would like to shout so that all the world could hear me, "Praise the Lord!"

—Journal, *Friends Review*, 1867

50. Willing to Be Made Holy

The whole thing seems so simple to me now, that I am perfectly astounded at my old darkness and am overwhelmed with astonishment that every Christian does not know all about it. It is just trusting Jesus that is all that can be said about it. It is to consecrate—a "willingness to be made holy." That is what is really meant, because to be willing to give up sin is after all the only dedication we can possibly make, and even that willingness must be the work of Jesus and we must trust Him for it, just as much as for anything else. The only necessary steps are, first, being brought to see our own utter inability to help ourselves in the slightest degree, even to dedicate ourselves, and second, being enabled to exercise faith in Christ to do the whole work for us. They are just the same steps as are necessary in justification, the only difference being that in the one case it is for the forgiveness of sins, and in the other for victory over sin.

—Journal, *Friends Review*, 1867

51. Implicit Faith

The whole matter lies in this—trusting Jesus to do for us what we cannot do for ourselves. It is taking Him to be our daily, hourly, momentary Saviour from the power of sin, just exactly as we took Him to be our Saviour from its guilt. We have actually no more to do in the one case than in the other. He assumes all the responsibility and accomplishes all the work. Our only part is to commit ourselves to Him, and trust Him with implicit faith. All you can do is to commit yourself to Him this very moment to begin the work from now and carry it on in His own way. Just say to Him continually, "I trust you, I trust you." And you will find that your faith will grow wonderfully. Try the plan of handing over your temptations to Him to conquer, and you will be astonished at its success. In short, trust Him with your whole self, with all your life—every moment of it, with everything you are, or have, or do. Let Him, in short, be your life. It is a great trust, but He is worthy of it. He cannot possibly fail you in the least particular. He is infinitely trustworthy. No human words can set forth His worthiness to be trusted to the uttermost. It seems to me I never really trusted Him before, and it makes my heart ache to think of the long years in which I have dishonored Him so much, when He was so worthy to be trusted!

—To her cousin Carrie, February 26, 1867

52. The Answer to "Frustration"

The Methodists find themselves brought to a point where they are willing to give up every thing to Jesus and since its result is in reality dedication, they call the steps by which they arrive at it dedication. Then again, afterwards, they feel pure, they feel sanctified and they say so. I feel the same way, and the soul where Christ reigns cannot help feeling that way. The Epistle to the Galatians was written just to meet the legalistic life of Christians. It was written to believers, who were already forgiven and who evidently knew it, but who had gone back to observe the law for the purpose of working out their daily life of righteousness. And so they "frustrated," as Christians, the grace of God; for "if righteousness comes by the law, then Christ, as far as righteousness is concerned, is dead in vain." Christ really does become of no effect to any Christian who walks legally in the least way; that is, He is of no use to them in their daily life, but is merely reserved for the final victory. We have all been Galatian Christians, but I thank God now I can say "I don't frustrate the grace of God!" Can't we stop frustrating that grace by such legality from now on? Let's give up every effort, every thought even, of doing anything ourselves and commit it all to Jesus. Can't you trust Him? Isn't He worthy of trust?

—To her cousin Carrie, February 26, 1867

53. Jesus, Not Experience

I have found in Jesus an answer to all my questions, to all my longings, to all my needs! He is made of God unto me, even me—wisdom and right-eousness, and sanctification and redemption. Having Jesus I have all things, and by faith He is mine, and I am His, His only and His altogether. I find that I have been looking for an experience, instead of Jesus. My soul has been drawn out after the gifts of my Beloved, instead of after my Beloved Himself. But I trusted Him to teach me, and He has taught me that He himself is enough to satisfy my utmost need, and my soul rests in Him. Oh what a rest it is! Not only a rest of peace, but a rest of triumph also for "He always causeth me to triumph," and through Him I can do all things. Just this morning He has gained a victory for me that is wonderful. How can I praise Him enough? What a wonderful promise and what a full answer are contained in Matt. 5:6 and John 6:3: "Blessed are they which do hunger and thirst after righteousness: for they shall be filled." And the fulfilment of this: "And Jesus said unto them, I am the bread of life; he that cometh to me shall never hunger, and he that believeth on me shall never thirst." All our longings, all our hunger, all our thirst filled in Jesus!

—Journal, February 24, 1867

54. The Secret of the Christian Life

My soul continues to be satisfied in Jesus! Every day and hour of my life since I entered upon this way of faith in Him has only proved that He is more and more worthy of my complete confidence. He never fails me—never! I commit myself to His keeping continually and He keeps me, so that I can say from the bottom of my heart, "Thanks be unto God, who always causes us to triumph through Christ." Oh why did I never know this secret of the Christian life before? Why has my life been such a halting miserable one, when I might have lived in victory? What a striking proof I have been of the inherent legalism and unbelief of the human heart. For while I was trusting Christ alone for my justification, I have always been trusting myself for my sanctification. Of course I have prayed for help and for the influences of the Holy Spirit, but I always thought that they were to be given to me and then I was to resist my own enemies and fight my own battles. And consequently I depended upon my own efforts, my own resolutions, my own watchfulness, my own fervency, my own strivings to accomplish the work of holy living. This was legalism; as if I had trusted to these things to help save my soul in the first place. I was "frustrating" the grace of God as really in regard to my sanctification, just like those whom I have been used to condemning so strongly as "legalists" who were doing the same in regard to their justification.

55. Freedom from the Power and Guilt of Sin

I could easily see how they made the cross of Christ of no effect by their legalistic strivings, but I was blind to the truth that I also was doing the same thing they were. My striving to be sure was with a different end in view, but it was still, in both cases, striving; in both, it was self and not Christ. "For if righteousness came by the law then Christ is dead in vain." To me in those days His death, in regard to my practical sanctification, was literally in vain. But now, oh how different it is! Now I commit my daily life to Him as well as the saving of my soul, and I trust Him just as nakedly for the one as the other. I am equally powerless in both cases. I can do nothing—not even "I the new man," and if Christ does not do it all, it will not be done. But oh glorious truth, He does do it! His death purchased deliverance for me both from the power as well as from the guilt of sin. It made Him not only the One who gives me life, but the one who lives it too. It made me one with Him, so truly one, that it is no more I who live but Christ who lives in me.

56. One with Christ

All I can do therefore is to "abide in Him," and He does all the rest. And this satisfies me in my very soul. I am filled with Jesus and therefore I am filled with righteousness! I no longer frustrate the grace of God. I only desire that grace may have free course in me and be hindered by no legalism. I can leave all in His care!! And doing this, I have no anxieties. My cares, my temptations, my growth, my service, my daily life moment by moment I commit to Him, and He accepts the trust. Oh the rest and calm of a life like this! One with Christ—abiding in Him—what more can the soul desire?

Great joy and manifest and outpoured blessings would be precious it is true, but Jesus is enough without these, and I know He will give me just what He sees best. I only want to be like clay in His hands, to be used by Him or laid aside, just as He pleases. How can I have any will but His whole desire for me? He is such a glorious Saviour! How marvelously He has been working in me to will and to do of His good pleasure. When I look back at my experience and at all the darkness of my former life, I am lost in wonder at His marvelous working.

—Journal, March 12, 1867

57. Christ Our Life　　א٦

The work of the Holy Spirit is always to take of the things of Christ and show them unto us and not to reveal Himself. To me it is a real personal, living Jesus, who dwells within me and who is my life and not any vague idea of the Spirit. I am going to look up all the texts where the Spirit's work is spoken of and see whether they do not teach this. Another thought I would suggest to you, "Is our new nature anything more than Christ in us? Is He not our life, and our only life?" "He that hath the Son hath life, and he that hath not the Son hath not life." "God hath given to us eternal life." And this life is where? "In His Son." If this is true, how completely it settles all questions about our own abilities. If Jesus is our life, of course our only work must be to keep from living our own life and let His life work in us. It seems to me it is the triumph of faith to be able to reckon ourselves dead and alive only in Christ. But oh, when faith is enabled to take this leap, how glorious it is!

—To sister Mary, 1867

58. The Secret of Redeeming Love　　ל٧

Your letter filled me with thanksgiving and praise. How good, oh how good the Lord is! Your experience has indeed been a wonderful and a glorious one. And from all I can judge, you have received a manifested blessing which has not been bestowed upon me. But for all that, our experience is essentially the same; we have realized ourselves to be nothing, and Jesus to be all! With me it is more the calm resting in Him, than any ecstacies of joy, or any very great outpouring of the Holy Spirit. I have learned a secret of redeeming love that I never dreamed of before the wonderful glorious truth that Christ dwells in me, and is my life! That He it is who must will and do AND be everything in me; that I am dead, and that the only life I have now is His life. I know and realize the truth that "I bear about in my body the dying of the Lord Jesus, that the life also of Jesus might be made manifest in my body." He is my life! No words can express it more fully than this; and all His wisdom, and mine necessarily because of this. Therefore it is a perfect rest of faith. Nothing is wanting to me. I have Jesus, and having Him I have all things. I am content with just what He bestows. I am filled with righteousness, because I am filled with Him. And since all my ways are committed to Him, I have no cares, and no anxieties. My feet are truly set in a large place, and the yoke of bondage is broken.

—To Mary, March 8, 1867

59. Jesus, Simply Jesus   F 29

The future is in His care. I know that while I trust Him, He will never never fail me. It does not seem to me, however, that I have experienced so powerful a baptism of the Holy Ghost as you have, dear sister. But it is a subject which I am continually committing to the Lord Jesus. It is His gift and I know He will give me whatever He sees will be best for me. I confess I would love to be overpowered with such a baptism as yours; but not feeling sure that it is His will to baptize all so manifestly, I cannot exercise faith for it. I can only pray, and commit it all to Him. You know this subject of the baptism of the Holy Ghost has been much on my mind for a long time, and it may be I was putting it between my soul and Jesus, as an experience necessary before I could trust Him. And that therefore He is teaching me to be satisfied with Himself only, before He will bestow any of His gifts upon me. At one of the meetings on the subject of holiness Alfred Cookman said "Are there not some of you who have set up a desired experience between yourselves and Jesus, and are looking at it rather than at Him? You want a great shower, when perhaps it is His purpose to fill you drop by drop! You must lay down this strong will, this desire for the experience of a great blessing, and be content with Jesus, simply Jesus!" And this seems to me to contain my experience. I was determined to have a great outpouring but I am satisfied now with Jesus! And He helps me to exercise faith in regard to the guidance of the Holy Spirit.

—To Mary, March 8, 1867

60. Centered in Him   Mar 1

Still, I think there may be a fullness of blessing like this yet in store for me and I am waiting upon the Lord for it. Isn't there a special baptism for service, whereby one is endued with power from on high, which is given only to those whom God purposes to use more especially in His service? Or is it the privilege of all Christians? I feel so ignorant! But then Christ's Wisdom is all mine, and He will teach me what He wants me to know. Join your prayers with mine that nothing in me may hinder the full bestowal of every gift Jesus has in store for me. It is true, as you say, I never felt myself dead with Christ and risen with Him before. Intellectually I knew it was so, because the Bible says so, but as a living reality I never realized it before. In fact, dear sister, I knew nothing of my oneness with Him before, except judicially. I was trying to live my Christian life apart from Him, and no wonder I could not do anything. I thought "Without me ye can do nothing" meant merely "without my help." But now I see that all I have is centered in Him, and that I have nothing in any other way. Outside of Jesus I am nowhere and nothing. I am dead. "Nevertheless I live, yet not I but Christ liveth in me!" But words seem to fail before a reality so glorious! The more I say the more it seems I leave unsaid!

—To Mary, March 8, 1867

61. The Secret of Victory

Temptations have come in like a flood and the battle, as Anna Shipley says, has been fought in my presence, requiring me to be continually and moment by moment committing it to Jesus. But this means I am being taught to trust Him in a way that I could not do if I had no temptations, or if they were all removed at once from my sight, as is sometimes the case. And in the end Jesus does deliver! I have proved this beyond a shadow of doubt, and my faith in Him grows stronger and stronger. Do not be troubled then at any revelation of your own weakness, even though it may betray you momentarily to sin. We are but beginners as yet in this way of holiness and need much teaching. But we are in, thank God, and have learned the secret of victory, and what is to keep us from really walking worthy of the Lord with all pleasing? Do dwell on that text "He that abideth in me and I in him, the same bringeth forth much fruit." You are too sick now to do anything but abide, and it seems to me this might comfort you so much that in doing so, you will bring forth fruit. Not perhaps the sort of fruit that would please or satisfy your ambition, but the sort without a doubt that will satisfy Jesus, and His smile of approval is better than anything else.

—To Mary, Millville, N.J., March 8, 1867

62. No Independent Holiness

It seems to me life is far easier to live, and death far less to be longed for, now that we know the secret of abiding in Christ. With Him, we can be satisfied anywhere! Before, we have always rested on Him as it were, on His word, on His promises, on His faithfulness; but now we know what it is to be in Him and to realize Him abiding in us. We feel our oneness now, and it is so different! All we need now is to be utterly lost and swallowed up in Him to cease altogether from our own workings, and to abandon ourselves more and more to Him to work in us all the good pleasure of His will! I have not yet taken hold of Christ as a Power to overcome all sin. In the first place, I do not know yet how much I need Him for. Every day I get some fresh revelation of my weakness and I have to go to Him for some fresh need. Then, I often forget to trust Him and need to commit myself for this, as well as for all else. But this I have realized, that whenever I do trust Him, He does deliver, and now that I know the way and have entered upon it, I feel that there is no limit to the possibilities of holiness that are opened before me. What we have experienced, however, is not a gift of independent holiness which we can keep or lose. It is only that we have entered into the way of holiness. It is a way out of which we may step any minute, but into which we may step back as quickly. It is a way in which the exhortation to watch and pray is absolutely essential, a way calling for an absolute abandonment of one's self in every moment. Yet a way in which all this is possible, because it is a way in which Christ is our life in which we are dead, and He alone works our works in us. It is, in short, the way of "oneness" with Him. The Bible is full of expressions that describe it; so full, in fact, that it does not seem as if any other experience was supposed possible for the Christian.

—To Alice, March 14, 1867

63. Distinctive Commitment

We know, unfortunately, from sad experience, that there is another sort of life which many Christians can and do live, and that, in their cases, it is absolutely essential that they should distinctly step out of the one way into the other if they are ever to come up to a Scriptural standard at all. I say distinctly because I believe many Christians get a glimmering of the truth and mix the two ways, the way of works and the way of faith, because they lack clear understanding of the subject. And the result there cannot be any great degree of victory. The two ways are just as incompatible as it would be for a person to try sometimes to be saved by works and sometimes by Christ; and we can see plainly what a sad mixture that would be, and how utterly impossible it would be for such a person to attain any settled peace, or to teach others the way of life. Because of sometimes trying one way and sometimes the other way they suffer great loss both in power and in enjoyment. They are utterly unable to teach the way of abiding faith intelligently or distinctively. I want us all therefore to be very clear in our experience and to see plainly the contrast between our present and past way of living that we may not through ignorance fall back again into the old way, and that we may have the power to teach others concerning it. For this reason I think it is a great blessing that the Methodists make it a distinct experience, for among them a person cannot keep from knowing about it at least. I wish I could show the utter simplicity of this way of faith. It is just to trust Jesus, nothing more; and yet I know how mysterious and unattainable it seems beforehand.

—To Alice, March 14, 1867

64. Inexpressible Rest

The parallel is exactly the same as that between the way of justification and the way of sanctification. In both cases it is just a blind trust in Christ to do the thing we need. With this difference, that justification is an accomplished thing, and sanctification is a thing continually being accomplished, requiring therefore a continual exercise of present faith. There is no other difference, I think. In both cases we have to come to the end of self, and in both cases it is hard to believe that Christ will do the whole work for us. But in both there is no other way but absolute and unlimited confidence in Him, a casting ourselves upon Him as it were in naked faith and leaving ourselves utterly in His hands. But oh it is worth all the previous wandering, to know the unutterable preciousness of rest in Jesus! It seems as if I wanted to sound His Name over and over everywhere. Nothing is to be compared with Him, just Himself! Even the idea of glorifying Him is lost sight of beside Himself. And we have such a promise in John 15:5: "He that abideth in me and I in him, the same bringeth forth much fruit." If we only continue to abide, we may be sure of bringing forth much fruit without any effort of our own! I think this gives us a rest which words cannot express!

—To Alice, March 14, 1867

65. Baptism in the Spirit

Your letter has helped me to realize that what I have experienced has been truly the baptism of the Holy Spirit, although not with such manifest distinctness as in your case. But, however we may express it, the experience and its results are essentially the same with everyone. I feel, for instance, that although my experience was so very quiet, it must have been a real baptism of the Holy Spirit, because I find in myself the results which follow that. As you say, this very revelation of Christ as dwelling in me, which fills my soul with such joy, could have been given to me in no other way than by the Holy Ghost. And this renewal of all my spiritual activities and this burning desire to proclaim the blessed truth of a full salvation in Jesus and this concern for the souls of others—from where could they come but from the Holy Spirit? Baptized souls long to confess Christ. They welcome the chance to open their mouths to speak for Jesus. My sorrow is that I have so few opportunities. But then I have found a most precious promise in John 15:5: "He that abideth in me, and I in him, the same bringeth forth much fruit." I don't have to trouble myself about fruitbearing, for while I abide in Him, He will take care of this just like He does everything else. And I know very well that I will need a great deal of training in the school of Christ before I become a servant fit to do his work. I feel satisfied, therefore, that I have been baptized with the Holy Ghost, and need nothing now but obedience and faithfulness to His guidance.

—To her sister Mary, March 16, 1867

66. One with Christ

I wanted very much to tell you more about the new and blessed truth I have learned lately respecting the real and living oneness of the believer with Christ and the power over sin that the realization of this gives to us. It is a genuine Quaker experience I am sure, that is, it was a truth which the early Friends, and especially George Fox, rejoiced in; and it was the secret of all their lives of devotedness and power. I have always of course known intellectually that I was, in a sort of judicial way, one with Christ, because the Bible says so, but now it is a reality to me, and oh so glorious! It seems to me that this is the secret of holiness, for which I have searched so long in vain. To know that Christ is living in me and working in me to will and to do His good pleasure, certainly has to be in the way of holiness, and the progress in it may be infinite! How precious is that text, John 15:5, "He that abideth in me and I in him, the same bringeth forth much fruit." If we only are abiding in Him, we need have no responsibility about anything else for He will do all the rest. It is this which I have discovered lately, that Jesus is just as much my Saviour from the daily power of sin, as He was long ago from its guilt. I never knew that He would do so much for me as this that He would fight my battles and conquer my enemies, that He would live my life for me in short, and that my only part was to abandon myself to Him, to abide in Him and to leave all the rest in His hands. Oh what a rest of faith this is!

—To Mother, March 18, 1867

67. Christ the Deliverer

It is an experiential truth to me that Jesus is a perfect, complete and present Saviour from continual sinning. I am happy to confess His wonderful love and marvelous grace whenever I have the chance; for surely such a sinner as I have been was never loved and saved before! And I wish that every one could know the blessed reality and practical value of the truth—that Jesus does save and does deliver, in a most marvelous way, all who simply put their trust in Him! I trust, dear friend, that it is an experiential truth to you too, now, and that the breathing of your soul is, "Thanks be unto God, who always causeth us to triumph through Jesus Christ!" If this is not the case, I want to urge you just to try this way. Take your next temptation to Jesus and give it up totally to Him to fight and to conquer for you and see if it doesn't give you marvelous triumph and victory. Our Christian warfare is definitely a fight of faith and not a fight of effort. The only thing we have to struggle for is to trust Him. "All things are possible to him that believeth" and to that individual only. And the reason for this is that we are dead, really and truly dead, and the only life we have is "Christ living in us." "He that hath the Son hath life, and he that hath not the Son hath not life." How this answers all questions about our individuality, and the independence of our will etc. As Christians, we are nothing apart from Christ; we have no more independence of being than the branch has apart from the vine, or the hand apart from the body. We are one with Christ! All those questions therefore belong to the old life, before we were crucified with Christ and had risen with Him to newness of life, even a life hid in Him. They have no significance. Real peace and triumph will never be yours until you are brought to the end of self in all of its aspects. My prayer is that Jesus may be revealed to you in all His fullness!

—To a Friend, March 27, 1867

68. Christ the Meeting Place

With regard to the work of the Holy Spirit in sanctification, my conclusions have been very much like yours; I cannot give the prominence to the thought of the indwelling Spirit. To me it is the personal presence of a real Jesus Christ living in me, and the part the Holy Spirit plays, as you say, is to reveal Him there. I believe this is always the Spirit's work, from first to last, to speak not of Himself but of Christ, to take the things of Christ and show them unto us. He is not the Light, but He opens our eyes to see the Light, just as at first He opened our eyes to see the Saviour. The central point of all revelation, the resting place of God's love, the end of our faith, the one meeting place between God and men and women is Christ! And the Holy Spirit is only the Revealer of Him. I am sure the early Friends understood this, and when they spoke of "the Seed" & "the Light" etc. they meant Christ, and that all the mistiness of their descendants on this vital point and all their wanderings into error and darkness, have arisen from their having substituted the Holy Spirit in Christ's place. The moment we let go the thought of a personal Jesus, we step into a path which may lead us into unitarian darkness which has misled thousands. But while we cling to Him, I believe it is impossible for us to go far wrong. If we are "strengthened with might by His spirit in the inner man," it is that "Christ may dwell in our hearts by faith," and that we may comprehend the heights and depths of His love. Not that we may know or realize anything special concerning the Spirit Himself. And I feel almost sure a critical examination of every passage where the Spirit's work is spoken of, would prove Him to be as a revealer of truth, or something of that kind. It is an important question to be clear about I think.

—To a Friend, March 28, 1867

69. Alive in Christ

Aren't your questions about the will questions which belong totally to the old life in the flesh? And isn't the position in which we are now, one of death to all such things and life only in Another, so that we no longer have to speak about any totally independent existence—any will of our own, or reason of our own, or any faculty, in short, except His? It seems to me it is the triumph of faith to reckon ourselves dead as to our life in the flesh and alive only as to Christ who is our new life. Therefore we can do nothing but completely ignore all those faculties of the old life which continually try to assert themselves and abandon ourselves to Him, become truly lost in the life of Christ. The question has suggested itself to me in this connection, as to whether the new nature in us is anything more than Christ in us. I have always heretofore looked upon the new nature as an independent sort of divine seed begotten in us by God; not Christ, but a separate and independent existence, joined to him in some mysterious way, but still apart from Him; and it was in the strength of this new nature that I used to seek to live. But now it seems to me that apart from the life of Christ in me I have no life, none whatever, but am literally dead, and that every energy in me which is not the energy of Christ is but the galvanic twitchings of a dead man and of not the slightest more account.

—To a Friend, March 28, 1867

70. One with Christ

Someone says, "I am lost whenever I think of Christ and myself as two," and it seems so to me now. Think over the expressions "Christ, who is our life;" "Alive in Jesus Christ;" "He that hath the Son hath life, & he that hath not the Son hath not life"; and many other like them, and tell me if you don't think they teach a most marvelous and glorious reality? Our only life is Christ, and in Him "dwelleth all the fullness of the Godhead bodily!" It almost takes my breath away to think of anything so glorious! Surely this will answer every question about our individuality, our independent will, our fighting etc. The grand fight of all our lives is, as you say, with Amalek and other enemies which typify the flesh. It is not the temptations of the flesh we are to resist, so much as the flesh itself, the legal element in our natures, which is continually turning us back to reliance on the flesh. Our fight is emphatically a fight of faith, not a fight of effort. It is a fight to cease from effort in fact and to suffer another life to be fully worked out in us. And I think a deeper typical meaning than has ever been discovered yet, must lie hid in Israel's old contests.

—To a Friend, March 28, 1867

71. Lost in Jesus

I am beginning to learn more and more of the depth of meaning in the teachings of Christ. I find myself, since this new life in Jesus has opened before me, turning far oftener to His own words, than I used to for revelations concerning it. I never before gathered any meaning from that passage in John 6 about eating His flesh and drinking His blood, but now it is full of precious truth. The 56th verse is the key to it: "He that eateth my flesh and drinketh my blood dwelleth in me and I in him." And again John 15:5 really sustains my soul, especially now that I seem to be cut off so much from active service, "He that abideth in me and I in him, the same bringeth forth much fruit." It seems to go down to the deepest cravings of my soul and to satisfy them fully, when I realize that if I only continue to abide in Him, I shall without fail bring forth fruit of just the kind, and just the amount that pleases Him, and it shall be "much" too. All responsibility as to service seems taken away by this thought, for the responsibility is His. You ask for beautiful thoughts, I have none to give you but Jesus. He is the sum and substance of everything—the Life, the Light, the Strength, the Joy! All I ask is to be lost in Him. It seems to me that I never knew Him before as the personal Friend. I now feel Him to be all—my cares, His; all my joys, His; all my life, His; nothing is mine apart from Him! But here words fail to express the glorious meaning of Christ in us? And I can only repeat over and over the dear name, Jesus!

—To a Friend, March 28, 1867

72. Christ Works Through Us

I do not doubt that my Lord means to teach me that He Himself is sufficient for all of my every need for support and fellowship; and I want to learn the lesson without complaining. Isn't it strange that there should be any temptation to complain? But the walk of naked faith is always, I suspect, a trying one to the natural man, although we know from the experience of so many that it is sure to end in blessedness. Just to trust Jesus simply and alone, though so simple, is so hard. I have many a fight in trying to do it. It often seems to me as if the "old man" were continually lifting itself up, and my big problem is to keep him down. While I was with my sister Sally, together we looked up the subject of Israel's conflicts and victories and found it very suggestive and instructive. In most cases we found that all Israel did was "to go through the motions," while God did the actual fighting. And we suggested that in the same way we also must "go through the motions," that is, that we must do just what we would do if the whole burden lay upon us, knowing all the while that it is only God who finally works. I mean, of course, in regard to outward action. If, for instance, we are asked to speak for the Lord, we open our mouths, and He speaks through us. Just in fact as the man with the withered hand stretched it out at the command of Jesus—"going through' the motions—" but Jesus performed the miracle.

—To a Friend, April 16, 1867

73. Going Through the Motions

How often Israel marched out in battle array, and found the Lord already fighting their enemies and putting them to flight. And what a striking instance Jericho was of this. They did nothing at all towards conquering that city, except to go through some apparently utterly useless motions, and yet it is very evident that unless they had gone "through those motions," God would not have given them the victory. Doesn't this teach us a little something of what our part in the great work is? But I feel as if I had everything to learn and could teach nothing in this new life of faith, which is so different from my old life of effort and legalism. There was a very interesting field of typical teaching opening before us in the books of Judges and Kings and Chronicles. In Judges aren't we taught the causes of our failure in this life of faith and God's remedy of constantly intervening? Then wasn't David's reign the time of conflict and Solomon's the time of rest from all enemies and of peace and enjoyment and, above all, of the fullness of love? Do look over these books with this life of faith especially in view, and tell me what impression it makes upon you.

—To a Friend, April 16, 1867

74. The Battle Is His

O for more of Christ consciously manifested to my soul! What shall I do to get this desire of my heart? It is not enough to know the secret of victory, I must also live in the momentary practice of it, and this I fail to do. It seems to me that I need a divine work of the Holy Spirit in my soul. Something is lacking somewhere; I know there is everything lacking on my part, but this I cannot remedy, and where is the failure? It is not in Christ. Perhaps I am not yet helpless enough for Him, and He is only bringing me to this. Oh Lord Jesus, reveal yourself! "Lord, you have declared that sin shall not have dominion over your people. I believe your word cannot be broken; and therefore, helpless in myself, I rely upon your faithfulness to save me from the dominion of the sins which now tempt me. Manifest your power, O Lord Christ, and get yourself glory in subduing my flesh with its affections and lusts" (Romaine). I feel more and more utterly cast on Christ and more and more bereft of anything of my own. My wants are many and they are continual, but I know that His supply is far more mighty, and it is promised to me moment by moment, and therefore I can trust all to Him. All! I leave the whole battle to Him, because I must. Wisdom, courage, armor, strength, patience and victory all to be found only in the Lord. I have nothing, literally and truly nothing. But Christ has all, just as literally and truly all and He is mine. Oh, can I doubt that every need will be fully supplied? No no a thousand times no! let me wait then patiently His own time, and commit everything to Him continually. "For they shall not be ashamed that wait for thee." Isa. 49:23. I want to know that I am one with Jesus and to know that He is dwelling in me and working in me to will and to do His good pleasure.

—Journal, April 26, 1867

75. Fashioned for His Purposes

This is just one of those things where the working of my indwelling Saviour can be made manifest in a special way, and I do commit it continually to Him. It seems to me that every day I experience more of the rest of faith. And also I realize the joy of consecration. It is most blessed to feel that your will is consciously given up and that there is actually nothing, so far as one knows, to hinder the working of God's grace. I love to feel just like a vessel of clay in His hands which He is fashioning for His own purposes. Not but what my will may rise up again soon in all its old force, but it seems to me in this life of faith we speak only of present experiences. I do long for more feeling for more of the manifested presence of my dear Lord, but I can wait on Him for this and there is a promise which says "They shall not be ashamed who wait for thee." Do write me about your Bible class, and call on me for any texts you may want. I should love to help you in that way.

That lesson from Joshua is very impressive, but we are safe are we not if we commit the discovering of this accursed thing to the Lord Jesus? The very thought of self examination seems so hopeless to me, but it is precious to have the Lord examine you.

—To Sally, April 1867

76. Prayer for the Holy Spirit

I long to be "filled with the Spirit," and it seems to me this is my privilege. Yet I feel very ignorant about it. Since I last wrote, the Lord Jesus has continued to be sufficient for all my needs, and the life of moment by moment faith in Him has only become a greater reality, and a more lasting experience. I see indeed that I have never before even dimly comprehended the truth of my oneness with Christ. I have known Him as a transitory refuge and a hiding place from overwhelming troubles, but I have never known Him as an abiding place. Oh how wonderful and precious it is! But still I am not satisfied. Perhaps it is impatience on my part, and I ought to be willing to wait and watch until His own time comes for filling me consciously with His Spirit. Yet it seems to me that there are privileges which I could enjoy if I would, and my soul longs to be more manifestly filled than it ever can be by naked faith. But I can commit my ignorance in this matter to the Lord Jesus, confident that He will make all plain to me.

—Journal, April 23, 1867

77. The Lesson of Affliction

I do not expect you feel any less lonely as the days go on, but I trust you are learning the sweet lesson which I think affliction always teaches sooner or later to the child of God, that there is a joy in offering up our sorrows freely to our Lord as an alabaster box of costly ointment, just as a proof of our unquestioning confidence in Him, and our lavish affection. At first it is hard to feel anything more than simple resignation, but after a while it is given us to go deeper than this, and to rejoice that we have had something precious to offer up at the call of our Beloved! Are you learning more and more to make Jesus the life of your life—the one and only activity of all your nature? I have been rejoicing in an old book lent me by a Greenwich Friend full of some most precious truth concerning a life hid with Christ in God. Among other things the writer says, "Christ is in the believer instead of all created habits of grace." Just ponder this thought, dear Abby.

It seems to me our idea has always been, that we formed as it were habits of grace in the course of time, which we kept as a sort of stock of grace to draw upon in time of need. But I see now that Christ is; instead of all this, He is the only stock of grace which we ever possess. If we need to exercise meekness, or wisdom or any other virtue, it is not from any habits formed by us, or store of these things laid up within, that we are to draw, but from Christ, who is our meekness and our wisdom, and all righteousness to us.

—To Abby, Millville, N.J., May 28, 1867

78. Sanctified Wholly

Whatever the work of sanctification is, it must be what is meant in 1 Thessalonians 5:23 where it says, "May the very God of peace sanctify you wholly." And it must please God in its degree and kind and must be realized to the fullest extent that His death procured for me. I trust Him. It is Him I want to please and not to carry out my own ideas of what sanctification is or ought to be. And since I can do absolutely nothing, but have to trust Christ for everything, then God must be pleased with what Christ does and there I leave it. My only care is to hang moment by moment upon my Lord; to trust Him for everything; to abandon myself continually to Him and to leave myself in His hands for Him to work in me to will and to do His good pleasure. I confess it is a great mystery that Christ can be formed in me (see Galatians 4:19), but my very ignorance concerning it is a comfort to me, for if I cannot know what it is, I certainly cannot accomplish it, and I am therefore forced to leave it to God. I am inclined to think it is in reality no change in me, but only my being "filled with the Spirit" being made "strong in the Lord and in the power of His might" being "strengthened with might by His Spirit in the inner man." In short that it is the Baptism of the Holy Ghost.

—To Sally, August 1867

79. Fill Me Now

The longing of my soul to be filled with God is not satisfied yet. I have seen and realized much of the joy and rest of a life of faith since last I wrote in this book, but I am sure there is still a greater work of grace which it is my privilege to experience by faith. I want the conscious indwelling of the Spirit. I want the manifested presence of my Jesus in my soul! I want, in short, to be filled with all the fullness of God! This is my privilege, I am not sure what is it that holds me back. Oh my God, sanctify me wholly. I don't know what this means exactly—I am ignorant of the extent to which the cleansing blood of Jesus can purify, but whatever it is, oh my Saviour, grant it to me to the very utmost limit! I lack wisdom on this subject, and I come to you in faith to teach me. Let me know your own mind fully and let nothing keep me from entering in to all the rest of faith that you have in store for me. Oh! don't let me frustrate your grace. This is my longing cry—don't let me in any way or in the slightest degree frustrate your grace. Oh Lord, fill me now! Fill me now! Shed abroad your love in my heart now! Sanctify me wholly now!

—Journal, September 3, 1867

80. After the Red Sea, Jordan

The Red Sea passage, it seems to me, simply typifies the death of Christ as it conquered Satan judicially and released the sinner from the guilt and judgment of sin. It separated the children of Israel from Egypt and introduced them into a life of pilgrimage and trial, just as we are separated from the world and made pilgrims and strangers there. But it did not lead them into the land of rest, nor put them into such a position where they could build a temple to their God. And so a Christian who has known the death of Christ only as deliverance from the guilt of sin is not introduced into the full rest that remains for the people of God, nor is such a Christian the temple of the living God in the wonderful reality and power that is meant by such passages as John 14:21, 23 etc. The passage over the Jordan, I think, typifies this last and higher aspect of the death of Christ. It introduced the Israelites into a new country and a new life and shows the believer as seated in heavenly places with Christ, as walking in "newness of life," as having not only been separated from the world but as being also introduced into a resurrection life. With regard to the Red Sea passage, we read that although every Israelite made it over Jordan, there were two half-tribes who chose to stay on the wilderness side of the river because "it was a good place for cattle." Also, the enemies destroyed in the Red Sea never returned to harass the Israelites; they never even saw them anymore; and this is true of Satan when he is viewed as having power to make us his slaves again; but it is not true of him as having power to cause us to err.

—To Anna, September 4, 1867

81. After the Wilderness—Rest

It seems to me the "Reckon ye yourselves to be dead to sin" cannot be found in the Red Sea passage but rather in the passage of the Jordan. There they were commanded to "sanctify themselves" (Joshua 3:5). There, at Gilgal, they were called to a second circumcision and there we are told that the Lord "rolled away the reproach of Egypt" from off them. Does not all this signify far more than the scene of the Red Sea tells us? Have we not in Romans 6:11 Gilgal reckoning, in Romans 6:12 Gilgal separating, and in Colossians 3:1 Gilgal dwelling? We can easily see how an Israelite must have felt his separation from Egypt when he was circumcised like this in the land of promise; and we can only know the manifest rolling away of the reproach of Egypt, as we stand by faith in heavenly places, and walk even as Christ walked in newness of life. Then too the manna ceased after they had crossed the river and they ate the old corn of the land. So when we realize ourselves as a heavenly people, it is Christ who belongs to heaven that we feed upon, a risen Christ seated at the right hand of God, ever living to make intercession for us. Certainly the land of rest was a better place than the wilderness, and it was only the failure of the Israelites, or rather their unbelief, that kept them out of it so long. So that they were practically walking in sin during all those forty years, delivered from Egypt it is true, but very far from being in the place or the position that God had called them to. Both passages were types of the death of Christ, but of that death viewed in two aspects. And does not this way of viewing them run parallel with the experience of nearly every Christian? First we know redemption from the guilt of sin merely and deliverance from the bondage of Satan; then we wander in a wilderness truly having God with us, as He was with the Israelites and sustained by His bread sent down from heaven, pleasing Him sometimes, grieving him often, needing strict discipline, and growing foot-sore and tired. Then at last we see that our crucifixion with Christ has a fuller meaning and leads us into higher privileges and we cross the Jordan and enter into the rest of faith, into the life hid with Christ in God, and all our wanderings are over forever.

—To Anna, September 4, 1867

82. Definite Faith

I think my faith has never been definite enough. I have never actually trusted Christ to do for me the work which the Apostle speaks of when he says,

"The very God of peace sanctify you wholly." I do not know now what that work is either its nature or its extent. But the Lord Himself knows, and whatever it is, it must be what pleases Him, and for this I trust Him. My faith reaches out for all the sanctification that His death has purchased for me, because it is the purchase of His blood I know it must be mine now. Therefore I am able to "reckon myself dead to sin and alive unto God in Jesus Christ." And now I am waiting for what the Methodists call the "witness" or the "evidence;" that is, the inward conviction which God gives by His Spirit of the reality of all His work. I believe without having this, but it seems to me it would be so precious to experience it that I cannot be satisfied until I know something of it. It seems to me that I know more of what naked faith is now than ever I did; just to trust God without one thing to go upon except His bare word! And I am gaining a tremendous view of the nature of faith and of its possibilities. How omnipotent it is, if I may use the word; how "all things are possible to him that believeth." There is something better than merely moving the battle to another field. There is such a God-given confidence in the Lord Jesus and in the efficacy of His atoning blood, that the battle is absolutely turned over to Him, and the soul does nothing but stand still and see His salvation! "Look to Jesus, look to Jesus; Just now; just now. Jesus saves you; Jesus saves you Just now; just now!" Or this,

> All the way along it is Jesus
> All the way along it is Jesus
> And this, Glory to the Lamb, Glory to the Lamb,
> I shall overcome.
—To Sally, September 7, 1867

83. The Privileges of Holiness

My soul is waiting upon God to be filled with His fullness! The hand of faith had enabled me to grasp the utmost limit of the privileges of holiness that the Lord Jesus purchased for me with His precious blood. I do not know what they are either in their nature or their effects. I do not know what it means when we are told that the body of sin was destroyed by the crucifixion of Christ and when we are commanded therefore to "reckon ourselves dead to sin." But I do know that it means something which will enable us, from now on, not to serve sin, and will cause us to bring forth fruit unto holiness. And I know further that it must mean something which pleases and satisfies God. And since it is the purchase of the death of Christ, it must be my privilege to enter it now though so vile and unworthy, for my Bible says that "this is the will of God even my sanctification." Again, since it is the purchase of Christ's death it can be mine only by faith, not in any degree by works and therefore is mine now, if now I trust for it. And thanks be unto God I do trust Him now definitely to accomplish that work of His in me, therefore, now even I can "reckon myself to be dead indeed unto sin but alive unto God in Jesus Christ my Lord!"

—Journal, September 9, 1867

84. Dead But Alive

Since I have learned what it really means to believe and have seen how gloriously it exalts Jesus, and how it makes us hate the sin for which he died, I cannot bear the thought of any child of God being ignorant of it. And it is inexpressibly comforting to know that God commands us to exercise this faith, that his positive declaration to us is that we are dead and that our life is hid in Christ. So that in doubting it, we are committing the fearful sin of unbelief. I have been digging out the texts of "dead but alive" and I find they really confirm my faith. It is true that the flesh can never be made any better, that it must remain flesh to the end of the chapter; but it can be destroyed, the Bible says, and we can, in a sense, be free from it, for, "Ye are not in the flesh, but in the Spirit, if so be that the Spirit of God dwell in you." We are therefore reduced to the necessity either of believing that the Spirit of God does not dwell in us, or else that we are not in the flesh; and if not in the flesh, thank God we don't have to fulfill its lusts and "we will not," the Bible says! To my mind, it is something like this. Here is the flesh ,a rotten corrupted thing; there is Christ. And I may live and walk in either one or the other, but I cannot be in both at the same time. My feeling is that I must abandon the flesh and, as it were, run to Christ as a strong refuge, a hiding place, a rock, a fortress where I am safe from every enemy! For I may fail to guard myself, and I may step outside of Christ and go back again into the dead and rotten thing I had left behind before. But if I do, my only remedy is, the first moment I discover it, to abandon it again, and again plunge myself into Christ. I have no doubt this is just what the Methodists do when they believe that the "blood of Jesus Christ has cleansed them from all sin." It seems to go to the root of the matter somehow, and to deliver up the most basic issues of life into the hands of God.

—To Sally, October 17, 1867

85. Prayer and Watching

But oh! what a life of faith it is! And what a life of watching and praying it requires. I never felt the need of these disiciplines so much before; but now it seems as if every moment was a moment of danger, and yet thank God, a moment of triumph too in Jesus, my perfect and my present Saviour! The faith which brought us our justification was an easy thing compared to this faith, because that was something done in a moment and put away as it were in a closet with nothing continually to test it and bring it into danger. But this faith is being tried every moment, and every moment has to hang on to God. I am preparing a little book of Scripture texts on the subject which I am convinced will be far better than a book of any human arguments, to be divided something in this way: 1. Prayers for holiness. 2. God commands His children to be holy. 3. God shows us that it is possible for his children to be holy and to please Him, that it was for this very purpose Christ died. 4. God shows His children how to be holy; that it is to be accomplished by His power working in us and by our abiding and walking in Christ. Although we are dead, He lives in us, and works there to will and to do what He desires. 5. Personal experience of the possibility of pleasing God by the power of Christ working in us mightily. I am deeply interested in the search and am amazed and confounded at the former blindness of my soul!

    —To Sally, October 17, 1867

86. Christ Is All!

We can do nothing, but only continually keep committing everything to Him and leaving it in His hands. And so our lives will come to be lost in His, and we will realize that the "pure life of God" is over all, and that He will work in us whatever is well pleasing in His sight. Our only part in this great work is to stop working. Abiding, resting, believing,—these are our part; Christ does all the rest. Whether in temptation or in service, it is the same. If we cease from our own plans and our own activities and leave the whole care and ordering of our work to Him, He will plan for us, will work through us, and will use us as His instruments to accomplish His own purposes of love and mercy. The responsibility will be all His, the simple obedience only ours. And who can understand the peace of heart that we find in this, except those who have experienced it? Everywhere and in everything, we are nothing and Christ is all! Oh that this truth might be brought home to the heart of every child of God. The promise is certain that "they which hunger and thirst after righteousness shall be filled." But the fulfill-ment is all in Jesus. He in the believer instead of all the so-called created habits of grace which we ourselves may develop. So that we shall not be filled with any goodness of our own, nor with any righteousness to which we can lay claim as an independent possession, but we shall be filled sim-ply with Jesus and His righteousness. For He Himself says: "I am the bread of life; he that cometh to me shall never hunger, and he that believeth on me shall never thirst." Our hunger and our thirst are all satisfied forever in Him!

—Journal, 1867

87. God's Book

Today I have been looking up texts for our Bible class tomorrow night. The subject in order in the Book of Discipline is "Reading the Scriptures," and it seemed to me the right way to look at it was to consider first the duty of the Christian to search the Scriptures and to know and understand what the will of God is. And secondly to look at the texts which prove that unbe-lief and ignorance of God's revealed will are both a sin in His sight need-ing atonement. I was surprised at the number of texts I found. It seems to me that it is a precious and marvelous privilege that God is not only will-ing, but anxious to reveal His secrets to us who are so far removed from Him in status and intelligence. It is our usual human way, but how sad that we should be so slow to avail ourselves of such a privilege, that we should study other books so much more carefully than we do this Book, God's Book. The one book worth all our study!

—To Mother, 1867

88. The Power of Faith and Words

What you say about being as it were, "within Christ," is a most blessed experience, and, in measure, I do realize it continually. But oh, I feel that there are heights and depths of love which I have not yet seen that will swal-low me up in unspeakable joy. How are we to get into Christ except by faith? How can we abide in Him except by believing? How are we to "put Him on" except by our saying, "Lord! I do put off 'the old man,' and I do put on 'the new,' and I am abiding in you!" And isn't it possible finally, to be so established and settled in Him as to abide with him continually? I find it rewarding to obey the directions of that text, "Take with you words and turn unto the Lord." Whenever I go to him saying in words, "Lord I am dead to sin, and I would not dare to say so if you hadn't said it, for every evidence of my senses tells me the contrary, but you said it, and therefore, I believe it. I am dead to sin because I am in thee," I always find it becomes a very vivid reality. There is a lot of vagueness in our usual way of believing truth, and this is the cause of our being blessed by it so little. We cannot be vague when we tell God what we believe. I wish I had time to tell you of the wonderful discoveries that I am continually making about the fullness of Christ. The Bible is a veritable inexhaustible treasurehouse. Just look up what it says about coming to the light and walking in the light, what it is and what wonderful privileges are connected with it.

—To Sister, December 7, 1867

89. Abiding in Christ

I have been given unusual faith lately with regard to abiding in Christ. Have you ever noticed the three declarations made concerning those who abide in Christ: 1. He that abideth in Him "sinneth not." 2. He that abideth in Him, "the same bringeth forth much fruit." 3. He that abideth in Him "shall ask what he will and it shall be done unto him." Aren't they wonderful and glorious? And to think they are ours, yours and mine, if we only abide! It has strengthened my faith to see that we have God's word for abiding. He declares that we are in Christ, and becomes a practical reality to us as soon as we believe it. It is another one of those strange anomalies that God declares a thing to be ours, and yet it does not actually become ours until we believe it. I used to believe I was in Christ, but not that I was abiding in Him, which was actually saying that I had two lives, one in Christ and one in myself; whereas God says, "Ye are dead and your life is hid with Christ in God." In those days I called my life in Him "judicial," so that left me room for another life outside of Christ, a life of continual sin. Oh how unspeakably thankful I am that my eyes have been opened to see my glorious privileges.

—To Anna, December 14, 1867

90. Yielding the Inner Citadel

A life hid with Christ in God! How wonderful that this should be mine! Not judicially only but really and actually, so that I can truly say that God is working in me to will and to do of His good pleasure! Ever since the definite step of faith when I was made able really "to reckon myself dead indeed unto sin but alive unto God in Jesus Christ my Lord," I have had a very different experience from anything before that. It has seemed as if the center of my being was reached at last, as if Christ had taken possession of the inner citadel of my life and the strong man who kept the house before had been bound and his goods taken.

For the first time in all my Christian experience I can say, "I am abiding in Christ." And I find that in the same degree that I abide, God's promises made to those who abide are fulfilled in me.

1. He that abideth in Him sinneth not.

2. He that abideth in Him the same bringeth forth much fruit.

3. He that abideth in Him shall ask what he will and it shall be done unto him.

Oh what a blessed life it is to be really and actually "dead to sin," and "alone to God in Jesus Christ my Lord." I used to take this as altogether judicial, and of course it had no power over me. I knew well enough I was polluted in my own eyes, that I was alive to sin and under its dominion too, but I believed that God looked at me only in Christ, that He saw me pure, holy, just and righteous in His Son, although as a matter of fact I was not really like that at all. The only benefit, therefore, that I had received from the death of Christ was deliverance from the punishment of my sin, but not from the practice of it, which was to say in effect, that I might go on sinning, free of cost or risk, for there was no guilt connected with it.

—Journal, Christmas 1867

91. Whatever He Desires

But now, thanks be unto God, I see that the purchase of Christ's death was infinitely more valuable than this. That He died to give me actual holiness as well as judicial; that He died to make me really dead to sin, and really alive to God in Him, as well as judicially so; that He died in order that He might become my life; that He might be the only life I should have, and that living in me, He might work in me that which was well pleasing in His sight. I therefore die, voluntarily as it were, to myself and live in Him. I lay down my own life and declare myself to be dead, in order that Christ may become my life. With Paul I say, "I am crucified with Christ, nevertheless I live; yet not I, but Christ liveth in me; and the life that I now live in the flesh I live by the faith of the Son of God, who loved me and gave Himself for me." And so I am abiding in Christ and He is dwelling in me, and all I have to do now is to "yield" myself to Him as one alive from the dead, and to permit Him to do with me whatever He desires!

Not that I always abide like that. No, I am sorry to say that Satan sometimes succeeds in enticing me out, and makes me take up my old life in the flesh again and live and walk in that. But thanks be unto my mighty Saviour, His blood is there to atone for even this, and again and again He forgives me and cleanses me afresh from all unrighteousness.

Daily, more and more, I learn to cling to Christ by a naked unfaltering faith; and daily, more and more, I find myself established in abiding in Him. And why should not the time come, even for me, when I shall be so established and settled there, that I won't be moved again?

—Journal, Christmas 1867

92. Amazing Blessings

It is unspeakably blessed to know myself "dead to sin," and "alive in Christ." It is such a wondrous amazing blessing, that if God had not declared it I would not dare to dream of it. But oh, praise His Name! He has said it; He has declared that for this very purpose Christ died, that I being "dead to sins might live unto righteousness," and taking my place at the foot of the Cross I boldly dare to declare that what He died to accomplish, is accomplished, and I am dead to sin and alive to God in Him. It is all in Him.

Oh, how my soul hangs upon this! Christ in me and I in Him! All is in Christ; there is nothing outside of Him. I myself am nothing but death and corruption outside of Him. But oh wonderful truth, He died to make me one with Himself, to take me as it were into Him, and to make me die to every life but His. He died for this, and therefore I may claim it, and it is mine. And since He is living in me, He must be working there, and if He is working, it must be to will and to do of His own good pleasure. And I have nothing to do but to yield myself to Him as one that is alive from the dead and yield my body, soul and mind to Him as instruments of righteousness for His continual use. Oh, how I love that word "yield," and may it be my daily meat and drink to make it my practical life.

Oh may my Lord and Master keep me from taking any rest in only the knowledge about this blessed life, instead of in the life itself. How absolutely I need Him now; how vile and useless I see that I am, but He is all in all. Yes He is, and my soul knows it and can trust Him!

—Journal, December 31, 1867

93. Led by the Spirit

How inexpressibly comforting it is for us to be "led by the Spirit." And now that Christ is dwelling in our hearts by faith, it is our privilege to hear His voice and to know it. It just leaves nothing for us to do but to yield ourselves and our members up in childlike obedience to Him.

How different this is from the perplexing life of planning, and arranging, and consulting that otherwise would necessarily be ours. It seems to me I am almost overwhelmed at the wonderful thought of our being the temple of the living God, that He is dwelling in us and walking in us! It makes the flesh sink away into such absolute nothingness; or as a Methodist woman once expressed it, to "wilt down" before Him! I feel strongly that nothing is of any avail but the power of the Holy Ghost; no eloquence, no clear statements of truth, no touching appeals, nothing whatever can really accomplish anything except as it is energized by the power of the Holy Ghost, and the prayer of my heart is continually, oh fill me with your Spirit."

—To Mary, January 8, 1868

94. From Strength to Strength

I hope that you are able to abide in Christ by faith and to know in yourself experientially the fulfillment of the promises concerning those who abide. It seems so simple to me now that I am amazed that every Christian does not see the blazing truth. How can they live for a moment outside of Him? Of course I am speaking of the Christian life at a practical level, for as to any simply judicial or objective abiding, it is a mere mockery to speak of it.

"That Christ may dwell in your hearts by faith." If our Saviour shed His blood, then our faith doesn't need to vary, and we may go on, not from strength to weakness and back again from weakness to strength, but steadily forward from strength to strength, always abounding in the work of our Lord.

Oh it is so unspeakably blessed to have this faith, and so sweet to yield ourselves! I do not mean that there are no trials to the flesh, but beneath them all there is peace, and joy, and quiet rest!

—To Mary, January 8, 1868

95. God's Perfect Will

If God is working in me to do His good pleasure then it must be that I will what He wills, and therefore really want to do it although there may be many trials connected with it. In temporal affairs, how often the strength of our will carries us through obstacles and trials and even sufferings until we achieve the thing we were after; and we really do not even mind the trials for a moment. Now isn't this also the case in spiritual things? If God has taken possession of my will and wills His good pleasure in me, then the thing I will must be what He wills in me, and thus I actually want it. My will is set on it, and no matter what the obstacles may be, or the trials connected with it, I will to have it or to do it and therefore do have it.

Isn't this the true secret of the guidance of the Spirit? Is it not God taking possession of our wills, and through them carrying out His own will? And when He calls us to any work, underneath everything else, won't there be a strong desire for the very thing which will carry us through all opposition? And on the contrary, where the work is not what he wants, won't there be, at the very bottom of our souls, an unwillingness to do it which will completely cast doubt on what we want to do though every outward circumstance seems to favor it? Our blessed Lord and Master delights to do it if He is living and working in us to will and to do of His good pleasure.

—Journal, February 6, 1868

96. All on the Altar

As much as I have objected to it and disapproved of it in the past, I have been brought to the point of entire consecration. I find that the soul which wants to live the life hid with Christ in God must be entirely given up to Him—and definitely given up too. I must present my body a living sacrifice, holy and acceptable unto Him, which is my reasonable service.

And I do! Lord Jesus, here and now I definitely yield myself up unreservedly to you. All that I have and all that I am, both now and in the whole future of my life, I lay upon your altar. Everything is yours, and I am yours to follow you wherever you may lead me.

Oh Lord Jesus, let this be a reality! Bring this consecration about in me and through me, and keep it. You know my utter weakness, and to you I commit myself in this. Oh I ask you, let me never, never, never, draw back from the transaction of this moment. Let me never for a moment take back the slightest thing of all I have now consecrated or surrendered to you. Make it a reality.

—Journal, March 30, 1868

97. Giving God Our Future

I thank the Lord that He has made my consecration to Him a reality so far, and that He has given me more and more light upon the subject, both in respect to its importance and its effects. Now I see plainly that although I completely desired and intended, before this definite act of consecration, to give up myself wholly to the Lord and to lose my will in His, yet because of not having actually and definitely yielded myself up to Him, I left a little loophole for the flesh to exert itself, and whenever temptation did overcome me, it did not seem very bad.

But now, although I can't make any more promises for the future than before, yet I find a great difference in my way of looking at it. I feel that the future belongs to God as really as a present given to Him, and to think of taking back any moment of it into my own hands fills me with horror. Before, I might be able to say at any given moment, "I am the Lord's now, totally and unreservedl"y; but my will always took comfort in the thought of a future, when perhaps I would not be entirely His and, secretly and almost unconsciously, made a future provision for the flesh "to fulfil the lusts thereof." But now! Oh my Lord and Master, teach me the depth and reality of this giving up of my whole life to you!

Dimly I begin to see it, and I find that my will is slain in a manner I never before experienced. It can rest nowhere but in God, for in all my future I don't dare think of any moment when I will not be as unreservedly given up to Him, as at the present.

—Journal, April 17, 1868

98. Specific Consecration

Three things have come to be yielded definitely to the Lord without reservation: my reading, my tongue, and my thoughts. The first point was my reading, and the conflict of my will was there. It seemed as if I could not give up all control of my reading for my whole future life to the Lord, never to read anything against which His Spirit should witness, feeling sure, if I did, that my reading then would have to be in a very limited range. It was comparatively easy to do it for the present, but my will shrank back in horror from a future in which it might never again for a single moment have its way in this matter. And it was this very thing that taught me the need for a surrender of myself, which would include the future, as well as the present.

A hundred times I have surrendered that matter of my reading to the Lord, but it had never been a real surrender, for I always took refuge, in the bottom of my heart, that there would always be a point in the future when I could take it back again. Now however God showed me that the future was His as irrecoverably as the present, and He, not I, worked in my soul to make an absolute surrender. I felt that it was His work, not my own, and could only throw myself in utter spiritual weakness and nothingness upon His almighty strength to keep the sacrifice He had made. He conquered my will then and there in a way it had never been conquered before.

Since then the consecration of my tongue, and of my thoughts, have both been brought before me by the Holy Spirit, and I found no peace until these also were absolutely surrendered to my Lord's entire control. But there was no conflict connected with these, my will was already on the Lord's side, and my presenting them as a living sacrifice was easily accomplished.

—Journal, April 17, 1868

99. Absolutely the Lord's

I am the Lord's now, His only and His absolutely, not only by the purchase of His death, but also by the free consent of my own will, made willing by the working of His mighty power in me! Not for one moment, however, could I have the faintest hope or expectation of continuing in this state of entire surrender, if I did not trust my Lord Himself to keep me. But I can trust Him, and do. I am confident that He will keep that which I have committed to Him, and my only security lies in this—He is able, He is willing. He died to make it my privilege to trust Him like this, and with a sense of absolute giving up and sinking down into His will I abandon myself both for the present and for the future into His loving and wise care!

And now I wait for the baptism of the Holy Ghost! Several times since I have seen the way of holiness, and have more or less known the blessedness of walking in it, I have tried to believe that I was baptized with the Holy Ghost, and that I did possess all of His conscious presence that was my privilege. But all in vain. I could not work myself up into the belief, that I had ever experienced anything at all to be compared to the baptism of the Holy Ghost, which all the early church shared, not only on the day of Pentecost, but afterwards, all through the Bible times.

—Journal, April 17, 1868

100. A Personal Pentecost

I might believe I had the Spirit because I thought the Scriptures said so, but I could not but see that the gift of the Spirit was always there spoken of as a gift to be experienced, as a reality not an idea, or a belief as a proof and earnest of something else, and therefore necessarily something of which the soul should be conscious, and not merely which it should believe. My religious education has led me to ignore all this direct and conscious witnessing of the Spirit, and I don't doubt but that it is because of this that I haven't received it.

But oh! now my soul longs for realities, and I cannot be satisfied with only beliefs! The Lord Jesus has not taken away from His church this one gift of all gifts—this gift which He declared it was expedient for them to tarry for in order that He might bestow it. It is the purchase of His death, and I need it as sorely as ever did the early church. And therefore I come to Him for it. I believe He will give it to me. I believe I must pray and wait upon Him for it, and expect it soon.

Oh Lord Jesus, make a short work in my soul, and grant me this! It is your promised gift. I cannot be satisfied without it. I must have it. Oh! hear me and answer speedily, I pray you!

—Journal, April 17, 1868

101. Our Part and His Part

The Lord is leading me on step by step, having worked in me a willingness and ability to consecrate myself to Him, to be His wholly and forever. I want to be His, not only in some of the special circumstances of my life, or in some of the activities of my soul, but to be His myself, to abandon my whole self to Him, with all my powers and all my circumstances, to resign my whole will to Him without any possible reserve. Since the Lord has, I say, wrought in me such a complete giving up of self as this, He has now taught me that He Himself has taken possession of me, and that He is having His own way in me to make me just what He pleases.

"This is His will, even my sanctification: therefore if He has possession of me it is impossible that He should leave me unsanctified for a single moment. It was only I myself who hindered the work, and if I give myself up, the work must be accomplished. I cannot but believe it. An actual transaction has taken place between God and my soul. I have abandoned myself to Him, and He has taken possession of me, and I must believe it, has sanctified me. A real work has taken place, on my part consecration, on the Lord's part sanctification. Oh praise His name! For it is all His work from beginning to end! I say my part because the conscious acting of my soul was to give itself up, but it was God who did it in me.

—Journal, April 20, 1868

102. God First

The Lord has shown me another step. Today the question has been presented to me whether I would be willing to lose my darling child, my little daughter Mary, for the sake of the revelation of the Lord Jesus Himself to me. It was a battle, but my Saviour has triumphed. It came simply to this point, Would I keep my daughter, and remain a cold and lukewarm Christian all my life, living at a distance from my Saviour, and unbaptized by His Spirit; or, would I give her up, that I might see Him in His beauty, and know Him to dwell in my heart in all His fullness?

Thanks be unto His Name, He has worked in me to choose the latter! I desire Him even more than I desire my precious, my darling daughter! And now surely the last link to earth is broken, for, without my daughter, life would be desolate indeed. I am wholly the Lord's now.

Oh what hinders Him from blessing me! Still I wait and pray that He will reveal Himself, that He will baptize me with the Holy Ghost!

—Journal, April 22, 1868

103. Doubt and Blessing

I am suffering under a great temptation, one which never before has assaulted me since I was a child of God. It is to fearful unbelief—to doubt the reality of anything divine; to doubt the reality of any religious experience; to doubt almost the existence of any God. But oh! my Jesus keep me! Keep me Lord, keep me! You do exist; you are an almighty Saviour; you do manifest yourself to the soul that waits upon you. I will trust you. I will set my face as a flint, and I know I shall not be confounded!

Oh that this may be a forerunner of some great blessing. Come Lord Jesus, come quickly and show me yourself so that I will doubt no more!

—Journal, April 23, 1868

104. Hindrances and Unbelief

It is three weeks since, on the 30th March, I presented myself a living sacrifice unto God, feeling that it was indeed my reasonable service. And then I began definitely and intelligently to pray for the baptism of the Holy Spirit. But as yet I remain unbaptized!

My soul asks, why is this, and I cannot find any answer. That it is all right as far as my Lord is concerned I am sure, and I can only pray that He will speedily remove whatever hindrance on my part frustrates His grace in this matter. Today He has been shown me that one hindrance lay in the fact that I have never been able at any given moment to ask God to bless me now, but always put it off into the indefinite future. This was simply unbelief, for if ever God blesses me it will have to be in some now, and now is always His time. I believe He has taken this unbelief away at last, and I can come to Him with confidence for a present blessing.

But another hindrance I am afraid will delay me now. So many who have been baptized with the Holy Ghost have made fools of themselves in the eyes of others, have acted, as they did on the day of Pentecost, like men "drunken with new wine," that I am afraid there is at the bottom of my heart a little shrinking from being brought to the same condition, I who have always prided myself on my self control, and whom nothing of a devotional nature ever moved! But, oh Lord, you can remove even this weakness and this shrinking, and I do give it all up to you. Glorify yourself in me and through me without regard to me. Let self be obliterated, and let your power and your will have full control over my body, soul and spirit.

Oh I beseech you, let nothing on my part hinder the full manifestation of your power in me and through me! Make me a spectacle to men and angels, if that will get you the most glory, and me the most of the blessed Spirit. Oh, do not, do not, let anyone or anything frustrate your grace!

—Journal, April 24, 1868

105. Filled with the Spirit

The Lord has answered my prayer and taken away my unbelief. Last night, as Carroll, Frank's tutor, and I waited on Him together, He gave us each the conviction that He could not withhold the gift of His Spirit from any soul, that really came to Him in sincerity for it. We say that this gift of the Spirit was a part, and a very essential part, of the salvation procured for us by the death of Christ, and that therefore it was our right, if we came with no other plea than that of His death. We saw that God had promised to give it to every one who believed on the Lord Jesus. We saw that He had declared Himself more ready to give it than parents are to give bread to their children. We felt that we dared not doubt Him any longer.

That text in 1 John 5:14,15 was especially sealed upon our hearts "And this is the confidence that we have in Him, that, if we ask anything according to His will, He heareth us; and if we know that He hears us, whatsoever we ask we know that we have the petitions that we desired of Him." We could not doubt that it was according to His will to baptize us with His Holy Spirit, and He gave us such a feeling of confidence in Him that we knew He heard us; and knowing this we did not dare to doubt that we had the petitions we desired of Him, even the baptism of the Holy Ghost, the full indwelling of the Spirit, whereby we became, not judicially, but really and actually the temples of the Holy Ghost, filled with the Spirit!

It was not so much that we believed this, as that we did not dare to doubt it, for it presented itself before our minds as an actual fact, something which must be from the character of God, and from every revelation of Himself that He has made as a God who hears and answers prayer. We were forced therefore to return thanks together for a present and actual answer to our prayers, and had to believe that we had the baptism of the Holy Ghost.

—Journal, April 29, 1868

106. Show Me Yourself

Oh my soul is sore within me! Continually I cry out, "You are a God that hides yourself." I dare not doubt Him. I must believe that He has heard and answered my prayers; but oh the dreariness of a life that has to believe only, and can never feel; that longs for a sense of the presence of its Beloved and may never have it; that longs to see Him in His beauty and is never satisfied! As the hart panteth after the water brooks so panteth my soul after You, oh God! and yet you hide yourself! I feel after you and cannot find you. I draw nigh to you and it seems as if you withdraw yourself. My soul is breaking because of the longing it has for your manifested presence. But there is no light.

The old judicial life seems all coming back upon me, a life of faith, which believes everything God says, and all the record concerning the Lord Jesus but which never grasps any tangible realities, a life of beliefs not of realized possessions. That life that my head lived, but not my heart, that was full of truth about Christ, but that never laid hold of Christ Himself as my very own present, living and manifested Saviour! Oh my God, I cannot live this way! I must have my Lord Himself! I must see Him, I must feel Him, I must be conscious of His personal presence with me. Beliefs are not enough; I must have tangible realities. Oh! what shall I do.

Oh I implore you, reveal yourself to me. I beg you; I entreat you, show me yourself. Whatever hindrance there is remove it at once, and let me know you as a present and manifested Saviour! I must have you; I cannot live without you; oh, show me yourself!

—Journal, April 29, 1868

107. Believing Promises or Trusting Jesus

I have trusted Jesus at last. I have cast myself wholly on Him for all the benefits of His death. I trust Him for them, and they are mine—all— including the baptism of the Holy Ghost and the sanctification of the Spirit! I was brought at last to this point—"I must trust Jesus, and I must trust Him now, for all that He died to make mine," and I was obliged to believe that then and there He actually gave me what my soul had been seeking.

Now there was this difference between my faith and the faith I had exercised in my entry April 29th. Then I believed promises, now I trusted Jesus, and while the intellect could do the former, it could not grasp the latter; therefore, I felt and knew it was the work of God.

Carroll and I both came to the same point—that we must cast ourselves utterly on Jesus for all the benefits of His death, and must really and truly trust Him to bestow them upon us. It was a desperate venture of faith, but He worked it in us, and we did trust Him. What was the result? No great outpouring of the Spirit, no especial manifestation, such as we had hoped for, but instead, a revelation of Jesus as a perfect and complete and present Saviour. Such a revelation of Him as compelled an implicit confidence in Him, and a peaceful resting in His love. It was very sweet and comforting, and I could not but praise and bless His dear name!

—Journal, May 10, 1868

108. Trusting His Infinite Love

But after all it was only a glimpse, and my soul was not satisfied. Nor is it satisfied yet. This was two days ago, and I thought that perhaps this glimpse would widen out into a full and glorious sight of my Saviour. The most I could say then was that I trusted Jesus, and that I knew He could not fail me and that I knew He did give me all the gifts that His death had purchased for me, including that longed for gift of the Spirit in His fullness and His power.

And this is all I can say now. I dare not doubt Him. He is a perfect Saviour, and His salvation is a complete salvation, and I do trust Him and therefore it is mine. I dare no longer pray for the Spirit, for, I am certain my faithful Saviour has revealed Him to me, and I must now only yield myself up to His working, and expect to see the fruits manifested in my life.

But while I do really believe this, and do trust Jesus, I am not satisfied. I wanted a real and manifested display of Divine power—something that would force from me the confession, "this is the working of God and of none other—this is more than the natural results of faith, it is in very deed the mighty power of the Holy Ghost." I wanted some tangible experience to silence forever all the reasonings of my intellect and to convince me with unmistakable authority that God Himself was at work. But this is not granted, and I must still live by naked faith alone, resting on His word, and trusting in His infinite love.

—Journal, May 10, 1868

109. Unanswered Prayer

Yesterday and today my soul has been almost breaking for the longing it has had after some manifested token of the presence of my Beloved! I have felt like prostrating myself in the very dust before Him, and holding Him as it were by the feet until He would grant me a satisfying portion of His manifested love. With strong crying and tears I have asked Him to show me the smile of His face, to make me joyful with the sense and feeling of His presence. But as yet these prayers remain unanswered. I must believe that the Jesus I have trusted will not and does not fail me. I dare not doubt Him, and I am forced to give Him thanks for His unspeakable gifts. But I am walking by naked faith still, and my soul is not satisfied!

And now the question arises whether I can continue to trust Jesus if He allows me to go on very long in this state of aridity and absence of all emotion. Haven't I, even today, had some hard thoughts about Him?

—Journal, May 10, 1868

110. Doubting Jesus

I have to confess tonight with deep humility of soul before God that I am a poor miserable sinner in His sight! The question I asked myself last night revealed to me the unbelief and rebellion of my heart. I found that I could not trust Jesus unconditionally for the future; and further and worse, that I was cherishing hard thoughts of Him because He did not bless me as I desired! I have passed a day of intense wretchedness. I seemed to lose my hold of everything, and to be cut adrift upon a fearful sea of unbelief and sin.

I doubted Jesus and nothing else was of any account. None of my past experience seemed worth anything, and Satan urged me to throw the whole thing up, and to turn to the world for that satisfaction which he tried to persuade me I had not found in Christ. So dreadful a thing is the slightest unbelief! But my faithful Saviour would not let the Devil carry off one of His sheep like that, and He has delivered me from his snare.

—Journal, May 11, 1868

111. Syrophoenician Faith

After entering into the solemn covenant recorded last evening never to doubt Jesus again, almost involuntarily, the prayer arose in my heart, "Lord test my faith." And now I believe He is testing it. Oh my God keep that which I have committed to you!

Almost immediately I felt that although I had cast myself on the Lord Jesus to trust Him forever, even through the darkest seasons, yet still that it was not really His will to lead me in darkness but that He desired to manifest Himself to me and to give me the joys of His salvation. The Holy Spirit gave me that blessed promise, "Ask, and ye shall receive that your joy may be full." And I seemed to be able simply to believe it like a little child, and to lay hold upon it as the promise of that Jesus, whom I had now trusted, never to doubt again. Then I felt pressed to ask that my joy might be full, and my heart rested in the promise that it would be.

I prayed with a faith and a fervency I never felt before, and was enabled to believe confidently that I should indeed receive a fullness of joy now. I prayed and waited like that until between three and four o'clock in the morning, but no answer came, and it seemed I ought to go to bed, because, just now I am especially burdened with household responsibilities that I can't escape. I woke up, however, with the same prayer of faith, and all day long it has been the breathing of my soul. I feel that it is the test of my faith, for which I asked.

It seems as though the Lord were turning a deaf ear to my entreaties, as though His promises were not going to be fulfilled. But I know that He who has promised is faithful, and I will trust Him. Yes I do trust Him. He has said, "Ask, and ye shall receive that your joy may be full;" and I know that if I do not grow weary in asking, nor become discouraged with my Lord's delay, I shall receive.

He Himself has taught us that importunate prayer which will take no denial is the prayer that prevails—in Luke 11:1–13, and He teaches this in answer to the express request of the disciples, "Lord, teach us to pray." In the case of the Syrophoenician woman also He has shown us the value He sets upon faith which still claims the blessing even though apparently repulsed. Yes, my Lord Jesus; I will trust you; I do trust you. Oh! keep me trusting thee, you keep me pleading with an importunity that will take no denial for your promised joy!

—Journal, May 12, 1868

112. The Blessing of Sanctification

I owed you a letter, in fact two or three, but I wanted to wait until I could tell the good news of my soul having been filled and satisfied. But it has not happened yet, and I will not wait any longer. You would say, I suppose, that I never will be; but I have Scripture against you, and God is true, even though every man's experience may seem to make His words false, and I will and do trust Him! One single promise of my Lord's is enough for me to found my faith upon. "Ask & ye shall receive that your joy may be full." That would satisfy me, to have fullness of joy and I dare not stop asking until He gives it to me.

The lesson taught in Luke 11:5–13 is one which we need to learn. The disciples ask, "Lord, teach us to pray"; and He at once tells them that illustration of the man going to his friend's house at midnight for bread, and refusing to give him any rest until he gave it to him; plainly showing, that importunate prayer, which will not take any denial, is the prayer that will prevail. I pray that He may teach me this lesson effectually. It is so hard to persevere in prayer when no answer seems to come, and when even the Heavens seem as brass.

Though I cannot say that this is quite my present extremity. The Lord has answered my prayers in this that He has I believe given me the blessing of sanctification to the full extent of all that His death purchased for me, and has revealed Himself to me, giving me as it were a glimpse of His trustworthiness, and enabling me to feel a confidence in Him far exceeding any I have ever known before.

—To Sister, Millville, N.J., May 19, 1868

113. Step by Step

The cry of my soul for some weeks has been "Lord make me a living witness of your power to save to the uttermost," and now I feel enough confidence in Him to trust Him to do this very thing, and can thank Him beforehand for such great mercy. Surely He has revealed Himself to me to some degree, or I could not possibly trust Him this way. I thank Him, therefore, for these revelations, but press on after far more full and satisfying ones. I will not despise His present appearances to my soul, although as old Isaac Pennington says, they have not been at all comparable to my expectations. But delighting myself in these, I still expect Him to give me the desire of my heart, which is, a full and satisfying sight of Him in His fullness and His beauty.

I find I must walk very softly. What absolute dedication of soul is required from one who would be as clay in the hands of the Potter, and who desires to have no will but His! Oh do pray for me that I may never for one moment look away from Jesus, nor cast away my confidence in Him! My own weakness is utter, but his strength is sufficient, and I do trust Him.

—To Sister, Millville, N.J., May 19, 1868

114. Pray and Don't Faint

I wish I had time to tell you more about his dealings with my soul. He has led me and is even now leading me in ways I don't understand. Satan is seeking to sift me like wheat, but Jesus is enough, and I have Him, and therefore cannot fail. I am clinging to Jesus. I dare not look at experiences, either my own or others, but can only cast my soul in its utter weakness upon Him, and trust Him for everything. Twice since I saw you I have stayed up nearly the whole night to pray, and it seems as if I could hardly do anything else in my leisure moments.

This has been one reason why I have not written to you. I feel as if glorious privileges are just within my grasp, if only I will pray and not faint. And oh! if I should lose them through lethargy or negligence how dreadful it would be.

Dear sister, you know what a perfect Saviour Jesus is. Do trust Him to make you a living witness of His power to save to the very uttermost. Living witnesses are what we want. There are plenty to preach the doctrine, but so few to say, "I have tried & proved it." Let's commit ourselves to be proofs of the almighty power of our Saviour, that He may get great glory in saving us!

—To Sister, Millville, N.J., May 19, 1868

115. Open My Eyes

My whole soul is going out in one agonizing cry for my Saviour's manifested presence! I cannot live without Him! I have given myself up entirely to Him; I have consecrated my whole self—body, soul and spirit—to Him. I believe that He receives me, and that I am wholly His. "This is the will of God even your sanctification," and I do believe that He has sanctified me, even me. But oh! how trembling and weak my faith is, in the absence of any manifestation of the presence of my Saviour.

I have suffered so much in my past Christian life by stopping short at an intellectual belief that I now feel very distrustful of my faith. I can only cast myself upon Jesus to make it a real living faith and entreat Him to fill me with His own glorious presence and powerful life in such a way that I shall know, beyond the possibility of doubt, that He is in actuality living in me; and that all I believe is in fact a divine reality. I do ask Him to let me die rather than let me draw back or vacillate any more. I am willing to die, but I am not willing ever again for a single moment to wander away from a fixed faith in my Lord Jesus, and a grateful acceptance of His full salvation.

But I feel that I must have some manifestation of His presence to sustain and strengthen me. I love Him, and I cannot live without Him! Oh my Jesus, show thyself! Open my blind eyes to see thee in thy beauty! It seems as if it was all just here, all the life, love, power, and joy that my soul longs for, only my eyes are blinded so that I cannot see it. O my Jesus, open my eyes! I believe that I have your full salvation; I trust you for it all; but I cannot rest until I know and see it. Oh show me, show me!

—Journal, May 26, 1868

116. Free Gifts of Love

Last night my agonizing prayers for the realized presence of Jesus seemed to reach a climax. It seemed as if He had to hear and answer, and when ten o'clock came and there was no sign, my heart sank lower than ever. And I felt that there must be some mistake somewhere. His gifts cannot be so hard to get; the Bible declares just the opposite, and I prayed earnestly that any mistake, whatever it was, might be revealed to me. Carroll also, who has gone with me through all the conflicts of the past months, and who has seemed to be led in much the same paths, felt that there must be some solution to the perplexing questions which are troubling our souls, and we both spent most of the night in prayer and waiting upon the Lord.

The result was that we came to a clear and settled conviction that the difficulty lay in the simple fact that we were trying to obtain God's blessings by our own efforts, instead of trusting the Lord Jesus to obtain them for us. We had been fasting, and praying, even spending almost the whole of several nights wrestling with God, thinking that, in this way, we could obtain the blessings which He has so emphatically declared are the free gifts of His love.

But we saw last night that this was legality; that it was as much legality as for us to try to conquer sin by our own efforts; and that the only thing we could do or ought to do was to commit to the Lord Jesus the procuring of these blessings for us in just the same way as we commit to Him the conquering of our temptations. The battle is not ours but His, and we can do nothing but hand it over to Him and then stand still and see the salvation of God.

—Journal, June 3, 1868

117. Not in Our Strength

He is our High Priest to make intercession for us and in us, and His intercession will avail, so that we may be confident of getting what we ask. We can no more pray in our own strength than we can fight in our own strength. He must do it all. He must pray in us with groanings that cannot be uttered, and God will not fail to hear and answer the prayers offered by the power and virtue of the life of Christ in the soul. We become more and more absolutely nothing, and Christ becomes all in all!

It was a very precious experience. Our souls sank into Jesus and by faith lost themselves in Him, and we took Him as our Life in a deeper and more comprehensive sense than ever before. And now the battle is His. He must obtain for us the blessings our souls so sorely need, and He will. We trust Him. Yes, we trust Him with an implicit confidence, and can even beforehand sing a song of praise for the rich blessings which His availing intercessions are certainly going to procure for us. Oh what a perfect Saviour He is, to carry the whole burden of our lives, both spiritual and temporal this way. And how sad it is that our legal spirits have deprived us for so long of this privilege of casting them totally upon Him.

And now, Lord, can't we look for a very speedy answer to your prayers in us? Now that it is all in your care, may we not expect you will make short work of it and that our souls will soon be rejoicing in the revelation of yourself, and therefore in all the fullness of God? Oh we long for this; we pant after it, we cry out for you! Your gifts are not enough, unless you yourself are given; we must have you.

—Journal, June 3, 1868

118. Power In Prayer

We must wait on Him moment by moment for the fulfillment of His promised blessings and must trust Him to obtain them for us. So that in a fuller sense than ever before we are nothing and Christ is all. I feel that this is a very important lesson to learn in regard to prayer. The only prayer that accomplishes anything is that which was offered in "the power and reality of the life of Christ in the soul." The Spirit must make intercession in us, if we expect to have power with God.

So I have come to feel that true prayer is wholly out of my own power, as much as any other good work is, and I am utterly dependent upon the energy of the life of Jesus in me for it. I do not know how I can express it any more clearly; but it is only a further insight into my own utter nothingness and the all sufficiency of Jesus, and I thank Him for it. There is more to know about this, but His time is not yet, and I know he is leading us by the "right way to the City."

—To Lizzie, June 4, 1868

119. Naked Faith in the Naked Word

I have felt my soul stirred up again this evening to trust the Lord Jesus for His full salvation with a naked faith, and have covenanted with Him to have that kind of trust, even if He should never manifest His presence to my soul by any sign or token. His bare word is enough for me, and I will trust Him not to let me be deceived about it. This has been my great fear— that my faith might prove to be only an intellectual faith, and therefore would fail to actually grasp the promised blessings. But I have cast myself upon Jesus for my faith, as well as all else, and do trust Him to give me a real and living faith of His own power, and I must believe that He does.

In the very most effectual way that I can, I do present myself to Him as a living sacrifice and I do believe that He receives me. I ask Him to sanctify me wholly, and I do believe that He does do it. I trust Him to preserve my soul, body, and spirit blameless until His coming, and I do believe that He will do it. And this confidence I will hold fast until I die, trusting to my mighty Saviour to keep me steadfast in it, even though no other proof than the naked word of God is ever granted me.

—Journal, Evening, June 6, 1868

120. The Proof of His Presence

My soul is hanging upon Jesus for the fulfillment of His gracious promises in reference to the gift of the Holy Spirit. The more I examine the Scriptures on the subject, the more thoroughly am I convinced that the Holy Spirit is not an idea or an influence merely, but that He is a real and manifested presence in the soul—the witness to the soul of the divine reality of the things it believes and trusts. His presence is the proof that all we believe is indeed divinely real and actually true. Therefore, His presence must be consciously known and felt, and not merely believed in, because of some statements in the Scriptures.

And I feel that this witnessing of the Spirit is the great need of my soul at the present time. I have Jesus, by faith, and I trust Him for His full salvation, and I do experience a wonderful daily and hourly deliverance from sin; but I need also the infilling of the Holy Ghost. And Christ has promised to give me this, and I may come in confidence to ask Him. And now I am trusting Him continually for the fulfillment of His utmost promises in this respect.

Oh Lord Jesus! since I am to be a living witness of thy power to save to the very uttermost, you know I will need a very large measure of the Spirit, and I come to you in childlike confidence for this. Hear me speedily!

—Journal, June 9, 1868

121. The Fullness of God

Still trusting, and praying, and waiting. Today that prayer in Eph. 3:16–20 has been impressed upon my soul, with the solemn question whether I do really believe that the Lord can and will grant me the wondrous blessings which Paul prays for—to be strengthened with might by His Spirit in the inner man, according to the riches of His glory; to know the love of Christ that passes knowledge and to be filled with all the fullness of God! Yes and even more than this, even exceeding abundantly beyond what I can ask or think.

Now can I trust the Lord for all this—do I believe that He surely will give it to me? Faith answers triumphantly yes—yes I can! When I look at the Lord Jesus and at Him only, I can trust, I can believe! Oh God, keep my eye single to Him!

My faith has been sorely tried this evening. We had a little meeting in our parlor, and I saw others around me filled with the Spirit, and rejoicing in the manifested presence of the Lord, while I sat there unfeeling and unmoved. But my mighty Saviour did not allow my faith to fail, but enabled me to praise Him, through it all. He is faithful, and I will trust Him!

—Journal, June 14, 1868

122. Something that Will Last

It is important to get ahold of something that will last. I have learned a great deal about that lately and feel sure that there are lasting blessings and a continuous fullness of joy for those who look for them.

If a child cries, its father does not always go himself at first, but waits to see if it will quiet down without him. If it continues to cry, he may send someone else in the family to comfort it, or give it something to cheer it up, and if it is satisfied with this, he himself may not have to take care of it himself. But if it still continues to cry for its father and will not be satisfied with anything else, then the father himself goes and takes care of the child and lets it know his love.

And so it is with God. If His children will be satisfied with the company of His children or with having His gifts, He often leaves them to these and keeps His manifested presence for those souls which cry out for Him continually and will not be satisfied without Him. And I thank Him that He has given me this feeling of longing for Himself that nothing but His presence continually with me can possibly satisfy. I must have a Bible experience!

—To Sister, June 15, 1868

123. Faith Not Feeling

I have trusted the Lord Jesus for the full results of His redemption—for His present and perfect salvation! Exactly as I trusted Him on the 8th of May, I trusted last night again. I was made to see that in Him and in Him alone are treasured up all the blessings I need, and that my only resource was in trusting Him unreservedly for them all. I have done this several times before, and always with the result of quiet assurance and peace; but I have failed to "hold fast the beginning of my confidence." Because I have been called to walk by faith instead of feeling, I have grown discouraged, and have let go my grasp of Jesus as a perfect Saviour, and have tried to supply what seemed lacking in Him, by my own prayers and strugglings, and efforts.

By a simple, childlike, present faith in Him and His full redemption from all iniquity, I have entered into the life hid with Him in God several times, and have walked in it for awhile. But because my feelings have not been like I thought they ought to be, I have always let unbelief in, and consequently have wandered away from God. Then, I have been tempted to murmur at the darkness in which I walked, and have felt as if God did not prove faithful to His character as the hearer and answerer of prayer, because He did not give me the things for which I was asking, when I ought instead to have been trusting Jesus for them. I was like a person refusing to take an offered gift, and at the same time entreating and imploring the Giver to bestow it.

—Journal, June 24, 1868

124. Not Feelings or Experiences

As yet my walk is one of naked faith, and the conflict at times is almost fearful. My temptation now is not to doubt Jesus, but to doubt myself. If I had a real living faith wouldn't the results be different? But Jesus is my Saviour from every sin, and every weakness, even from an imperfect faith, and I can do nothing else but trust it all to Him. And I do! Oh my Lord, I do trust you like a little child. In utter ignorance, and weakness, and foolishness, and blindness I throw myself on you for your full redemption. You are the Saviour of the lost, and I am lost without you. Oh! keep me trusting you moment by moment!

If I look at my feelings, or at my experiences, and at what seem to be the practical results of my trusting, I would despair. But I will look only at you. You are able, you are faithful, you shed your blood to redeem me, and that blood is sufficient to cleanse and sanctify even me! I trust you; the continued cry of my soul is "Jesus, I am trusting you!" It is all I can do, and I am sure He cannot fail me.

And now, oh my loving Saviour, I am in your hands. Do with me as you will. Glorify yourself in me! Lead me in darkness or in light—only keep me trusting you!

—Journal, June 26, 1868

125. Not Your Gifts Lord, But You

Surely you are touched with a feeling of my infirmities, and know just how hard it is for me to trust you in the absence of all feeling, and of all apparent results, and you will not suffer me to be tempted above that I am able to bear!

Carroll, Frank's tutor, who also has trusted Jesus for His full salvation, has had a good deal of joy since then; this makes my coldness harder to bear. But I can thank God for his happiness, although I do not share it. This evening, while writing to a friend and urging her to cast herself fully and unreservedly upon Jesus, and while telling her of His fullness, not as I had felt it, but as I see it revealed in the Scriptures, the Lord gave me a little glimpse of Himself dwelling in me, and filling me with His fullness. It was the first glimpse since I have been trusting Him, and it was only a glimpse. But it was real, and oh! so blessed! And I thank Him for it. I did not deserve it, but He saw that I needed it.

And now, Lord, for more! This little glimpse of you only makes my soul hungrier than ever for the full manifestation of yourself! Your gifts are not enough, unless you give yourself. Oh Lord, show me yourself!

—Journal, June 26, 1868

126. Secrets of the Life of Faith

I believe I am slowly learning the secrets of the life of faith—especially with regard to temptations—that I must not look at the temptation, but right away to Jesus, and that I must just do this continually, never stopping to examine as to whether I have yielded to the temptation or not, but trusting, trusting, trusting moment by moment, and moment after moment until deliverance comes.

As Isaac Pennington said, I must "look up to the Lord to keep out the temptation, if it be not already entered, or to thrust it out, if it be already got in. And if He do not so presently, or for a long time yet do not murmur or think much, but wait till He do. Yea, though they violently thrust themselves upon thee, and seem to have entered thy mind, yet let them be as strangers to thee; receive them not, believe them not, know them not, own them not; and thy bosom will, notwithstanding, be chaste in the eye of the Lord, though they may seem to thee to have defiled thee."

Now, if I had done this yesterday in meeting, I would not have been so totally defeated. But instead of continuing to look at Jesus, I let my eyes turn towards my experience, and the temptations which only He could thrust out established themselves at once in my soul. I see that my only safety is in looking at Jesus continually. He is a perfect and a faithful Saviour, and His blood does cleanse and keep clean all who walk in the light and have fellowship with Him. And I must trust Him; trust Him nakedly, trust Him blindly and look at nothing else.

Oh Lord Jesus, as a very little child I cast myself on you. I do not know anything, I cannot understand anything; but you are my perfect Saviour and I can and do trust myself to you implicitly, believing that now, even now, you redeem me from all iniquity with your own most precious blood! I am complete in you! Oh keep me, keep me trusting you like this! No one so weak and wavering ever trusted you before, but because of this I need you all-the-more, and all-the-more you can glorify yourself in saving me! I trust you Lord, I do trust you!

—Journal, June 29, 1868

127. "The Promise of the Father"

I am sure it is my privilege to have a Bible experience. The salvation which the Lord Jesus suffered so much to procure is something far more complete than I have yet proved it to be. I am sure it is something that will last, something that grows better and better and stronger and stronger, something very different from the quavering, wavering thing I have yet found it to be!

And whatever others may say, my soul cries out for a lasting reality and I cannot be satisfied without it. I believe it is the "Promise of the Father" I need. I am sure I have never received the Holy Ghost in the measure, nor in the power that He was poured out upon the Bible saints; and if I am to have a Bible experience I must have Bible power to make it possible. I do not suppose you will understand how a soul could have so much knowledge of truth without the corresponding power and life of it. But the head can grasp a great deal which the heart has never comprehended; and I solemnly believe that if my head were cut off there would be very little of my religion left.

All this may be of little comfort to others, and yet, I have nothing else to say. I do get glimpses now and then of what a life in the Spirit would be and see how one would move from strength to strength and from glory to glory in such a life with none of these dreary and wretched wanderings and backslidings. And my soul presses on to know its full experience and realization. Our Jesus is a perfect Saviour and I do not want to dishonor Him any longer by realizing only an imperfect salvation. He will save me to the uttermost, and, although in darkness, I can sing a song of victory and triumph as I look forward to the consummation, which in His own time, I know will come.

—To "An old friend," August 9, 1868

128. Helpless, Hanging upon Jesus

My last entry in this little volume! Would that it could be a different one! I have just been looking back at the opening records, and have realized how much there was of the intellect in all those first rejoicing experiences. I chose to believe that I was "abiding in Christ" because I thought the Bible said every believer was. I chose to believe I was "dead to sin and alive to God," because I came to the conclusion that the Bible said this was the case with every believer. And for awhile, believing these things had an effect; but of real Holy Ghost work there seems to have been none!

The whole matter seems to have been a transaction of my reasoning powers. The Bible stated certain things of believers, and knowing myself to be a believer I came to the conclusion that they must consequently be true of me, and I took what I called a "step of faith" and believed them. But God was left out. The Holy Spirit was ignored. I believed in things accomplished 1800 years ago; but of any present work accomplished now by the Holy Spirit in sanctifying my soul I had no conception.

The result was, I never got hold of any realities—never of anything that lasted! Always I felt that after all I had the whole management of my religious life in my own hands, and that it all depended upon my believing, and my apprehending, and my taking steps of faith, and my praying, and my consecrating, and my waiting upon God. God Himself never seemed to get hold of me somehow. The Holy Ghost never seemed to work. And this whole volume has been a record of my fruitless struggles after a Divine reality and I have felt that it is no longer a belief in the indwelling of the Holy Spirit that will satisfy me, but I must have the Holy Spirit Himself. It is no longer either a belief that I am "abiding in Christ" and am "dead to sin," but the real experience of this that can quiet the cry of my starving soul! And I must have this, or I shall die!

—Journal, September 25, 1868

129. Hopeless, Helpless, Holding On

Since my first entry in this book another little daughter has been added to our family, making three little girls all under five years of age, and one little boy. They are sweet children—the joy and delight of my life. Mary, Lloyd Logan, Alice, and Rachel—Ray.

I had prayed, and even fondly hoped, that during the time of my daughter's birth I might receive the answer to all my many prayers of the past six months. And my soul went out in one continuous cry to God that it might be so. But alas! in vain. As yet He has answered me not a word, and I am heartsick and well nigh despairing! Oh my God my God, why is it thus? What is the hindering thing that frustrates thy grace? God has said, "Ask and ye shall receive;" His word is full of promises that those who hunger and thirst after righteousness shall be filled; Christ died and ascended to Heaven that He might pour out this gift of the Holy Spirit for which I have been seeking—and all Scripture has led me to think it was His will that every believer should receive it, and that, without delay.

And yet I have prayed, and prayed, and wrestled, and tried to exercise faith, and have in short taken every Scriptural way which seemed pointed out to me, in order to obtain this great and sorely needed blessing, and it does not come! And now, utterly worn out and weary of my strugglings, despairing of any answer to my prayers, hopeless of any result from my believing, I can only throw myself in my utter helplessness at the feet of Jesus and holding up in one hand my unanswered petitions and in the other His unfulfilled promises, cry, "Lord, behold!"

—Journal, October 29, 1868

130. Sunday, Monday

The perplexing question as to how I can hope to experience the blessings I am seeking for has finally been settled. I have found, ever since this subject of the baptism of the Holy Ghost has engrossed my attention and filled my soul with such a hunger and thirst for God, that whenever I cast myself on the Lord Jesus in complete ignorance and helplessness and trust Him to give me the full salvation He had died to secure for me, I have always had peace and rest. But no sooner have I given myself over totally to Him, than the question has invariably come up as to whether after all this was the best and Scriptural way; as to whether there don't have to be definite acts of faith for definite blessings, and that I have to have definite gifts. And at once I have been plunged into darkness again.

And in this way I have been driven from one side to the other, making no progress of any kind. But some dear saints of God have helped me to settle the question and have shown me that however it may be with others, my only resource is to cast myself upon Jesus in the most ignorant sort of way, defining nothing, and almost as it were believing nothing, but simply trusting Him to accomplish the whole work from beginning to end in His own way and time.

I feel like that poor woman, who knew no English words but "Sunday, Monday" and who, longing for the rest and peace she saw depicted in the faces of some English Christians, and supposing their God could understand no language but English, went by herself and prayed in these two words "Sunday, Monday; Sunday, Monday," over and over, until He heard and answered, not her words, but the desire of her heart! Jesus knows what I want, and I trust Him to give it to me; and here I rest. My helplessness is so great! Only an omnipotent Saviour will do for me!

—To Sally, December 16, 1868

131. The Pentecostal Promise

Would it have been right for those disciples gathered in that upper room before the day of Pentecost to have given up their seeking and waiting for the baptism of the Holy Ghost? It was God's will to give them the fullness of the Spirit. He had declared it to be so, and could they have dared even for a moment to think of doing without it? You might as well tell sinners to resign themselves to being lost if that was God's will. It could not be God's will, and to entertain the thought of such a thing is treason against Him.

He has commanded us to abide in Him. He has declared that it is His will that He should abide in us forever. He has told us that the Lord Jesus shed His blood for this very purpose, that we might be dead to sin and alive only in Him. And how can we dare, in the face of all these things, to resign ourselves to a lower experience? I know what it is to be tempted in this way, and I know that it is one of Satan's subtlest temptations. It seems to bring a great rest after struggling just to settle down into resignation with our present condition, but it seems to me it is the rest of lethargy or sleep, such rest as the bride in the Canticles was enjoying when she found her Beloved was no longer by her side.

Rather than such rest as this, I would wander forever around the walls of the city, seeking for my Beloved! I do not doubt that Satan stops many souls just here, and cheats them out of their rights and deprives the Lord of His glory by this counterfeit resignation which is, after all, a resignation to Satan and not to God. For God's will is that we should be filled with His fullness, and to be resigned to anything short of this, is not to be resigned to Him.

—To Anna, 1317 Filbert St., January 26, 1869

132. Deliverance from Sinning

I am convinced that there is one definite result at least, which I must claim as the necessary consequence of consecration and faith, and that is a present and complete deliverance from sinning. If my soul is really entirely surrendered to the Lord Jesus and if I am really trusting Him to work all the good pleasure of His will in me, I must be delivered from sinning. There is no alternative here. Where Jesus reigns, sin cannot, and therefore my faith must claim this as a present experience, as a necessary result of faith in Him.

And I believe until this point is fully and definitely settled, God can bestow no other blessings however much the soul may hunger and thirst for them. The temple must first be made pure, before the King will come in to reign there gloriously! And the attitude of my soul at present is that of consecration and faith for this very thing. I feel I must experience deliverance from sinning even though every other blessing should be denied me! If I can only be sure the Lord has worked this deliverance out in my soul, then I am sure the Lord will continue His further work in my heart and will satisfy every desire of my soul, revealing Himself to me as my abiding indwelling Saviour, who will never leave me again!

As yet my faith is but weak and wavering, but oh my God, do thou make it strong!

—Journal, February 16, 1869

1334. God's—Wholly and Forever

I feel that perhaps it will help me to write out a definite consecration of myself to God so that I may distinctly grasp the reality and irrevocableness of it.

Lord, I am yours, yours wholly, and yours forever! I am yours by the purchase of your blood, and I present myself to you now as a living sacrifice, body, soul, and spirit to be as clay in your hands.

I give you my heart, Lord, to love only what you love; to hate what you hate; to endure all things, to suffer long and be kind, to be not easily provoked; to think no evil, not to seek my own. Help me, oh my God!

I give you my intellect to be wholly devoted to your service, and perfectly under your control to think only those thoughts that will please you, to devise only such plans as you suggest, to yield the management of all its affairs to you! I give it to you that you may fulfil the purposes of your grace by casting down in me imaginations, and every high thing that exalts itself against the knowledge of God, and bringing into captivity every thought to the obedience of Christ. Help me, oh my God.

I give you my body to be used by you. My eyes to see only what you would have them see, my ears to hear only what you would have them hear; my feet to go only where you lead, my hands to do only what can be done in fellowship with you, my tongue to speak only words that please you. I give you any appetite to be under thy control and regulation. I give my time to you, Lord, to be all employed for you.

I leave my reputation in your hands. I give you my children, my husband, and everyone whom I love to be disposed of according to your will. I leave to you the ordering of my whole life, and with your help will follow you wherever you lead. I will give you the control of my feelings and of my prejudices.

I submit, in short, my whole being and life, all that I am and have and will be to your complete control and only ask that your will may be perfectly done in me, through me and by me! Take me and keep me oh my God!

—Journal, May 31, 1869

134. The Cleansing Fountain

Thank God it is the blood that cleanses, the precious blood of Christ! It is not discipline, nor effort, nor prayer, nor fasting that cleanse the heart and make it a fit dwelling place for the Father and the Son; it is the precious blood alone. And it can cleanse in a moment; yes, can make, even out of my heart, a holy temple for God to abide in!

And I thank my God that I do believe that it has cleansed me, that it is even now cleansing me, so that God can come now at any moment and manifest Himself to my soul! Glory to the Lamb! Praise the name of Jesus! "I've washed my garment white in the blood of the Lamb."

> Jesus thine all victorious Love
> Shed in my heart abroad.

Then shall my heart no longer rove?
Rooted and fixed in God.
—Journal, May 31, 1869

135. The Condescending God

The Lord has stirred up my soul again to a sense of my utter need of the baptism of the Holy Ghost, or in other words, my need to know by a living experience what it is to have Christ formed within me, to have God coming into my heart and abiding there forever! And about ten days ago I began by prayer and fasting to seek after a realization of this blessed experience. The Lord has been teaching me many things during this time. He has made my consecration far more complete and thorough than it ever has been before; and He has given me a sense of the glorious awfulness of being indwelt by the living God!

Just think of it, Frank, that God, who made all things—the great, and mighty and omniscient God condescends to stand at the door of our hearts and knock for admittance; and if we will open to Him will come in and abide with us forever! It seems too glorious to be true, and yet the Bible promises it, and Jesus died to make it our privilege.

But God is of purer eyes than to behold iniquity, and before He can take up His abode in a heart, it must be cleansed from all sin. And the precious blood of Christ does cleanse the heart and keeps it clean, so that our hearts, vile and polluted as they are by nature, are made fit temples for the Lord to dwell in.

I feel, dear Frank, that this precious blood cleanses my heart, and I am waiting on the Lord now for Him to reveal His glorious presence there!
—To Son, The Barracks, June 8, 1869

136. Christ Formed in Me

The Lord has answered my prayers and has come into my heart to take up His abode there! As yet I have not great joy, or light, or glory, but only a simple consciousness of His presence, that is different from any thing I ever felt before & that is filled with a divine certainty! Father, brother James, and I all felt impressed last night to stay up all night and wrestle with God for the victory; and although we none of us mentioned it, we found ourselves with one accord continuing in prayer and supplication, and about three o'clock, after a severe conflict to have and to keep a steady faith, the Lord came into His temple, and consummated the everlasting union of my soul with His. Oh, praise and bless His holy name! I am waiting and expecting to be filled with joy, and with glory but meanwhile I know that I must confess boldly what the Lord has done for me; and must hold fast the confession of my faith without wavering.

And oh, Frank, it is most blessed to know that Christ is formed within me, and that He has set up His kingdom there! Bless God!

—To Frank, June 10, 1869

137. Trusting in the Cold and the Dark

I am still hanging on by naked faith. Satan fills my soul with the most despairing suggestions, but I know that to entertain them a moment would be to plunge myself into the blackness of despair, for if I should allow myself to think that the Lord had failed me now, I could never trust Him again, and certainly could never hope to be more sincere or earnest myself. No! No! I will believe, I will trust straight on through all the coldness and darkness of my soul! Jesus is a perfect Saviour and His salvation is for poor lost sinners just such as I am, and His salvation included the very things I long have sought.

I have not asked for any extraordinary blessing or privilege, but only what the Bible declares to be the common possession of all who believe in Jesus. Does it not say, "Whosoever confesseth that Jesus is the Son of God, God dwelleth in Him and He in God?" Whosoever—surely that includes me. And again, "For the promise (of the Holy Ghost) is to you and to your children, and to all that are afar off, even as many as the Lord our God shall call." Is not the command universal, "Be ye filled with the Spirit;" and was not the exhortation, "Abide in me and I in you," addressed to every believer? Did not our Lord Himself pray—"That they all may be one; as thou Father art in me and I in thee, that they also may be one in us. I in them and thou in me, that they may be perfect in one."

Oh no, I cannot doubt, I will not! My Jesus is dwelling in me; and now I have only to let Him work there to will and to do of His good pleasure, in order to experience all the glorious fullness of His mighty salvation!

—Journal, June 14, 1869

138. Confessing Christ in the Hard Times

Again today I have tried to witness a good confession to the work the Lord hath wrought in my soul. But it is hard to testify where there is so little feeling, and Satan tries to hinder me by every possible suggestion he can bring forward. He tells me it is all a lie, and that I had better have had my tongue cut out before I ever presumed to say such a thing of myself, and tries to induce me to stay away from the meetings and from every place where confession could be made. But my indwelling Saviour keeps me from yielding to these suggestions or from entertaining them for a moment, and enables me to set my face like a flint that I will hold fast the confession of my faith without wavering, because faithful is He that hath promised.

Yes, I will believe, I will trust; even though the Lord should never again show me the light of His countenance, nor manifest Himself to my soul! My Jesus is dwelling in me, and has established His Kingdom there, and I am altogether and only His! Oh praise His holy Name!

One blessed result I do find, and that is that I love His will now with a genuine love that makes a cross borne for His dear sake filled with an untold sweetness.

—Journal, June 15, 1869

139. The Power of Testimony

The Lord has helped me to witness a good confession during the last two or three days, and my faith has been greatly strengthened. But still it is faith not sight and my heart longs for some more manifest tokens of my Saviour's presence and love! Yet I must and can praise the Lord for the comparative freedom from doubts of the last few days, and that He has kept my faith throughout this sharp trial.

I have found one of the most helpful means to drive away Satan with his awful suggestions is to begin defying him at once by making a bold confession of all the Lord has done for me; if possible in public, or if that isn't possible, in private, or by writing a letter, or even in prayer and thanksgiving to God. The last and sharpest conflict was on the evening of the 16th when it seemed as if the very gates of hell were yawning open to swallow me up, and I was walking the floor in an agony of soul. When suddenly in desperation I turned around and in my agony almost shook my fist in his face with the boldest confessions I have yet made of the work the Lord has wrought. Satan was silenced and has not dared to trouble me much since. I find it very helpful to say to myself continually in the intervals of conversation and when at work, "Oh my indwelling Saviour, I am wholly yours, and yours only. You have taken up your abode in my heart; you are dwelling there."

Now, oh Lord, manifest your presence. My faith is greatly strengthened by this, and Satan is kept at bay.

—Journal, June 16, 1869

140. Purpose in Suffering

"My flesh and my heart faileth, but God is the strength of my heart and my portion forever." Yes, oh my soul, God is your portion!

Again Satan is busy with his suggestions to doubt my whole religious experience, and it seems as though they hardly were doubts, but the very truth. I feel like a poor miserable self-deceiver! But, oh my God, save me from entertaining these feelings for a single moment. Oh, be my Keeper, now, in this time of sore need! You are dwelling in my heart and I am wholly and altogether yours. I dare not doubt—I will not! Oh Saviour of the helpless. Save me!

I have been crying to the Lord and lately He has given me a text which greatly comforts and sustains me, 1 Peter 1:6, 7: "Though now for a season, if need be, ye are in heaviness through manifold temptations; that the trial of your faith, being much more precious than of gold that perisheth, though it be tried with fire, might be found unto praise and honor and glory at the appearing of Jesus Christ." Since my Jesus is to get praise and honor and glory through this trying of my faith, I am willing, yes, even thankful for every moment of it!

—Journal, June 21, 1869

141. Hearing His Voice

It has seemed to me today that I must hear the voice of my Beloved or I would faint and fail! And I went to Him telling Him that I would be very confiding and childlike, and would receive any message He would give me without reasoning or questioning. I felt that up to now, I have been so full of my reasonings that His voice could scarcely make itself heard in my heart, and I told Him that from now on I intended to commit my thoughts to His keeping, and that I would believe He accepted the trust, and would receive every suggestion which was in accordance with the Scripture and which tended to glorify Him as being His voice speaking in my heart; while all suggestions of doubt I promised to lay to the door of my soul's enemy. And having told Him all about it, I then fervently asked that He would not allow me to be deceived.

My faith seemed to lay hold on the Lord Jesus, and I began to wait for His words. Almost at once this text was brought to my remembrance: "You are all fair, my love, there is no spot in you." My whole soul shrunk from appropriating such a text. I all fair? I to be called by the Lord Jesus, "my love;" no spot to be found on me? But I had promised to believe and to receive anything, and I dared not reject it, and oh what sweet peace and comfort I have drawn from meditating upon these blessed words. They have driven away all the dark clouds of unbelief that were gathering around my soul and have made me feel very near to my precious Saviour who speaks to me like that!

It is all because of the cleansing blood that such words can be spoken of one like me—the precious blood of Christ that can make even the foulest clean, yea, whiter than snow! Oh praise the name of Jesus, whose blood is thus availing! Bless His dear and holy Name!

—Journal, June 23, 1869

142. Confession

I am sure your conscience will not let you rest without making an apology. I know it always seems almost impossible to make an apology, but I have often done it, and I have always found that the hardest part of all was the thinking about it. Once you get the words out, all the trouble is over.

Be brave enough to do what is right. Before you go to bed tonight, clear up the whole matter. I know from experience how it is that we fail at this point. It is because we do not make confession when we should, and we never will have the strength we need until we are willing to do it. You know the promise, "if thou shalt believe in thy heart and shall confess with thy mouth thou shalt be saved; for with the heart man believeth unto righteousness, and with the mouth confession is made unto salvation." I think this means that we cannot be saved until after we confess. Don't be discouraged at your failure, but try again, and again, and again, if necessary, and your feet will at last be established firmly and immovably on the Rock.

Almost everyone, when they begin the pathway of consecration, has failures and perplexities, and they are apt to arise because of our refusal to confess our weaknesses because of a fear of future failure. And there is only one way to conquer this, and you know what it is. It is to obey the Lord totally, and when He calls for a confession from you, do it right away. Take this course, or you will be unhappy. I won't say any more, but just pray for you continually.

—To Frank, January 23, 1870

143. A Big Heart Full of Love

When Mary went to bed tonight and was going to say her prayers she said, "But mamma, I don't know what to say." "Just ask for whatever you want," I replied. "Well," she said, "I want dear Jesus to keep me from being like the children of Israel." I asked her why. "Because," she answered, "they did evil in the sight of the Lord." And then after a pause she said, "But mamma, I thought the children of Israel were good, a great deal better than us." "Oh no," I said. "Then why did Jesus save them?" she asked. "Because He loved them and chose to save them," I answered. "Well," she said, "I don't see how He could love them when they were so naughty." "Neither do I," I replied, "but then He did, and He loves us too though we are just as naughty."

"Don't He ever stop loving us?" she asked. "Oh no," I said, "never, and when we are naughty if we only ask Him, He always forgives us right away." "Oh mamma," she exclaimed, "if I was naughty every day and asked Him to forgive me every day, would He do it?" "Certainly," I answered. "He never gets tired of forgiving." "Never!" she exclaimed. "Does the Bible say so mamma?" "Yes," I replied. "Well why don't He get tired of forgiving us?" she asked. "Because He loves us so much; He has such a big heart full of love for us."

—Journal, February 11, 1870

144. A Heart as Big as the Whole World

"Oh mamma," she said, "is His heart as big as the world?" "Yes," I answered. "Well then I don't see how it can stay anywhere," she remarked. "Oh," I said. "His heart is not a thing, it is a feeling. Don't you know what a feeling is? When you feel happy that is not a thing, is it? It is a feeling." "Oh yes," she said. Then after thinking a minute she exclaimed, "Oh mamma, I'm so happy, I don't know what to do. I love Jesus so. I'm smiling at Him in my heart. I am so happy! I guess mamma, I'll have to pull my nose I'm so happy." Then I said, "Jesus is here daughter smiling on you and standing by you." "You mean," she said, "that He is in my heart. He often knocks at the door of my heart and I say, 'Come in Dear Jesus and don't let Satan in with you.'" Then after a pause she said, "Mamma, Satan often tells me to pray to him and to say, 'Please dear Satan make me do something naughty.' But I never do, I just resist the devil and he runs away from me. I feel as if he was afraid of me then. I can feel him running away mamma."

And now she continued, "Let's go on talking about Jesus. Oh I'm so happy. I feel as if I could cry I love Jesus so much. Do you know mamma, it makes me all tremble when I get near to Jesus, I'm so happy?" And after a pause she said, "Now I want to pray. Shall I just say what comes into my head?" I told her, yes so she prayed in the most loving of all loving little tones, "Dear Jesus, please make me always make you feel happy. This I ask for Jesus' sake!"

—Journal, February 11, 1870

145. Two Sides of a Mountain

With regard to predestination, I think both of your final arguments were unanswerable, and I believe the Bible leaves them like that. It seems as if the Bible says both things, and no one yet has ever reconciled its apparently contradictory statements. This is because of our ignorance. When we know more we shall see just how it all is, but now we must be content to take what God says about it, and believe it all even though one saying may seem to contradict another. God certainly is sovereign and not only knows all things past and future, but also arranges everything. And yet, man certainly has some freewill and can, to a certain degree, carve out his own destiny. Both are true. God knows how they harmonize, & one day we will too.

I suppose if a fly, for instance, could read our books and hear our statements, he would meet with absolutely irreconcilable contradictions, because of his ignorance; and we are less than this as compared with God. Guinness says predestination and freewill are like two sides of a mountain, the first being God's side, the second our side. He sees both and knows how they meet at the top; we see only one and think it must be all there is. But whatever our opinions may be about it, our faith ought to rest in an absolute confidence in God that He will do for us all that He has promised and that we need; and there we can leave it; for hasn't He promised to do everything, and don't we need everything?

—To Frank, October 20, 1870

146. His Strength Alone

Surely God has not given us all our life only to be quenched in death, but to grow and expand and become more and more vigorous. The lesson I learned in my own especial experience at Oakington Md. camp meeting is the lesson for us all I think—not to "frustrate the grace of God."

The one illustration that seemed to contain the kernel of it all was such a homely one that it hardly seems worth repeating, and yet my story would not be complete without it. One of the preachers told it one evening. Two little boys were skating when one of them broke through and breaking his way along the thin ice finally was able to hold himself up when he reached a solid part. He could hold, but he could not climb out, and his companion worked himself along on some rails to pull him out.

Before making any effort, however, he explained to the poor little fellow that it would be death to them both if he should make the least effort to save himself, that his only safety lay in being absolutely passive and letting his companion save him. The drowning boy promised to be still, and his friend reached out his arm to grab him, but in his intense eagerness to be saved the poor little fellow forgot his promise and tried to seize the arm of his friend. At once the friend drew back and threatened to leave the poor boy to drown unless he would remain absolutely still. Again he promised, and again an effort was made, and again the eager desire for life overcame him and he tried to seize the outstretched arm.

The friend saw it was a serious emergency and with feigned indifference he turned on his heel and threatened to leave him to his fate. The poor boy, now thoroughly frightened, promised faithfully to remain still if only his friend would make one more effort to save him. And this time, by a mighty struggle, he kept his promise and was pulled out of the water to safety.

Every effort we make to help Him save us only renders it impossible for Him to do it. Our only hope lies in being absolutely helpless and in our letting Him do it all! The lesson is a blessed one. And I believe that if we all would learn it as we ought, we would soon find ourselves, "living, free, and mighty, standing on our tombs!"

—To Anna, The Barracks, August 1, 1870

147. Your Will Be Done

The very thought of seeing Him face to face and sitting down in His presence to never leave again, thrills me with such a sense of eager anticipation, that I hardly like to think of the imperative claims of my nursery, which forbid every such longing! I can almost demand, as my right, some special and powerful manifestations of the presence of my soul's Beloved. And I surely thought I had the Scriptures all on my side. But now I have discovered myself to be so very important to Him, and am so sure that my Master always does just what is right that I can only say continually, "Your will be done—your will, not mine."

How thankful I am for this clause in the prayer our Master left us. What better petition could have been put into our hearts and on our lips? What could we ask or want beside? "Your will be done, and done too on earth here, just as it is done in Heaven." Why that would be a Heaven of itself at once!

—To a Friend, The Barracks, July 3, 1870

148. Love, Joy , and Peace

I am very glad you write to me so freely, although it makes me sad to see that the world has such a strong hold on your heart. I know it is natural, and I can sympathize with your feelings, but I see plainly where your mistake is. It is just because you do not know the joys of God's salvation yet, and therefore the duties connected with it appall you.

I wish, my precious boy, that you would just pray now for one thing that God will give you the joys of His salvation. I will ask this for you, and you must ask it for yourself. It is not a long prayer and you can easily remember to say it morning and evening, and when once your soul is filled with joy all the rest will come right. You are looking at the thing now in a dreadfully legal way, and making the Gospel out to be bondage, whereas, really and truly, it is the greatest liberty; and its special element is joy.

Dear Frank, the Gospel is good news, something to make people happy; not a law to bind them. You can never know all about it until you get hold of it at the right end, the end beginning with "Love, joy & peace." Just ask for joy, as I have said and let all the rest go. Say night and morning, and whenever through the day you think of it, "Dear Lord make me happy in you," and leave it there. All the rest will come out right when once you are happy in Him. And this happiness will be the beginning; remember: "love, joy & peace" are the first fruits mentioned.

—To Frank, November 14, 1870

149. Praying Is Always Right

A feeling of real need is always a good enough reason to pray. Whenever I go to any meeting I am always sure of one thing, that we always ought to have prayer soon after we begin. If anyone else prays my mind is relieved.

But if no one else seems inclined to do it, then I feel it is my duty. The command is for us always to pray, and I don't believe anyone ever goes wrong in trying to pray. Don't be discouraged about what others may think, and the Lord will hear.

He is trying your faith now. I am so glad you are beginning to know the joys of the Christian life. For my part I don't see how anyone who is not a Christian can be happy for a single minute. Children of God, who know their sins forgiven and who cast all their cares upon the One who cares for them, certainly have a right to be joyful and lighthearted. As to being so sober and solemn, it is all wrong. The merriest people I know are the most devoted Christians.

—To Frank, March 8, 1871

The way I know I ought to pray is this. We are commanded over and over to pray always, to meet and pray. And the only qualification that ever seems to be required is that we feel our need of something. If I feel a need, then it is my privilege to pray no matter where I am. And if it be in a meeting, and I feel that the meeting needs anything, then that is my qualification for praying, for asking, that need may be supplied. It is a mistake to think we must wait to feel good before we pray; we need to pray most of all when we feel poor, and empty, and weak. Never be afraid of praying, dear boy. It is always right.

—To Frank, March 14, 1871

150. Prayer Is Simply Asking

There is never a hint anywhere in the Bible that we are to wait for any special feeling in order to pray. Prayer is not a kind of religious performance. It is simply asking for something we want. And whenever we have a sense of need, that is the time for us to pray. When I go to a meeting, I ask God to show me my own needs and the needs of the meeting, and when I feel these, then I believe it is right for me to ask for Him to supply them, unless someone else has already done it; and I find it is very rare for two to ask for exactly the same things. But even if they do, so much the better, for God certainly does answer united prayer.

And if your conscience is uneasy about doing this, that seems to me a pretty sure sign that there must be something a little wrong about it. Let me advise you what to do. Tell the Lord exactly what your problem is at this point and just how hard it is to do it. Then ask Him either to put your conscience at rest about it, or else to make you willing to do what you should do. He will certainly do one or the other of these things for you, for you never can make yourself willing.

—To Frank, March 21, 1871

151. Happiness in Christ

There is no peace and no joy in a half-hearted religion. There is such a thing as having just enough religion to make one miserable, and as long as you hold back from a full surrender to His will, this will be the situation. Oh, do let Jesus have all of your heart! He will give you such a fullness of joy in Himself that will far more than repay you for any earthly pleasure you may think you may miss because of it. "In His presence there is fullness of joy, and at his right hand there are pleasures for evermore!"

—To Frank, March 21, 1871

Don't let those things that annoy you in life disturb your communion or interrupt your spiritual progress. Christians ought to receive everything as coming directly from the hands of our Heavenly Father, and consequently, bear them patiently. If the very hairs of our head are numbered, and He says they are, then we may be sure that He arranges all our affairs for us so He may educate and train us for His service and for His glory. And so, no doubt, He is permitting you to go through these trials in order to make you a better and nobler person. Only we must bear them in a right spirit in order to accomplish this result. Ask Him to give you the right feelings about them and to enable you to act like a Christian should. He can make you happy in spite of everything.

—To Frank, March 14, 1871

152. Discouragement and Victory

I feel inexpressibly thankful for the Lord's tender and loving dealings with you and am so happy that you have been able to give yourself up so completely to our Saviour. You will be a happy Christian as well as a useful Christian; and I am sure you will soon learn more and more about the simplicity of the life of faith, so that you will be able to look away from yourself and have your eyes fixed on Jesus. The soul can never be discouraged that looks to Him; never! For He is only love and tenderness and forgiving mercy.

When we look at ourselves, then there is never anything but discouragement. Don't ever expect to find any good in yourself; you never will.

And if you did, it would be a very bad sign. Our goodness, our strength, our everything, in short, is in Jesus. We are poor sinners and nothing at all, and Jesus Christ is our all in all! We pray for you that you will be kept resting in Jesus and with your hearts full of His peace! I feel sure now that He will make you a blessing to others. Remember George Fox's true saying, "All discouragements are from the Devil." All, every one, of whatever kind they may be, and never yield to them for one moment.

It is so sweet to be altogether His and His only. How totally peaceful and free from care we are, when we know that the Lord has taken us into His special keeping, and that His arms are round about us and beneath us. When I know this, I feel like singing, "Praise God from whom all blessings flow!" Don't let any sudden failure or temptation make you feel that the whole thing is gone. The very moment you discover your failure, go at once to Jesus, and have it all washed away in His precious blood, for His promise is, "If we confess our sins, He is faithful and just to forgive us our sins and to cleanse us from all unrighteousness." He does both. He forgives, and then He cleanses and makes us just as pure as before; and we need not be hindered by it a moment.

—To Frank, April 4, 1871

153. Don't Be Discouraged

But don't be discouraged. Remember, all discouragement is from the Devil. Discouragement is the first step towards sin. Just keep giving yourself up to the Lord over and over, and trust Him as much as you can. And like a child learning to walk, if you fall down, don't lie there and cry, but get right up and try again. You know that unusually helpful text, "If we confess our sins, He is faithful and just to forgive us our sins and cleanse us from all unrighteousness." He not only forgives, but what is better, He makes us just as pure and clean and acceptable as we were before. We are not put back by it one bit. So don't hesitate; and remember He has told us to forgive even up to seventy times seven a day, so He certainly will do the same.

Never be discouraged. If Satan trips you up, don't let him have the satisfaction of keeping you down. Just tell him that nothing he can do can stop you from going on again just the same as ever. Learn to walk by faith, and then any variations in feelings will not trouble you. Keep on giving yourself up to Him and trusting over and over if it is a hundred times a day, and it will get to be a life at last.

—To Frank, April 10, 1871

154. Learning to Walk

What you tell me about your religious experience makes me very happy. As long as you remain there, in the arms of Jesus, everything will be alright. The promise is sure, "Thou wilt keep him in perfect peace whose mind is stayed on thee because he trusteth in thee." It is such a simple and child-like way of living that many Christians completely overlook it and wear themselves out in trying to attain to some great height when all they need to do is to rest in the arms of Jesus. Some old writer says that "God's will is a pillow to rest on, not a load to carry;" and this is so true to the soul that is entirely given up to Him.

—To Frank, May 1, 1871

I do not think you need to be at all discouraged by your Christian experience. The life of faith is, in one sense, a gradual growth. That is, the habit of trusting grows, until it becomes as it were a second nature, and we trust almost without knowing it. In the beginning of the life of faith, the usual experience is very variable and sometimes faltering. But you have learned the secret. And if you always go back to the blood of Christ for forgiveness and cleansing, just as soon as you realize your failure, you will find that you will get into such a habit of continually looking to Jesus and His cleansing blood that you will not go astray any more.

I do not believe a perfect and complete victory ever comes just right away. It is like a child learning to walk; it may have many a tumble at first, but if it is not discouraged by its falls, but just jumps up and goes ahead, it will be able to walk after a while without falling. But if the falls discourage it and it gives up in despair, then of course it will never learn to walk at all. Just go on as you are, trusting as fully as possible, and when you fail, confess your failures at once, believing in forgiveness and cleansing, continually looking to Jesus and all will be well.

—To Frank, May 9, 1871

155. Spiritual Joy

As for joy, your joy is to be in the Lord, not in yourself. Spiritual joy is not a thing, not a lump of joy, so to speak, tucked away in your heart to be looked at and treasured. Our joy is all in Christ. We rejoice that we have Him for our Saviour; we rejoice in His love and in His power to save.

I once suffered a great deal because I looked for joy as a thing by itself, and I never found it. And that discouraged me. But now I never think whether I have joy or not. I have Christ, and that is enough. I am glad that I have Him, and this gladness, I believe, is the true Christian joy. It is certainly something to be happy about to know that we have such a Saviour and such a salvation, to know that we are heirs of God and are going towards our glorious inheritance.

So, give up looking for joy and just take all the comfort you can out of the gifts the Lord has already given you and be glad for your salvation and rejoice in Christ. Do you understand the distinction between rejoicing in your joy, and rejoicing in Christ? If you are entirely given up to Him, you will understand, because where He has His way with us, He cannot have us anything but right.

And yet this may not always be manifest to us. A lump of clay that is in the process of transformation of being made into a beautiful vase has to go through many different stages; and perhaps the earlier stages may not be very beautiful or attractive, but the Potter knows what He is about, and the lump of clay must be content to be just as He would have it, and not as it would like to be itself. You are that lump of clay, and your only concern should be to let the Potter have His own way with you. He will surely make a vessel out of you for His honor "sanctified & meet for the Master's use, and fitted to every good work."

—To Frank, May 9, 1871

156. Jolly Christians

Eph. 5:4 does not refer to that innocent playfulness which is, I think, perfectly legitimate for young people. The very best Christians I know indulge in it. Dr. Cullis, who has the Faith Home for consumptives in Boston is the jolliest fellow I know, always joking, and yet he is one of the most devoted Christians. All the Christians I am acquainted with, who have entered into this experience of abiding in Christ, are merry and lighthearted and fairly happy. One of them told me once that he felt just like a colt, as if he must go out into a field and kick up his heels.

This verse evidently refers to jesting on spiritual subjects for it goes on at once to say "but rather giving of thanks." It certainly doesn't mean to teach that the Christian is never to say a word except to give thanks! But it means that in religion we are to be continually in a thanksgiving spirit, and not to jest about it.

The Christian who wholly belongs to the Lord can afford to be natural. It is only the half-hearted Christians who have to walk on stilts. Like a child who is entirely obedient to its parents can go on at perfect ease and naturally until the parents tell it to change its course; so we may leave all responsibilities as to our course in the Lord's hands and go on at ease and naturally unless He speaks and calls for a change of course. The branch is not making an effort to produce fruit all the time; it simply bears it, and leaves all the labor of cultivation and of making it productive to the gardener. And we are the branches and our Father is the Gardener! Surely we can afford to trust Him!

—To Frank, May 16, 1871

157. Divine Life

I thank the Lord with all my heart for His great mercies to you. That revelation you had gives you a little foretaste of what it will be to pass an eternity with Jesus, and it has taught you how it is possible to be in ourselves poor sinners and nothing at all, but to find Him to be our all in all. It is a blessed thing to have such revelations of Christ; it is infinitely more glorious than any amount of telling about it by another can ever be. Don't you feel that you know now what before you only imagined, or rather imagined could not be?

But do not expect, dear boy, ever to find yourself any better or any nearer your ideal; for you never, never will. You yourself will always be utterly vile, and ignorant, and corrupt, but Jesus is your life now. It is with you "no more I" but Christ who lives in you. And isn't this glorious to lose your own life and find Christ's divine life put in its place? To cease to be of the race of the first Adam, and to become one of the race of the second Adam the Lord from Heaven!

It is far more glorious than for a dog to cease to be a dog and be transformed into a man. Never look into your own heart then for any sort of satisfaction or comfort. You will never find any goodness. There are no stocks of character laid up to draw upon. But your goodness is all in Christ and you must draw it from Him moment by moment as you need it.

Andrew Longacre says we Quakers are so thrifty that we do not like to live "from hand to mouth" as the expression is. We like a stock of goodness laid up ahead, and a stock of wisdom and of patience and of all the other graces. But he says God's plan for us is different. God has laid it all up for us in Christ, and we have to draw it each moment as we need it. If you feel that you are mean and foolish and completely vile, just look at Christ and say to yourself, "never mind, all I need is there ready for me whenever I have occasion to use it, and having Christ I have all things." Our views of our own hatefulness, therefore, don't have to discourage us. Of course we are hateful, but our life is in Christ. He is our life!

—To Frank, May 30, 1871

158. No Stock of Grace

I have had such a fresh and precious revelation of late of the all sufficiency there is in Christ for those who trust Him. It would take too long to describe it, but it is only a deeper revelation of what is meant by those dear old lines,

> I'm a poor sinner and nothing at all
> and Jesus Christ is my all in all.

I think that while realizing this before, I always had an idea that Christian graces were, as it were, things something apart from Christ, given for his sake but still separate from Him. So that for instance if I wanted patience, or spiritual power or wisdom, or any other grace, I expected to get a sort of stock of it, to be stored away in my heart, and looked at & rejoiced over. And if I did not get this stock, and of course I never did, I felt as if my prayers were not answered. But now I see that I already have all the graces I need in Christ, and that I only have to look to Him for the supply at the moment that the need comes and I will invariably get it.

—To a Friend, June 30, 1871

159. Living Hand-to-Mouth

It is a sort of living from hand to mouth, which does not agree with the thrifty ways we are taught in other things, and therefore we are slow to learn it. But the Bible is just full of it. "He hath blessed us with all spiritual blessings in Christ." It is already done; and the moment my faith apprehends any especial blessing as being mine, it is in reality in my possession. In Christ but not apart from Him. So that I shall always be as poor in all spiritual blessings as I was at the beginning, but I shall see more and more of the treasures that are in Christ, and learn how to appropriate them to myself in the time of need.

Do I make my meaning plain? It involves a great deal in the spiritual life, and puts an end to much of the struggling for blessing that we are inclined to value so highly. And it is so sweet to see everything in Christ! Now I understand what it means to sing

> Thou, oh Christ, art all I want
> More than all in thee I find.

He is all. But oh, how few Christians know it, and how slow we, who do know it, are to make it a practical reality!

—To a Friend, June 30, 1871

160. A Priceless Privilege

All day, I have had a happy undercurrent of peace while trusting in Jesus, and realizing the precious cleansing power of His blood. It seems so wonderful to think that such a heart as mine, so vile, so utterly worthless, and worse than worthless can be made pure, and yet there is power in His blood to make even the vilest clean, and I do thank God that this blood avails for me.

It is very sweet, dear mother, to realize the blessing of the pure in heart, and this is our priceless privilege, and I realize that it is mine tonight. But not because of anything in myself, oh no, a thousand times no! But because of Jesus and His precious blood.

> The cleansing stream, I see, I see,
> I plunge, and oh it cleanseth me,
> Oh, praise the Lord, it cleanseth me!
> It cleanseth me, yes cleanseth me!

—To her Mother, July 26, 1871

I want you to know that I am trusting Jesus more fully than ever before, and for much greater blessings. I believe that He does give me purity of heart through the cleansing power of His precious blood, and I think I have learned that I must go on believing this, no matter what may happen. My faith has been too wavering heretofore, but now I feel that I don't dare doubt. And peace and victory are the result thus far, for which I praise the Lord.

—To Sarah, July 28, 1871

161. Christ at the Center

The change in my experience at Round Lake Camp Meeting was a real one, and a very definite one. And ever since then I have recognized myself as being wholly the Lord's and His alone in a way that I never felt before. It seems as if it were inevitable now for me to obey His voice and to do His will. I must, even though I should die in the act! I dare not disobey for I belong to Him.

This was one step. The other was just as real and definite. It was in trusting the Lord definitely for the gift of a pure heart—made clean by the constant cleansing of the blood of Christ. I have trusted Him once or twice before for a little while at a time, and always sensed a mighty power in the realization of it. But I somehow never got the "grasp" on the blessing, if I may use the expression, that made it the reality it is to me now.

After trusting for it for a little while I would allow my faith to become dim and indistinct, and abandoning this central point, I would concentrate my faith on the outer works of the fortress of my heart, trying to trust Jesus to save me from each particular assault as it was made by the enemy, never knowing that his possession of the center gave him the throne and the kingdom which belonged only to the Lord, and upon which it was necessary for Him to be seated before He could save me. The result was, of course disappointment.

—Journal, September 3, 1871

162. Heart Cleansing

I consequently learned that the one important thing was to have the Lord possess the center and at the center He would possess all the rest and would guard and protect it all Himself. And I saw that the way to get Him to set up His throne in the center was simply to accept by faith that His precious blood really did cleanse my heart from all corruption, and make it pure in His sight, casting out the carnal nature and crucifying the old man of sin. So that one could truthfully say, "I have put off the old man which is corrupt etc." "I am dead to sin" "I am crucified with Christ" etc.

And to believe further that having made the heart pure, and a fit dwelling place for Himself, He does indeed come in and take up His dwelling there and sets up His kingdom and possesses all things. So that I can go on to say, "And I have put on the new man which after God is created in righteousness and true holiness. I am dead it is true, but also I am alive to God in Jesus Christ my Lord." "I am crucified indeed, but nevertheless I live, yet not I, but Christ liveth in me!"

I took this step of faith, and I'm standing firm. Discouragements are all around, but I don't dare pay any attention to them. God's unalterable plan is that "according to your faith, it shall be unto you."

—Journal, September 3, 1871

163. Not Only Legally but Truly Free

You say the 6th of Romans declares that our old man is "reckoned" to be crucified. But the text says emphatically without any reservation that "our old man is crucified with Him"; and it makes this fact the ground of the exhortation to us to "reckon ourselves to be dead."

An exact illustration of this is to be found in the history of emancipation during the late war. The slaves were declared to be free, and were urged, because of this fact, to reckon themselves free. We can see at once that their freedom, although an accomplished fact, could never have really done them any good so long as they did not accept it to be true. The government declared their emancipation, but it was necessary that they also should declare their own emancipation. If the freedom proclaimed by the government however had been only judicial, only a legal document of some kind, and not real and practical, their reckoning would have been a mockery; for nothing but an actual freedom would do for them. And if the experience described in the 6th of Romans is only judicial, it is worth but little to us practically in this life.

Yet the whole teaching of the chapter shows that it was intended for this life, notice verse 4 "should walk in newness of life" and verse 6 "that henceforth we should not serve sin"; and verses 12, 14 and 22. Such expressions cannot be applied to the life to come. Neither do they refer to our standing before God, but to our life here and now, our walk in this world, our deliverance from sin while still in the body. Indeed dearest Anna, if this chapter does not speak of real and actual things then I do not know of anything real and actual in the Bible, for even the forgiveness of sins is not declared in plainer or more emphatic terms. If being "dead to sin" is only judicial, then the forgiveness of sins is only judicial also, and our being complete in Christ, and our being seated in heavenly places, and our being translated out of the kingdom of Satan and into the kingdom of God's dear Son, all these are only judicial too, and we don't have actual possessions left at all.

—To Anna, September 6, 1871

164. Judicial or Actual?

In your statement of your own experience of this chapter, there seems to me a great contradiction. You say, "I knew myself to be crucified with Christ," and add, "I recognized my position as dead yet alive." Did you mean that this was judicial or actual? I judge your apprehension of it was simply as a judicial position true in God's sight, but not really true as an actual fact, because you go on to say that the "carnal nature" cannot be destroyed. And yet what is the carnal nature but the old self; and if the old self is crucified surely the carnal nature is crucified. Could stronger language be used than this: "Our old man is crucified with Him that the body of sin might be destroyed."

This "old man," this "body of sin" is what I mean by the carnal nature. It is the sinful nature that was put into me at the fall, and that Christ came to destroy. It would never have entered my head to think that it could be got rid of, if the Lord Himself had not said so, for I confess I should have thought it would have been too much for Him. But when He tells me that it is destroyed I do not see what else I can do but believe Him, even though it may seem to my own consciousness that I am believing a lie. I even can believe a lie on the authority of God!

—To use an illustration—that of Christ abiding in us. He cannot dwell where sin dwells. Before He can take up His abode in our hearts He must make those hearts fit for His dwelling place. He must cleanse them from all unrighteousness. Before we can put on the new man, we must put off the old man. His enemies must be subdued before the king can set up His throne and begin His reign.

—To Anna, September 6, 1871

165. The Carnal Mind

This brings me to your question as to which brings a conqueror more glory, to destroy or to subjugate. I answer that there are certain enemies whom God says must be destroyed, because they never can be subjugated, and of these the chief one is the carnal mind. "Because," He says, "the carnal mind is enmity against God, for it is not subject to the law of God, neither indeed can be." If the carnal mind could become the "loving and obedient subject of Christ," to use your own words, then it might remain, but it never can, for it is the offspring of Satan.

All my natural powers and faculties which God gave me can be subjugated by Him, and will be, as soon as they get rid of their natural master my "carnal mind." When this inward tyrant is expelled, the blessed Lord Himself takes the whole control of my inner man, and works in me to will and to do of His good pleasure. But while I insist upon the continual presence of my tyrant, I never know when I shall be at his mercy.

And I do not see, dearest friend, how with your faith, your experience could be any different from the one you describe with your carnal nature continually reasserting itself and bringing you into captivity. But those who have trusted Jesus to destroy and take away this "body of sin," this "old man" or "carnal mind" or whatever you may choose to call it, declare that they do not find it like that in their experience.

—To Anna, September 6, 1871

166. Christ Enthroned Within

Temptations come, but they come consciously from without and there is no inward traitor to admit them. Such believers abide in Christ continually, and always know what it is to have no will but His. Their victories are not intermittent and uncertain, but invariable and sure. They make no provision for the flesh to fulfil the lusts thereof. They may not always be filled with joy, but they always triumph. I know such Christians, and I know that what they are talking about is no cunningly devised fable.

As for myself, I will speak candidly. I never really understood this truth until this summer at Round Lake. I can see now that I had glimmerings of it before, but was not knowledgeable enough about it really to lay hold and to keep hold of it. My previous faith left this central point untouched, and I concentrated my energies on the outworks of the fortress, trying to trust Jesus to save me from each special assault as it was made by the enemy; not seeing and that the enemy's possession of the center, gave him the throne and the kingdom, which belonged by right to the Lord alone, and upon which it was necessary for Him to be seated before He could save me. The result of course was continual disappointment and I could not understand the reason.

With Christ on the throne at the center of my heart, temptation comes to me now consciously from without, and I am always forewarned of its approach. I do not find my carnal nature reasserting itself, but am conscious that it is dead as God has said. I know I have put off the old man and have put on the new, and my sky is without a cloud. My will is given over to Him in a way it never was before, and consecration is my perfect delight.

And this has all taken place without one particle of emotion & without any conscious outpouring of the Spirit. It has been the result of a simple naked faith, that saw in Jesus a perfect Saviour, and that trusted Him for His full salvation. I stand humbled and amazed at His wondrous grace to one so utterly unworthy.

—To Anna, September 6, 1871

167. Continuing Acts of Faith

Oh, what a Saviour He is. Words can never express His mighty power to save! I never felt so utterly weak in myself, but Jesus is strong, and He is mine, and He saves me now. Praise His Name!

You ask if by an act of faith this great work can be done for you? I answer it can be done for you at this moment by an act of faith, and the next moment by a renewed act of faith, and the next, and so on all through life. "Every moment, Lord I need the cleansing of your blood. And every moment, Lord, I have the cleansing of your blood." I do not mean here cleansing from the guilt of sin, but cleansing from the sin itself, that cleansing which makes me "pure in heart."

And now for the texts, although I have touched upon them all through. They have convinced me that Jesus died to do this work for sinners. Take 1 Peter 2:24, Titus 2:14, Col. 3:3, Eph. 4:21–24, Gal. 5:24, Col. 3:9–12, 1 John 1:9, Rom. 8:2, 8, 9, 10.

Take also all those texts which speak of purity of heart; surely they cannot only mean a judicial purity. Now if out of the heart are the issues of life, then in the pure heart the issues of life must be pure also, and what is this but the destruction of the carnal nature and the old man cast out? I will refer to these texts on heart purity: Acts 15:9, 1 John 3:3, 1 Peter 1:22, 1 Tim. 3:9, 2 Tim. 1:3, Matt. 5:8, Titus 1:15, 2 Pet.3:1, 1 Tim 1:5, 2 Tim.2:22.

These texts prove at least that there is such a thing as a pure heart. And since God tells us that by nature our hearts are deceitful above all things and desperately wicked, if in another place He tells us they can be made pure, He must mean that all this deceit and wickedness is in some way gotten rid of and this is by the cleansing power of the blood of Christ. And this can only be appropriated, as all the other benefits of His death are appropriated by faith. And if by faith, then it may be now!

—To Anna, September 6, 1871

168. Present Cleansing, Present Purity

There is a difference between purity and maturity, but of course you understand this. The rosebud is perfect, but it is not a perfected rose. And it has to be a rosebud first, before it can be a rose at all. And so we must first be made pure, before we can become mature. A heart made pure by faith in the blood of Christ is what the Methodists call the "blessing of holiness," and it is the entrance upon the highway of holiness. It has to be a definite experience, because there must come a moment when we begin to trust for it, if we have not been trusting for it before. It is this trusting for something for which we have not trusted before that we call an "act of faith."

But you would not think for a moment, would you, that we mean our hearts are made pure once for all, and that from then on we go on carrying a pure heart as we would a watch, or some other acquired possession? No, our hearts are made pure by the present application of the blood of Christ, and they are kept pure only by a continual application. Lose sight of the blood, and nothing but impurity remains.

You may ask, "How can we sin if we are made and kept pure in heart?" I answer, just as Adam did, who certainly was created pure and holy. But we need not sin, and we will not so long as we definitely trust Jesus to keep us pure. And as I said, temptations will come to us from without, and we will be forewarned of their approach.

—To Anna, September 6, 1871

169. God's Secret of Security and Peace

And now for my experiences at Round Lake. I believe I had learned before the lesson that everything is in Christ, and that apart from Him I have absolutely nothing. But I had not yet found out what there is in Him. Like a person who knows that all their treasures are stored up in the different chambers of a beautiful temple, but has not yet opened some of the chambers, and consequently is in ignorance of the full extent of his possessions, so I had never apprehended one part of my riches in Christ, and that a very important part. I think my theological notions had stood somewhat in my way. I had never believed that the carnal nature could be utterly cast out of a soul. I knew it could be kept under and conquered; but I supposed its presence was an unavoidable necessity while on this earth. I learned at Round Lake that it might be cast out!

Let me illustrate. Here is a man in his castle with strong walls and massive gates. An enemy from without is seeking to gain an entrance. The castle however is impregnable and the enemy would be forever baffled, but for the presence of a traitor inside the castle, who, no matter how closely he is watched, will find means every now and then to steal down and open the gates and admit the enemy. What is needed to make security invariably safe is to have this inside enemy cast out of the castle, and the gates barred against him. The justified soul is in this castle, and his inside enemy is the carnal nature, or the "body of sin." While that remains inside he never can get a complete or continuous victory.

But can this inside enemy be got rid of? Is he not an inevitable companion of our life in the body? I have always thought he was. I see now that he is not. I see that Jesus died to rid us of this very enemy, and that those who trust Him for this wonderful deliverance, do really experience it. They are made "pure in heart," through the cleansing power of the blood of Christ.

I do not think I ever taught this, and I know I never trusted Jesus for it before, because I was ignorant of its being a part of the purchased salvation. But I thank God that now I do trust my mighty Saviour for even this great deliverance, and that it has brought me "perfect peace."

—To Anna, September 6, 1871

170. Sanctification, Not Self-Satisfaction

Don't you remember how I used to complain because I felt such a capacity to do anything? It seemed so wrong for a Christian? Well, it is just the opposite now! But I need not go into particulars, for I don't want even you to know me as Jesus does. And since it is "no more I but Christ," it is no matter any way.

Only what an utter mistake they make who think this life of sanctification makes people satisfied with themselves! It does make us satisfied with Jesus, and our souls feel very free to make our boast in the Lord, and to tell of what great things He has done for us. And when we do this, we have to say "I," and then people complain. But we are His witnesses; and a witness is not worth anything unless he can say, "I." His testimony would not be received in a court of law; and I am sure the effectiveness of our testimony very much depends upon our ability to say, "I have tasted that the Lord is gracious."

This is just where we have always been lacking. Oh, may the Lord give me such a rich experience of His grace that my mouth will continually show forth His praise!

—To a Friend, September 20, 1871

171. Full Salvation Now

As regards your own experience, I expect, darling Frank, that your lack of peace comes from a lack of faith. You don't believe enough. You trust Jesus for His full salvation, but after all you don't quite believe that He actually does give it to you, and this uncertainty about it gives you unrest. Suppose now you were to come right to Jesus, and give yourself up altogether into His hands, trusting Him to save you fully; then you must believe that He accepts you, and does save you fully at that very moment. "Whatsoever ye ask when ye pray, believe that ye receive it; and ye shall have it." This is God's unalterable plan.

I expect you never get further than to believe that you will receive it sometime. But that won't do. Believe that you receive it now, and then you shall have it. And I am sure it must bring peace to any soul to believe that Jesus does, even now at this very moment, save him with a full and complete salvation; that He does even now make him pure in heart through the cleansing power of His precious blood. Try this present faith, darling boy, and I think you will find a present peace accompanying it.

—To Frank, September 20, 1871

172. Confidence in Christ and Confession

That your prayers may be availing, dear boy, keep your own heart with all diligence. Keep it, that is, by abandoning it to the care and keeping of the Lord. I am so thankful you are finding the rest of faith. This can only come from a childlike confidence in Jesus, which clings to His word, and does not give heed to any doubt. Of course He will save you! This is just what He is for. And when all your cares are cast on Him, He will keep your heart and mind in perfect, perfect peace.

I am glad you spoke in the prayer meeting about it. You will invariably find that confession will greatly strengthen your faith. And the clearer and more definite your confession can be, the better for your own soul. I find a bold clear confession one of the surest ways of baffling Satan, when he comes with his suggestions of doubt and discouragement.

—To Frank, October 2, 1871

173. Deliverance and Victory

The way of faith grows more and more blessed to my soul. And I find that this definite trusting for the casting out of my carnal nature, for having my heart made pure by the precious blood of Christ, brings me the deliverance and the victory which every other kind of faith has always failed to do. Jesus does save me, even me, fully!

I do not mean for a moment that I am satisfied with myself now. No, no, a thousand times no! I never felt myself to be so utterly vile and worthless in myself; I dare not look at myself for a moment. But I am satisfied with Jesus. He is my perfect Saviour, and He does save me from all this vileness and corruption, and does work in me that which is well pleasing in His sight. The Lord Jesus does it, it is all His work, and He has all the glory! Oh praise and bless His holy Name!

I have many a sharp battle with the enemy to hold the beginning of my confidence steadfast, but the Lord has kept me this far, and will keep me, I believe, to the end. I dare not doubt. And when I am tempted to do so, I have learned that the quickest way of deliverance is to assert in a more positive manner than ever my absolute trust in Jesus as my present and perfect Saviour. I find a speedy deliverance by simply declaring over and over again, "The blood of Jesus cleanseth me from all sin." It seems as if Satan cannot endure the mention of that name; he always takes his flight.

My service for the Lord is opening up before me in a wonderful way. I feel utterly unfit for it, and incapable of performing it, but I can trust Jesus.

—Journal, October 6, 1871

174. Definite Faith

I know there cannot be the fullness of blessing in your own soul nor to others, until you apprehend and trust Jesus as a perfect Saviour to keep and to purify. Please don't be indefinite about this. Nothing is ever given to an indefinite faith. Vague generalities will not do in such a crisis as this. The Lord Jesus has offered Himself to you definitely as a Saviour to the very uttermost, and if only you will accept Him, the far reaching extent of His salvation will astonish you. But I feel sure you have accepted Him even in this uttermost sense; and I am only waiting to hear from you that I may rejoice with you.

Oh, it is such a glorious salvation! And the poor world is so hungry for it. Let us rejoice to spend our life and strength in proclaiming it everywhere, and in compelling them to come in!

—To Anna, November 10, 1871

175. Uttermost Salvation

I am thoroughly convinced that the same necessity exists for definite teaching on this subject of sanctification as there exists on the matter of justification if we want to lead others on to an experience of the power of Christ to save similar to our own. And I confess I do want to do this. My heart yearns over the church. I feel the tenderest sympathy for every child of God whose feet are still wandering in the wilderness, and I long unspeakably to show them the way to the promised land and to help them over the Jordan that lies between.

I believe the first thought that always comes into my mind when I meet a Christian, is the question as to whether they know about Jesus as able to save to the uttermost. I do not suppose you can feel this yearning quite so strongly, from never having had the experience of any other kind of Christian life, but those must try and have charity for those of us who have suffered the weariness and the distresses of the wilderness journey, and who are continually filled with thanksgiving over our blessed escape from it.

And now, my darling friend, can you see any objections against a definite confession of Jesus as your present Saviour to the uttermost, cleansing thy heart and keeping it pure by the application of His most precious blood?

—To Anna, November 10, 1871

176. The Christian's Secret

Still I am trusting, and still Jesus saves me! It grows better and better. I have got the secret at last. It is a life of faith, and I have learned how to live it! It has been a most blessed winter. My own experience has been one of perfect rest in Christ. I trust Him, and He does all the rest. Oh, what a Saviour He is! I am so thankful now that He led me by the way of faith, and that He would not grant me the emotions I sought so long.

I am perfectly satisfied now, and would not raise my hand to change anything in all of His dealings with me. I have had a bitter grief, and a cause for sharp anxiety pressing on me all winter, but I have been enabled to say a continual "yes" to His sweet will; and my soul has been kept in perfect peace. Oh praise the Lord, praise Him, praise Him, for such an amazing Salvation!

—Journal, March 12, 1872

From the time of his conversion in the "Layman's Revival" of 1858–59, Robert Pearsall Smith's enthusiasm for lay ministry continued unabated. At the same time he was still active in his business ventures. His experience of the fullness of the Spirit in 1867 intensified his zeal and enlarged the scope of his influence. But we now know that along with this great and apparently whole-hearted dedication to God, he had within him a physical time-bomb. The Smith family carried the genetic strains of a manic depressive syndrome, and his son Frank's sudden death from typhoid fever in 1872 pushed him over the edge into a stage of manic euphoria. It was his second attack following an earlier one brought on by a head injury some years before. An effective, highly sought-after lay evangelist, true to the syndrome of the illness he was heir to, he felt himself indefatigable in whatever he set himself to do. Frantic religious activism that threatened to destroy him and his family drove him from speaking engagement to speaking engagement. Finally, with the help of the family's doctor, Hannah got him to consent to a trip to Egypt and up the Nile. It was designed to get him away from any place he might hold a meeting of any kind and break this threatening cycle of exhausting activity.

But it was not to be. During a stopover in England, friends invited him to address breakfast meetings with British evangelical leaders. Within a two-and-a-half year period, the candlelight of his holiness\higher-life witness in these small, but influential evangelical circles sparked a firestorm of deeper-life evangelism that swept across England and the Continent.

177. Live the Moment

I wish you could learn the secret of living a moment at a time as thoroughly as I have. I am sure it is God's way for us and it is the only way that life is at all bearable. The present moment always brings with it a supply of strength for present needs, but nothing beyond, and as soon as we try to endure even the next hour before it comes, we are out of God's order and are powerless. Do try to make this practical. Don't look ahead at the distant future. But take each moment as it comes and try to dwell only on the blessings it brings.

This is my only resource, but it is an effectual one; it preserves me in peace without anxiety, and enables me to say continually, "Thy will be done." It may be that this is one of the lessons the Lord means to teach you by this trial; and I suppose the quicker we are in learning our lessons, the sooner our discipline will be over.

It is not a lack of feeling that makes the Christian happy, even under sorest trials. But it is the peace of God that passes understanding, that keeps the heart through Christ Jesus.

—To Robert [in England], April 13, 1873

178. Peace Without Intermission

The way of faith grows better and better. Nearly a year has passed since my last entry. It has been a year of earthly sorrow, but a year of heavenly joy. Our darling precious Frank, our noble boy, was buried on his eighteenth birthday last summer, after an illness of ten days with typhoid fever. Through all my life, however, there runs an undertone of gladness that my boy is with the Lord—forever housed from all that could trouble or weary him. I have had the sweet pleasure of writing his life, Frank, the Secret of a Happy Life, and it has just been printed. It seems sometimes as if in this cup the sweet has so outweighed the bitter that I can hardly recognize there was any bitter in it.

I have been given a cup to drink, however, during this last year of almost unmingled bitterness. My husband's nerves have given way. I have only been able to endure by living moment by moment in the will of God, saying a continual "yes" to Him, and casting all my cares every moment upon Him. And as the result of this, through it all, I have known almost without intermission the peace of God which passeth all understanding to keep my heart and mind through Christ Jesus.

—Journal, April 25, 1873

179. Faith Not Emotions

This past year, therefore, has been a time to prove the reality of my doctrine concerning the life of faith, and from the depths of an overflowing heart I can testify that it has stood the test! The Lord has kept and does keep me in perfect peace. I am more than conqueror through Him. And I realize more fully than ever before that I am all the Lord's, and that He has taken upon Himself the whole burden of my whole life both inward and outward, spiritual and temporal, and that I have nothing to do but continually to yield myself to Him. I find it unspeakably "sweet to lie passive in His Hands, and know no will but His." I have no cares and no anxieties; the

Lord is my Shepherd, and therefore I know I shall not want. Oh it is a blessed happy life; who could dream earth had such liberty?

I rejoice more and more that the Lord has led me by the way of faith, instead of by the way of emotions. Faith is the key to God's secrets, and He is teaching me wonderfully. Tonight I am trusting in Jesus, and tonight He saves me fully.

—Journal, April 25, 1873

180. A Bitter Grief

Still the way of faith grows better and better. I am passing through a time of deep trial, but recently I have come to such a new awareness of the suffering which His own sympathy for our suffering must cause Him, that I feel like bearing it all cheerfully and bravely, making Him believe, if it were possible, that it is not so very hard to bear! There is some fierce necessity somehow for all this sin and misery, which He sees, but which He knows we cannot see; and it seems to me as if His heart of love must be ready to break at times with the thought of the mystery it must seem to us, and our misunderstandings of His love.

To have all power both in Heaven and in earth, as He has, and yet not to use it for the relief of His poor suffering world, must be a bitter grief to our loving Saviour; and I have a feeling that we who love Him ought to try and make as little of our sufferings as possible, for His sake! And this helps me to be cheerful now. I know every pang I feel is felt more deeply by my Jesus, and I want to spare Him all that I can.

This is fanciful, I expect, but it is my genuine feeling and helps me. I love Him, in my poor way and with my small measure, and I will cheerfully take up the cross He appoints, and bear any suffering He permits. I can say over and over with rejoicing, "Thy will be done."

—Journal, June 14, 1873

181. Chastening Love

We have so much to be thankful for; and if our Lord sends some sorrow, surely we can say, "Thy will be done." He can overrule even our very sins for our good and make our chastisement the means of greatest blessing to our souls. I feel that he has done this with me. I often think of that scene in *Pilgrim's Progress*, when Christian and Faithful had wandered out of the way and became entangled in the net of the Flatterer, One came to them

127

with a whip of small cords in His hands, and, after freeing them from the net, commanded them to lie down and then chastised them, saying as He did so, "As many as I love I rebuke and chasten." And when He had finished, they got up and went on their way softly singing.

I am sure it is in love that he chastises me, and I cannot murmur. But I want you to be happy, darling. I cannot bear for you to suffer and be sad. And if I could only make you happy, I would be unspeakably thankful.

—To Robert, June 19, 1873

182. Content

I cannot write about anything but the life of faith, for I do not know of any other. I am sure the Lord has a meaning in leading me, as He is, in the way of faith. Perhaps it is that I may teach it thoroughly first before I begin to teach the way of manifestations. It is surely needed to be learned by Christians. And I am content. If the Lord is better pleased and more honored by my walk of faith, it satisfies me, and I would not ask to have it different. He loves me, and I can leave it all to Him. It doesn't matter much anyhow how this life is passed; it must end sometime and I can wait. And meanwhile I do find the knowledge of the fact that Jesus is mine and I am His enough to make me happy.

As to my approaching trial, as it is called [the birth of another child], it does not disturb me in the least. I scarcely ever think of it even. When the time really comes I have no doubt everything will be all right; and, if not, then will be time enough to worry. Sometimes it comes over me with a rush of joy that then may possibly be the time for me to go home, but I know this is not the least likely, and I am perfectly content with the will of God.

—To Robert, July 10, 1873

183. God's Justice Is a Bed

I have been thinking for the last day or two about the justice of God, and it seems to me that this is after all almost a greater rest than the thought of His love. Faber says,

> God's justice is a bed where we
> Our anxious hearts may lay;
> And, weary with ourselves, may sleep
> Our discontent away.

I have used the thought for my bed for two or three nights, and my sleep has been sweet! The thought came to me one day when one of the children said, Alice I think, that she wished she had made the world and it belonged to her, and I replied, "Oh Alice don't wish that, for if you had made it, you would be responsible for it, and just think how unhappy you would be if things went wrong like they do." Then it flashed on me, "God made us, and therefore He is responsible for us, and his justice demands that He cares for us." And oh it was such a rest!

> Muse on His justice, downcast soul
> Muse, and take better heart;
> Back with your angel to the field,
> And bravely do your part.

—To Robert, July 20, 1873

184. Unquestioning Acquiescence

I trust I have learned a lasting lesson in regard to permitting myself to dwell and brood over my troubles and grievances. I am sure for me it is wicked and would end always in utter misery to myself and others. While if I number my blessings and the good things in those around, I find myself happy and able to make others happy.

The dear Lord knew the secret of our needs when He told us to forget the things that are behind and to take no thought for tomorrow! The present moment is always bearable. Having laid all my cares, therefore, onto the Lord afresh, I am at peace and can rest in His will in happy submission. I am not called upon to glorify Him by any especially fervent or delightful emotions as some of you are. My mission is to glorify the Lord by the steadfastness of my faith in the midst of a storm of doubts and reasonings and by my unquestioning acquiescence in His will in circumstances of peculiar trial.

The one continual cry of my soul is "Lord I believe" and "Thy will be done." Beyond this I cannot go. It would be very nice to be emotional and to have the wonderful outpourings that you have, but I have to be content without them; and, after all, there is an evenness about a life of faith that has its compensations.

—To Robert, August 16, 1873

185. In the Hands of God

Anything that makes you happy will satisfy me. I have handed my whole life over into the hands of God and must leave it with Him, or I should go wild. Unless the Lord undertakes for me, there is no hope. I am at peace because I have given myself to the Lord in this way, and I know He will take care of me. He may lead me through fiery trials. He is; but He is with me, and I have His promise that the flames will not hurt me. I have fought the battle of submission and have conquered, and now I rest in Him and His sweet will. I will try my best to please you, my dearest husband; I do want to make you happy. I shall ask the Lord to help me in this, and if I fail you must try to forgive me and be patient with me. In my poor way I love you truly, and could I know you were happy, I would be at rest.

The Lord is keeping me very quiet under His will. I live a moment at a time, and I find that grace comes as I need it. I trust now that I shall be carried through the nervous time that always follows childbirth and will be able to rest in the Lord.

—To Robert, August 28, 1873

186. God's Will, Our Pillow

[After a miscarriage]

I suppose I used up all my vitality in the Lord's work, and in bearing the burdens necessarily laid upon me by my dear husband's state of health and there was not enough left for the baby. It has been an inexpressible disappointment to me, and I do not care to dwell on it. I thought I sorely needed the comfort a baby always brings to me, and I had looked forward to it with the most intense longing.

But I know God's will is best, and I am satisfied! I do not permit myself to dwell on what might have been. And in the lonely night hours, when sorrows and losses and anxieties are so sure to come and claim a hearing, I can only turn resolutely away and say over and over and over to myself and to God, "Thy will be done, Thy will be done!" until the sweet refrain lulls me to sleep when nothing else would. And so I have learned to make the sweet will of God literally my pillow; and upon it I often realize with Faber that "no cradled child more softly lies than I."

—To a Friend, September 2, 1873

187. Undisturbed Confidence

The Lord knows, and He loves us, and what more can we say? Or what more do we need? All must be right, even that seems most wrong, if it be His sweet will. This is my unfailing resting place and I have no other.

You pray that I may have manifestations of God's love, darling Carrie; but that does not seem to be God's way with me, and I have settled down now to being content without them. A blindfolded reckless faith is my religious life and it sustains me. If the manifestations should be given, I know they would be very precious, but I can trust the Lord without them. I have grown to have such unbounded and undisturbed confidence in the love of God that I feel a sort of abandonment of trust that does not even require a promise to sustain it. That God is God is enough for me.

—To Carrie, September 10, 1873

188. Take-It-For-Granted Faith?

One of my chief subjects of interest just now is the simplicity of faith. I do not believe we even yet begin to know how simple a thing it is. It seems to me that the most effectual faith of all is that take-it-for-granted kind that never dreams of anything else but that God will of course do the thing we ask. It is a faith that is so sure of all good things that it hardly feels the need of asking, and would not at all, only that God has said, "Make your requests known."

I have found as a matter of positive experience that the things I pray the most about are the things I do not get, and the things I just take for granted, as it were, are the things that turn out right. A great many other Christians have told me that their experience has been the same. And when we think of the sort of faith we like our children to have in us, the analogy is very teaching. I should be grieved enough if my children teased and worried and agonized for things as I have sometimes teased God. I would not wonder but that the true secret of availing prayer may lie in this direction. There seems to be something in our very natures that always recoils from a demand, so that things we can give with ease and joyfully, if the gift is spontaneous, become impossible to us when they are demanded.

And I cannot but think that this development of our own natures teaches us something of the nature of God, and that the demanding system is not the way to prevail with Him. However, I have not developed the idea yet.

—To Robert, November 1, 1873

In her lifelong drive to test out spiritual experience for herself, Hannah met all kinds of exotic spirituality which she discovered led to all kinds of fanaticisms because they were centered in subjective guidance led by purely emotional impulses. Out of all of this she learned to turn more and more to the clear truths of Scripture, the advice of trusted Christians, and her own common-sense reasoning to discern God's direction for her life.

189. True Guidance?

Speaking of meetings, Sarah F. Smiley has fully adopted and endorses the "Boston Party" as it is called. My impression is that it is an awful delusion, the outgrowth of Dr. Foster's idea, but carried to a great excess. I told Sarah at Lynn that while she endorsed that party she and I must separate. She says they are far ahead of all other Holiness meetings she has ever attended in spirituality, direct guidance, etc., etc.

I am more and more convinced that a doctrine of emotional guidance such as theirs is a very dangerous delusion and sure to lead into fanaticism at the very least. I never want to hear anybody say again, "The Lord led me to do this," or "The Lord led me to do that." Not that I do not believe in His leading, but I am convinced it is more through our judgment and reason than through our emotions that He leads, and such emotional persuasion does not make us infallible.

—To Robert, December 4, 1873

190. United Faith

In view of the blessings promised to those who "agree" as touching anything that they ask of their Father in Heaven; and of the great gift received by those who "continued with one accord in prayer and supplication" some of us as the Lord's children who desire richer blessings for ourselves and for the church do hereby band ourselves together, as though present in spirit although absent in body to devote a half hour daily to united prayer. The needs we have felt are these:

I. Full and definite consecration as the Lord's children and servants to be what He wills and to do what He wills. Col. 4:12. 1 Thess. 5:23, 24.

II. The laying aside of every weight and hindrance whether of sin, infirmity, weakness, or folly, that no hidden sin like Aachan's keeps us from victory. Ps. 139:23, 24.

III. A clearer knowledge of the truth of the gospel wisdom, sound judgment, and discretion with such an understanding of the times as to know what we ought to do. Prov. 2:19 Jas. 1:5, 6.

IV. Simplicity of heart, a single eye and to be strong and very courageous. Josh. 1:6–9

V. More power from on high and more of the Lord's evident blessing upon our work. A marked bestowal of His Holy Spirit upon us.

VI. More hearty Christian fellowship with the whole church of Christ and with each other, each remembering the needs and interests of one another in our prayers. 1 Sam. 12:23

VIII. True and constant faith in our Lord and Saviour Jesus Christ that we as a "little band whose hearts God has touched" may be consecrated, sanctified, enlightened, encouraged, strengthened, and united in Him!

—To [?], 1873

191. Possessing the Land

I do so hope that your faith has dared to go up and take possession of the land to which the blessed Spirit has evidently been calling you. Doesn't the Bible tell you that it is already yours in the mind of God and only needs your step of faith upon it to become actually and experientially yours also? Isn't purity of heart what is meant by Rom. 6:6 and 11? And isn't it necessarily true that just as the presence of light drives out the darkness, so the indwelling presence of Christ must drive out sin? But just also as the room cannot presume on the absence of darkness and think it need no longer admit the light so neither can the soul presume on its purity and think for a minute it can do without the presence of Christ.

> Every moment, Lord, I need
> The merit of your death
> And every moment, Lord, I have
> The Merit of your death.

I cannot tell you how much I long to see you enter into all the blessedness of this life of perfect trust. The absolute submission of your will is the first step and that is accomplished. Now let the precious cleansing blood of Jesus do its perfect work in your whole being, by faith claiming His life as your own. Let Paul's reckoning be yours: "I am crucified with Christ: nevertheless I live; yet not I, but Christ liveth in me."

—To Priscilla Mounsey, March 15, 1874

192. Confession Brings Joy

Oh, how he must love us, to take so much pains with each one of us in seeking to unite us to Himself! And now, dear friend, you are altogether His. You have cast yourself on Him, and from your own weakness may look only at Jesus and His mighty strength. He has promised to supply all your needs, and His word cannot fail. You may trust Him, therefore, with the most childlike simplicity, leaving everything in His hands, only seeing to it that day by day you yield yourself up altogether to His working. The habit of trust will grow more and more easy, and your soul will find itself kept by the peace of God which passes all understanding through Jesus Christ.

But do not forget that the Lord needs you to witness for Him; and that He has given you the promise that if you will confess Him before men, He will confess you before His Father and the Holy Angels. This is too blessed a privilege to be neglected, and the Lord has connected it so intimately with our joy in Him that the soul always languishes which shrinks from entering upon it. I know, dear friend, it is hard at first, and my heart feels deeply for you, especially, because your lifelong habits have been so different. But you must be willing to endure hardness for your Lord who endured so much for you, and very soon you will find even the hardness turned into a precious joy. I cannot plan for you how the confession must be made, but I am sure that your own family and your own immediate circle ought to know, and to know soon, of the step you have taken in your soul's experience. The Spirit will guide you and you need not worry or plan, only obey.

—To Priscilla Mounsey, May 7, 1874

193. The Secret of Guidance

There must be a complete submission of your will to God, that where He leads you'll follow; and then you must leave it altogether to Him and don't worry about it. If the thought comes that you ought to speak or to pray, say at once, "Yes, Lord, I will; only give me something to say if I must speak, and, if I must not, let me forget all about it."

Don't indulge in self-reflective acts, either of congratulation because you did well, or of distress at having done badly. Let the whole thing go at once, and let your soul return to its rest in the will of God. The Lord will lead you by a right way, and, what if he should call sometimes for things which are hard for flesh and blood to follow, I do believe that now you will not shrink back.

This rule of guidance applies to everything. The guidance of the Spirit is generally by gentle suggestions or drawings, and not in violent pushes; and it requires great childlikeness of heart to be faithful to it. The secret of being made willing lies in a definite giving up of our will. As soon as we put our will on to God's side, He immediately takes possession of it and begins to work in us to will and to do of His good pleasure. You have proved this in your own experience, for since the moment when you gave up your will that night, a willingness to do God's will has come to you almost unconsciously. And, like trusting, it will grow and grow, until God's will really does become to you the most precious thing in all the world.

—To Mary Beck, May 14, 1874

194. Restoration

The Lord is leading you rapidly onwards in His paths, and I believe He will soon restore the years that the canker worms of doubt have eaten, and will cause you to be well-fed and satisfied, and to praise the name of the Lord that has dealt wondrously with you!

I felt that night when we were together that this struggle through which you had just passed would probably come to you sooner or later, and I do praise the Lord that He has enabled you to fully surrender to Him. Yes, now you are His, wholly and entirely, no longer your own in any sense, and you indeed do His will and follow Him wherever He leads you! And His ways are truly so pleasant and peaceful that I am sure you will never regret the decisions of the past few weeks. Already your soul has experienced some of the blessing the Lord gives, and infinite riches of peace and joy are stretching out before you, all awaiting for you to move ahead and possess them.

And now you must lay this burden about any public service to which you may be called wholly upon your burdenbearer. If He wants you to do it, He will supply all the needed strength and wisdom, and you don't even have to think of it or worry about it for one single moment. Only see to it that you yield yourself up to Him perfectly, and then leave it with Him. It is marvelous to see what He can do with even the poorest and the weakest instruments that are pliable in His Hands!

—To a Friend, May 31, 1874

195. The Higher Christian Life

Your promise to me and to the Lord that night involved not only trusting Him for deliverance in the future, but also trusting Him now and continually for your daily and hourly needs. It meant that you started out then to live by faith. And this, dear friend, is the Higher Christian Life. I am sure that you entered it then, and I see that you are being continually taught many precious lessons about it, and that your soul responds to the voice of your Master.

Never mind the doubts and questionings that are sure to come. Satan will not let you escape from His bondage without a struggle. But if you will continue to hold fast the profession of your faith without wavering, victory is sure. I emphasize the word "profession," because often all we can do is to say we believe, and to say it even when we feel as if we did not. I am sure this is what is meant in that command that if we confess our faith with our mouth God will give us the victory. For, "whosoever shall confess that Jesus is the Son of God, God dwelleth in him and he in God." Many a time I have held fast to my confession, when I felt as if I were a hypocrite almost, so did little. I feel as if it was true. But never once at such times has my God failed to give me the victory.

—To a Friend, May 31, 1874

196. The Power of Profession

You have put yourself wholly in the Lord's hands, now you must claim continually that it is true. When it seems to be the most untrue then claim and assert it with the greatest boldness. This is what it means to lift up the shield of faith, and this is the way to overcome by faith. But then, when making such a profession, there never must be any indulgence in an unsurrendered will in any respect, for this would bring darkness at once, as you have proved. I do not think the Lord will permit it in your case. He will follow you and draw you and keep you restless apart from Himself, for you are altogether His now. It will help you tremendously to let your friends know that you have entered on the Higher Life. In nothing is confession so absolutely necessary. For we are to overcome not only by the blood of the Lamb but also by the "word of our testimony." I am sure your confession to me on the 25th was a great help to you in your battle with Satan that same evening. Wasn't it?

And the Lord needs your testimony, therefore, I am sure you will not hold it back. It is so comforting to know that you are in His Hands.

—To a Friend, May 31, 1874

197. Simple Prayer

First of all with regard to words in vocal prayer. Doesn't some part of your difficulty come from your desire to make a good prayer, one that will sound well? If you could be content to use ordinary language and just express the needs of your own soul and of those for whom you are praying, as they come to your mind, it seems to me you'd have the words you need.

For myself, I found it necessary, when I began to pray vocally and also to speak, to be willing to be extremely simple in my way of doing either. In prayer, for instance, to talk to God as though He and I were alone together, and I were telling Him in everyday language the things I wanted; and to ask for the same things over each time I prayed, if they were the things that came into my mind as my needs at the time. We must remember that there is no human being with whom we may be as free as with our Lord; and it is not beautiful prayers He wants but just for us to tell Him our needs. If you only need one thing, ask for that, if two, ask for them, and then stop. Never try to make a prayer. Some of the most effectual prayers I have ever heard, have been just two or three sentences spoken in the utmost simplicity. I think a willingness to be simple and direct will help you. If not, then you must obey the will of God in this matter, and must be willing even to be a fool for His sake, if He requires it. Do not at any rate let the lack of words make you disobedient. If the Lord puts it into your heart to pray you must be willing to kneel and say what you can, and be humbled and mortified, if needs be. I expect your long disobedience lies at the root of your difficulty after all, and that a prompt and cheerful obedience now will bring the quickest deliverance.

But however this may be, my dear friend, still you must obey. You have given yourself to the Lord to be His completely, and there is no alternative now but obedience. I am sure the Lord has been trying for a long time to make you into an instrument for His own purposes, but up to now you have hindered Him. Now, all that is past, and if you are only totally pliable in His hands, He will, I am sure, soon restore the years the canker worm has eaten.

—To Priscilla Mounsey, June 29, 1874

198. Planting and Harvesting

As to power, dear friend, you must simply trust for it, and be satisfied with whatever measure God gives to you. It is not the place of everyone to reap the harvest; some must plant, and some must water, and all such services are equally necessary and acceptable. Often the reaping seems to me the least valuable of all. You may be sure of this that if you yield yourself wholly up to God to be used by Him as He pleases, He will certainly make you just the kind of instrument He wants you to be. And this is all you could possibly want, isn't it?

To get rid of self requires a continual act of faith. Satan is sure to come to us continually after any work for the Lord with either one of two forms of temptation. Either he tells us how well we have done it, or else how poorly. We must meet him always with a steady determination not to look at either side of the question but to commit the matter completely to the Lord and leave it with Him. We must never indulge in self-reflective acts of any sort. By an effort of faith we must ignore the very existence of this kind of concern for self.

—To Mary Beck, July 13, 1874

199. Conscious Trusting, Conscious Doubting

In asking you to promise never to doubt I did not mean quite as much as your sister seemed to suppose. I did not mean that there might never be a momentary failure in your conscious trusting. That would have been to promise too much. But I meant that there should never be any conscious doubting. I meant that even if for a moment a failure should come that you should not be led into doubting by this but should begin to trust again harder than ever. The promise was not always to trust, but never to doubt, and there is a great difference between these two.

Of course I believe that it is right always to be exercising a conscious trust, but I would never ask anyone to promise this, as it would be almost sure to be broken. But to indulge in a conscious doubt is so obviously wicked, and it is so very easy to avoid it, that I would like to persuade every Christian in the world to give it up definitely and forever. And I trust you will hold on to your promise about it without any wavering.

—To Priscie, September 16, 1874

200. Baffling Satan

Confession does not mean going around telling everyone about God's work in your heart, nor doing it every moment. But it means taking such a stand among our friends and in our circle that everyone will know what our position is. You are quite right in saying that having once committed yourself, you can't draw back and don't need to be continually repeating it. And yet it does help us tremendously to put our faith into words sometimes, and I believe we are often able to baffle Satan in this way.

If I find my faith becoming dim and my experience vague and indefinite, I am generally brought back into clearness and definiteness by making a confession of my faith to someone; or, if no one is at hand, by making it aloud to my Heavenly Father.

—To [?], 1874

201. Conscious Union

Don't be discouraged at any form of temptation which threatens you, but always look to Jesus, and ask Him to meet and overcome it by His own wisdom and power. I think I am learning more and more of what utter trust means. Having naturally some feeling of personal ability and good sense, it has always been a temptation for me to rely on these and to feel that I wouldn't be likely to lose my balance whatever happened. But I have seen recently that even my natural abilities must be laid aside in this life of death to self, and that I must really and practically have all my resources in the Lord only.

I do not know whether I am making myself clear, but in my experience this has been very real. It has cost me something to lay aside my old dependence upon my own judgment and good sense, and to let myself be helpless in the Lord's hands. But it is unspeakably sweet when it is done. And I believe it is to me the opening up of a life of conscious union with my Lord such as I have never know before. I seem to have sunk into unfathomed depths of littleness and nothingness, and to have found the Lord there in a more real and actual consciousness than ever before.

Only, dear friend, ask the Lord to fulfil John 14:16, 21, 23 in you, and open up your whole being to receive His manifestations.

—To a Friend, December 17, 1874

202. Delayed Answers

Ray had quite an experience last night. You know about her two burdens being afraid and another one, and how the other evening she told me she was going to lay them on the Lord, and I explained to her how to do it. Well, since then she has been waiting and expecting to find herself delivered but seemed to think she had to wait a great while, and told me once that Logan said he heard of a woman who had to wait for twenty years before she got her prayers answered, and asked me if I thought Jesus would make her wait that long.

Last evening when I went to kiss her farewell in bed, she burst out most triumphantly, "Oh mother, I have learned how to trust now, and I am not going to be afraid any more. I truly am not! For I believe, yes, I do really believe, and I know I never will be afraid again. And oh mother, I am so happy I don't know what to do." And then she began to turn somersaults, and kick and scream in a fair ecstasy of delight, interspersing it with such expressions as, "Yes, I do trust now, I really do believe," etc. etc. "Tell it out loud," she said, "so that Alice can know." And then Alice joined in the rejoicing and there was a real private "Methodist shout" for a little while in the bedroom.

Soon they subsided, and then Ray began to moralize. "I'm just like bubba," she said, "only bubba got his thing the very next morning after he trusted and I have had to wait ever so long. I expect that was because I didn't know how to trust and Jesus had to keep me waiting to teach me how. But bubba knew how, so he didn't have to wait." Then she turned over on her pillow and cuddled her little head down, and said with such an air of comfort, "Now I am going right to sleep without being afraid one bit." It was lovely.

—To Robert, March 2, 1875

203. Sorrow in the World, Peace in Jesus

My little baby girl was born dead! [1873] And though my heart longed after it, I was glad for its sake that it was spared the pain and risks of life. My husband remained in England, and his health continued the same. It was a summer and autumn of sorrow in this world, but of unfailing peace and rest in the Lord Jesus. I fairly learned to revel in His most lovely and lovable will!

In January 1874 I went over with our four children and joined my husband in England. My volume of copied letters describes all our outward life there, and the wonderful openings the Lord gave us for preaching the Higher Christian Life to rich and poor. My inward experience continues, through it all, to be one of perfect rest and peace. My husband's health was mercifully restored, and the strain of my earthly sorrow was removed. The Lord saw that I had learned the lesson and He delivered me. And my earthly happiness has been unclouded since, except for the separation from my country, and from my dearly loved family and friends.

We returned last Sept. 1874 to America and this winter has been a time of busy work in Philadelphia for me. In March 1875, my husband went back to England, and in a week, I sail with the children to join him. A great work is opening before us there for this summer in large conventions calling for the promotions of Scriptural Holiness [at Brighton, England], at which I have to take a prominent part, both in holding ladies meetings, and in giving "Bible readings," as they are called to save the feelings of the dear brethren who are afraid to call it preaching.

—Journal, May 6, 1875

204. Endless Song

I find the life of faith grows better and better every month I live. I can truly say my life flows on in endless song above earth's lamentations and can add most heartily that, "Day by day this pathway smooths Since first I learned to love it." It is better and better the further I go. Oh what a wonderful salvation! What a perfect Saviour! The blood of Jesus cleanseth me from all unrighteousness; this is my confession for today.

I henceforth take Jesus Christ to be mine. I receive Him as a Husband to me. And I give myself to Him, unworthy though I am, to be His spouse. I ask of Him in this marriage of spirit with spirit, that I may be of the same mind with Him, meek, pure, nothing in myself and united in God's will. And, pledged as I am to be His, I accept, as a part of my marriage portion, the temptations and sorrows, the crosses and the contempt which fell to Him. I rest in His love.

I am now writing a life of my father, for private circulation only. While I am so occupied with writing, I have to turn down most of the numberless calls that come to me for preaching or giving Bible readings here in Philadelphia and in all parts of our country. But I am presently giving weekly Bible Readings here in Horticultural Hall, and, now and then, address a meeting where there seems an especially urgent need. Our children are all developing nicely, and all of them are trusting Christians. Mary is taller than I am, and is unusually bright. She is at Howland School in New York State. Logan is as good a boy as ever lived, and is growing up just like Frank. Alice and Ray are sweet and good and full of fun. As to my inward experience, I am still living the life of faith, and I have found it a very blessed life. But after trying it for some years, I still find myself going back to the old need of the conscious baptism of the Spirit, about which my soul has been exercised so often in the past. I am convinced that faith on our part is not the whole of our salvation. There must be the Divine response to the heart as well.

—Journal, May 6, 1875

205. Harvest Time

My last letter was sent off from Brighton [England, where Robert Pearsall and Hannah Whitall Smith addressed thousands of British and European Christians] on the 30th of May. Since then I have not been able to write a word. I can't begin to describe the meetings; the whole thing was too wonderful. The days all began with morning prayer meetings, often with four thousand people, and an overflow meeting of two or three thousand in another room, and they would be in the room waiting at half past six. Then at 9:30 would be various other meetings led by different people. I always had one for ladies exclusively generally two or three thousand in attendance. We did not allow any report to be made of these, but they were very blessed occasions. Part of the time I devoted to answering questions, and part, to hearing experiences.

We had some lovely testimonies, among the rest, Miss Macpherson, the friend of the poor little London matchbox makers etc. who takes so many over to Canada. She had been a very violent opposer of what she supposed to be our views, and purposely avoided all intercourse with us. But she attended the meeting we held in Devonshire House last June and there had her eyes opened somewhat to see the truth. And then she began to read our books, and finally in Canada she met Mr. and Mrs. Varley, and the last difficulty was removed, and she entered into full rest. She said she immediately got a green pencil, and went all through her Bible marking every verse that touched upon this life of trust with green, until, she said her Bible was full of green spots. Her testimony was deeply moving and so were several others. But the time was so short and so many wanted to speak, that at last I had to ask for a few lines of written testimony, and I think I must have received at least two hundred and fifty from people who had definitely entered into rest at Brighton besides a continual stream of people coming up to me whereever I went to tell me in person of the wonderful blessing received during the Conference.

—To Father and Mother, "Glebe Lands," Woodford, Essex, June 9, 1875

206. One in Christ

It was simply wonderful! Just as at Oxford [a previous conference in 1874] a great wave of blessing seemed to sweep all before it, and people could not help being carried along by it. Among all the thousands who came, there did not seem to be one who did not receive some definite spiritual help, and some of the testimonies I have are really most beautiful.

Besides the ladies meeting of about two hours in the morning, I had to address two immense audiences every afternoon, one from three to four and one from four to five, each one three or four thousand. And as I was determined everybody should hear me, I fairly had to shout, which has made me as hoarse as a crow. There were so many people I knew at the Conference, that I actually had to drive to & from the meetings, in order to get along at all, I was so constantly stopped.

And all sorts of denominations and nationalities, and conditions of life met and mingled in the most happy and blessed union and fellowship. One of the German pastors said to me, "These are the days of Heaven! We all love one another, and we forget every difference. There is no more any time, nor any place!" These foreign pastors were very interesting. We had German, French, Spanish, Italian, Swiss, and several other nationalities represented, and the overflowing love of Christ seemed to unite all as one. Sometimes they would pray in their own languages or even sing, or give their experiences, sometimes in broken English, and it was most touching. The Germans and French came with some bitter feelings in their hearts towards one another, but they soon confessed it all and gave it to the Lord, and embraced each other in the most genuine Christian love.

One German Pastor the last morning said, "I came over with our Pastors to report the meetings, very unwillingly, and with my whole mind full of prejudices against this new heresy. I did not believe it was according to good German theology, and for a day or two I did nothing but criticize and get vexed. But now all is changed. I do not know indeed whether it yet is good doctrine or not, but I do know the experience is true, and I have got it!" Such things were continually occurring. But I might as well attempt to

143

describe a whirlwind, there seemed to be such a perfect storm of blessing almost.

—To Father and Mother, "Glebe Lands," Woodford, Essex, June 9, 1875

207. Waiting on God

And yet all the meetings were so very solemn & quiet. Everybody cried out for times of silence. Five then, and even twenty minutes were eagerly begged for. Some meetings were held expressly for an hour of silent waiting on God, and hundreds flocked to them. It was to me one of the most remarkable features of the whole week, this hunger for silent waiting. Meetings were held for it every day. And so many testified to receiving the light and blessing during these seasons, that it reminded one of the days when George Fox saw people "convinced" as he called it during the "living silence" of his meetings. Ours was truly living silence. The truth was continually set before the people in the clearest simplest manner, and then they were entreated to make these times of silence, times of definite transactions between their souls and the Lord.

Sometimes a verse of consecration or of trust would be sung softly, while we were thus bowed before the Lord. Sometimes they would be closed by all repeating together a promise in faith, all who could, of course I mean. Dear Rachel Buxton said it seemed to her just like the wonderful Yearly Meetings that used to be held in the days of Elisabeth Fry and Joseph John Gurney etc. Oh, it has been altogether a marvelous time.

The watch word of the whole meeting was "Jesus saves me now." And finally we got a chorus all to sing together, in our different tongues. Jesus saves me now, Jesus saves me now, Yes, Jesus saves me all the time, Jesus saves me now. You cannot think how lovely it was to sing it all together in our own languages. The words were on everybody's lips. The Earl of Center made me write my name in his Bible and underneath it this sentence, "Jesus saves me now." He and Lady Center were very much impressed, and are very anxious for us to go to Scotland, which we quite expect to do in August. There were so many grand people at the conference that I cannot begin to tell you about them; but the wonderful baptism of love that was upon us all quite swept away all the social distinctions for the time, and made us one in Christ Jesus. A dear Dutch countess became quite my intimate friend, and never seemed to think of any difference between us in rank.

—To Father and Mother, "Glebe Lands," Woodford, Essex, June 9, 1875

208. His Ministers

We stayed with Fowell Buxton, uncle of the present Sir Fowell. His wife is Mrs. Barclay's sister Rachel, and they have eleven children. They are a most delightful family, and certainly did exercise the most royal hospitality. They gave Robert leave to invite any friends he pleased to meals. I warned them of the rashness of such a permission to him, but they persisted, and the result was enough to have appalled an ordinary mind. Robert would come in to dinner with thirty, forty, and even fifty foreign pastors, and the rush and crowd were something wonderful. Altogether Mrs. Buxton paid for 1317 meals during those ten days, and it was all done with such princely hospitality as made it delightful. Dear Mrs. Buxton sat at the head of one of the tables, and always saved a seat for me beside her, and was as calm through the whole bustle and the confusion of foreign tongues, as though in a little family circle. It was certainly very interesting.

Sometimes at the close of the meal we would have a German or a French hymn which was grand. Mr. Buxton very often waited on us all, and one day a Norwegian pastor paid him such a pretty tribute at the end of the dinner. He said, he thanked God that the good English householder had given his foreign brethren such a beautiful picture of Christ, who came not to be ministered unto but to minister, for we had not seen the good householder sit down to his own dinner at all, but he had been all the time serving us. But everybody was blessed! Every face was shining, and every eye was filled with tears of joy. I never saw anything like it. And the numbers made it really marvelous.

—To Father and Mother, "Glebe Lands," Woodford, Essex, June 9, 1875

Glowing reports of Pearsall Smith's 8,000–10,000-strong convention for the promotion of scriptural holiness held at Brighton, England, in May 1875 came from all quarters. As the meetings had begun, Dwight L. Moody had sent greetings with his belief that it could prove to be one of the most significant meetings in the history of the church. Those who attended felt that it was just that and that evangelical Christianity in England and on the continent was poised for a new era of spiritual renewal and expansion.

The whole venture seemed to be like a giant rocket for a brilliant moment arcing against the night sky and then just as quickly plunging to earth again leaving nothing but darkness all around. Rumors about moral and doctrinal deviations involving Smith began to spread. In spite of Smith's immediate open discussions of the charges with his sponsoring committee, they panicked and summarily dismissed him.

Hannah always supported him against his accusers. The incident did not in itself end his ministry in other circles, but it threw him into his third manic-depressive attack; this time into its depressive stage. Hannah found him huddled in despair in a Paris hotel room where he had fled in his collapse. In the classic pattern of that disease, it was the end of normal life for him and his family. He went back to America and to selling glass. His spiritual life degenerated. He never again had a heart for ministry or for God. He retreated to a world of Buddhist meditation and died in 1899 a broken man.

With Smith's fall, the Higher Life Movement was severely wounded but did not die. Its influences and impulses gave birth to the Keswick Convention, the Holiness Movement within the Evangelical Lutheran Church of Germany, and the German Free-Church Holiness and Pentecostal movements. Its essentially Methodist message of the possibility of sanctification by faith and a victorious Christian life came back to the non-Methodist evangelical churches in America through evangelists such as Dwight L. Moody, R. A. Torrey, A. T. Pierson, through institutions such as Moody Bible Institute and Columbia Bible College, and through periodicals such as the Sunday School Times and Moody Monthly.

209. Trusting Him in the Dark

After Brighton I was so worn out that I felt sure I must rest somehow, and as England could not afford me much quiet anywhere, I determined to fulfil a long cherished wish and go to Switzerland. A very kind friend, one of Sir Fowell Buxton's granddaughters offered to be my guide and caretaker, and on the 14th. of June, we started, this friend Miss Priscilla Johnston, a friend of hers named Blanche Pigot, my cousin Wm. Hilles, who came over with me from America, my Mary, and myself. We had a delightful trip of a little over two weeks, and I was returning home thoroughly rested and refreshed, expecting at once to plunge into work, as we had conferences arranged for the most of the summer. At Dover I was met by a telegram handed into the railroad car window saying that Robert was ill at Paris and I had better return to him at once! Of course I did so. But can you imagine the utter perplexity into which I was thrown? My last news from him had been so different. But amid all the uncertainty and perplexity I could rest quietly in the sweet will of God, and I felt as I travelled on through the night to meet I knew not what that whatever I might meet, I was sure I was going to meet the will of God; and this was always good. And I could sing continually our dear old Brighton hymn:

> Trusting as the moments fly,
> Trusting as the days go by,
> Trusting Him whate'er befall
> Trusting Jesus, that is all.

I found Robert at the Hotel du Louvre utterly broken down. He had left London intending to join us in Switzerland and keep us there with him for a month or two to rest and recruit. But he was taken too ill in Paris to go any further. And I soon decided that our only wise course was to go home.

It is a complete break down, and a threatening of the same dreadful nervousness from which he suffered so fearfully two years ago, and I am sure nothing but a long rest and thorough change of scene and occupations will be of any avail. This is the third attack, and past experience had convinced us that it is not a thing to be trifled with. I felt therefore that we must go straight home; and not only on Robert's account but also because of the dear children who of course are nowhere so well off as at home. It was very easy to convince Robert, and we at once wrote for staterooms which we secured on the S.S. Pennsylvania which sails on the 14th. of this month.

I then brought Robert on here to rest and be quiet until the day for sailing comes. He has lost 20 lbs. already, and is suffering very much from almost constant nausea, and from his head. At times even a few moments of conversation utterly exhausts him. But I trust the lovely air of this place will strengthen him so much as to make the voyage endurable. What the result will be it is impossible to say. I have always feared that a third attack would be very serious. But the Lord has taught me the lesson of living by the moment, and I am not anxious.

We are in the Lord's hands, and He loves us, and I can trust Him with everything. It seems a mysterious dispensation, but surely by this time I ought to know Him well enough to trust Him in the dark. And the change of plans is no disappointment to me, for it makes but little difference to me what I do, if only I am doing His will. I am delighted to be going home again. It was a great trial.

—To a Friend, Penmaen Mawr, North Wales, July 7, 1875

210. A Child in My Father's House

I have one great cause for thankfulness in the improvement of my dear husband's health. The most distressing symptoms have passed away, and although he is still unable to exert himself much mentally, and suffers a good deal at times, yet the improvement is so evident that I am greatly encouraged. And if he has no setback from our hot American weather, I cannot but hope his recovery will be more rapid than at first seemed possible. I hope to take him to our seaside home at Atlantic City soon after our arrival, and trust that this will relieve him from any danger from the heat. I am quite sure that coming home at once was the right thing for him, and to the rest of us it is such a joy to be going home that we can hardly believe it is true! I feel as if I never want to go a mile away from home again in my life! However, I have learned to live only a day at a time, and to take each day as it comes from the hand of my Father, and therefore changes that come don't affect me much. Each day brings its own strength, and its own comfort, and the Lord Himself makes everything smooth and easy. When life is lived moment by moment like this trusting the Lord, there can't be any very keen or bitter disappointments, for each thing received as the Lord's appointment is realized to be the best.

I am so thankful you have learned the happy secret of living by faith, and that you can testify for yourself to the peace and rest it brings. More and more the simplicity of being a child in the Father's house, or a sheep of the good Shepherd's flock, opens out before me, and I wonder at the ignorance and slowness of our hearts to come to such a place of marvelous privilege. Oh, may we who have learned something about it, so manifest the power of it in our daily lives that all who see us shall be drawn irresistibly to discover our secret!

—To Priscie, S.S. *Pennsylvania*, July 23, 1875

211. A Child in Its Mother's Arms

I think you can understand why I could not write to you until I felt sure you had heard of our severe trial. To write to you in a superficial way would have been impossible after our lifelong closeness, and to go deeper was equally impossible while you didn't know about it. Now, however, that your kind loving letter has come, I am very glad to be able to write to you freely.

I don't have to tell you I am sure that my dear husband is entirely innocent of the vile charges against him. Their only foundation consists in his tender fatherly ways with a lady whom he was seeking to help spiritually, and towards whom he had no feeling whatever but only an earnest concern for her soul's welfare. She was not even attractive to him personally. And no thought or dream of wrong ever entered his mind in connection with her. She had been used to being very free in her ways with him in the presence of others, looking upon him, as he thought as a father, even going up to him once after one of my Bible lessons and kissing him in the entry hall in front of the people who were going out, which surprised him very much. The consequence was that he never thought of offending her, nor of any harm whatever, when, in an interview that she had requested, he put his arm around her, and in a fatherly way soothed her as he tried to help her in her spiritual difficulties. It was a thunderclap when he found that she felt uneasy! But he saw at once and freely acknowledged that such a free manner was not right and apologized for it. And, dear friend, it is simply impossible for us to understand how any Christian men could act so heartlessly and cruelly as Mr. Blackwood and his colleagues have acted! It seems incredible to me every time I think about it.

As to the false doctrine they were concerned about, it was the teaching concerning the conscious union of the believer and Christ as the Heavenly Bridegroom. Robert thought that it was a very precious truth at the time, but he had been led to think since that it must be a delusion. For it seems impossible that anything can be the truth of God which is not fit to be publicly proclaimed. You may remember Miss Bonnicastle speaking on this subject at the Oxford Ladies meetings, and I believe it quite shocked a good many.

Well, dear friend, you will want to know where I am in all this storm. I am just a little baby in its mother's arms, a little chicken under its mother's wings. I do not know anything, nor understand anything. I cannot manage anything, I cannot alter anything. I have no sense, nor wisdom, nor power, nor any capacity for anything. I can only be a "little child" in its Father's house, or a poor foolish helpless sheep in the care of the Good Shepherd. I can only run into His fortress, and hide under His wings. And I am so completely a child that I have a child's lightheartedness and freedom from care and anxiety. I am not worried nor unhappy. My only trouble is the crushing effect this has upon my dear husband, who I fear will never recover from it. But the will of God be done.

I am thankful to tell you that our friends here all know Robert too well to believe for a moment that he could do anything really wrong, and they all stand by him with complete confidence and love.

All you tell me about yourself interests me deeply. Don't be anxious, dear friend, about your work. If we are conscious of yielding ourselves up fully to be the Lord's instruments, we need have no further concern. The

149

Lord will be sure to use us in His own way, and will make us fit for His use by His own means. I feel just as happy to be laid aside from my work now, as I felt when I was most actively engaged. What difference does it make, if only His will is being done?

—To a Friend, 1315 Filbert St., February 12, 1876

212. Under His Wings

I have not written to you because I did not know how to write without touching on the one all absorbing subject of my thoughts, and yet could not speak of that, while there was any hope that it should not reach you. Now, however, that hope is vain, and I may therefore speak freely of our trials, and of my dear husband's bitter suffering.

My dear husband has been most cruelly treated; and the Lord's cause has suffered a sad blow, through the mistakes of some whom he supposed to be his warmest friends. I do not however blame them. They have meant to do right, and they could have had no power at all against him, unless God had permitted it, so that I am able to overlook second causes and to accept all that has come to us as from the hands of God, and to say continually, "Your will be done." Our friends in this country all know my dear husband too well, to believe for one moment the wicked slanders that come from England concerning him, and they have all drawn closer to him than ever. This is a great comfort to him, but he is a heartbroken man, and will never I fear recover anything of his old energy or health.

As for myself, the effect of this has been to teach me to rest more utterly and more blindly than ever in the sweet will of God. No one ever committed themselves and their lives more completely to the Lord than we did; and since He has permitted this, it must be for the best, dark as it looks. I feel just like a little chicken that has run out of a storm under the mother's wings and is safe there. I hear the raging of the storm, and I am utterly unable to understand it nor to measure the damage it is doing. But I am safe "under His wings" and there I must rest. He can manage the storm, I cannot. Why then should I worry or be anxious?

—To Priscie, 1315 Filbert St., Philadelphia, Pa., February 1876

213. Temperance and Doctrine

I have just come home from my last Bible lesson. The attendance was large, and the farewells quite enthusiastic. I did try to put it to them as strongly as possible. Subject: the keeping of Christ. At the close Mrs. French made an appeal for money for our Temperance work — rather against the grain for me. But Sally thought I ought to "take up my cross," so I did, and I believe we got over three hundred dollars. Our work must have money. We have twelve men on our hands this minute to be taken care of and are aching to open a home for inebriate women, and money we must have. Sally is all on fire about it, and I am pretty well stirred up myself. I am praying for somebody to die and leave me a fortune that I may open a home big enough to take in everybody just as the Lord Jesus took me in, without asking a question or requiring a guarantee.

I spent last evening at Charles Gibbons' with the Rev. Dr. Curry to talk on our subject. The Lord gave me wisdom and utterance, and I think he was convinced of the scripturalness of our doctrine and of its extreme desirability. But he declared it was not for everybody in this life, only for a few especially mature ones, like me! The rest he thought would have to wait for it until they got to Heaven! I think the extreme want of logic and sense in this position will drive him out of it. But he was very candid, and I liked him.

—To Robert, April 22, 1876

214. Puzzlement and Wonder

And now about our Framingham, Massachusetts meeting sponsored by Dr. Charles Cullis. I am going to give you a plain unvarnished statement of facts, and you may make whatever theory out of them you please. I confess I am utterly nonplussed and cannot make out any. It was all a wearisome performance to us. We did it as if we had crossed over an impassable gulf. The flood had come since the last time when we held the Brighton meetings and changed everything for us. There was no interest, no enthusiasm. The meetings were a bore; the work was like a treadmill. We counted the hours until we could get away, and hailed the moment of emancipation with unspeakable joy. And all religious chroniclers or church historians would have been compelled by the force of Christian logic to have added to this record, "and no wonder the meeting was utter failure."

But still, to keep to facts, I must tell you that the meeting was a perfect success. There was just the same power and blessing as at Oxford or Brighton, only on a smaller scale because of the meeting being smaller. There was every sign of the continual presence of the Spirit. Souls were converted, backsliders restored, Christians sanctified, and all present seemed to receive definite blessings. Dr. Cullis and many others say that it was the best meeting ever held in that area.

And it really was a good meeting, even I, uninterested as I was, could see that. There was just the same apparent wave of blessing that swept over our English meetings. And Robert and I never worked more effectually. He had all his old power in preaching and leading meetings, and the same presence of the Spirit was with him as used to be in England.

—To a Friend, The Cedars, August 8, 1876

215. Someone Else Must Do It

As for me, you know I am not in the habit of speaking about my own successes, but in this case, in order that you may have all the facts, I have to tell you that I was decidedly "favored" as Friends say. In fact I don't believe I ever was as effective. All who had heard me before said so. And the fuss that was made over me was a little more than even in England. The preachers fairly sat at my feet, figuratively speaking, and constantly there kept coming to me testimonies of definite blessings received while I spoke. The second time I spoke a Democratic Editor was converted and consecrated on the spot; and I could scarcely get a minute to myself for the enquirers who fairly overwhelmed me.

I had to write all this, and you must tear it right up, but how could you know it unless I told you, and the facts you must have in order to see what a mystery all is. For who would have dreamed of such an outcome to the indifference and lack of every sort of proper qualification for Christian work, which I have described before? I must say it completely upsets all my preconceived notions, and I do not know what to make of it. I was completely unmoved; and both Robert and I came away more confirmed than ever in our feeling of entire relief from everything of the kind. We are done! Somebody else may do it now.

The one satisfaction of the meeting to us was this that Robert was treated with all the old deference and respect, and that no one even seemed to think of or remember the English scandals, and Robert felt that it was a complete reinstatement of himself in the eyes of the church and the world. Our object in going to the meeting was accomplished. There is a book to be issued about it, like the Oxford book, which Robert is preparing, and when that is out we shall feel that it will wipe out all the wretched English blot, and put him right once more. And then henceforth home and home life for us. To be a "good housekeeper" seems to me the height of honor now!

—To a Friend, The Cedars, August 8, 1876

Because of her long personal search for God out of the strongly non-creedal religion of the Society of Friends, Hannah's understanding of truth did not always match the formal doctrines of the evangelicalism of her day, doctrines which had been fashioned into evangelical orthodoxy after centuries of theological debate. Most Christians who knew her or of her were aware of these differences. Some had a real problem with her "broadness," but most did not.

Several factors contributed to the wide-hearing her spiritual counsels received among evangelicals in her time and up to the present time: (1) She never chose to ride a hobby horse or promote her differences publically. Total submission to God and following Christ were the keynotes of her writing and preaching. (2) Her readers and hearers were in a revivalistic tradition which was loyal to basic evangelical doctrine which believed that life not doctrine was the true test of pure Christianity. (3) She had the skill of a spiritual genius in getting to the heart of relational spirituality. Her God was the Omnipotent Lord, but above all, the Loving Father, and she was his devoted child. God was family, like her father, her mother, her sisters and her brother, only so much more.

Hannah's heresies have not been emphasized in these limited selections from the thousands of entries available. Many today who know her only through her writings know very little about them, or, if they do, like those who knew her best, they still accept her spiritual insights as valid in the same way that most evangelicals of her own generation did and for the same reasons. Like Job, God put her to the test. And like Job she put God to the test. Her ability to tell us about it is what still helps us home to God today.

216. Broad, Broader, Broadest

And now what do you think of it all? I think one of two things, but which one is right, I don't know. Perhaps you can tell me. Either I was awfully wicked in the whole matter, and God was not in it anywhere and all the success was because of our natural gifts and talents. Or else I was awfully good, so good as to have lost sight of myself to such a degree as to be only a straw wafted on the wind of the Spirit and so consecrated as not to be able to form a desire even, except that the will of God might be fully done. I waver about myself continually. Sometimes I feel sure I have progressed wonderfully, and that my present sphinxlike calm and indifference to everything whether inward or outward except the will of God, is very grand. And then again I think I am an utterly irreligious and lazy fatalist, with not a spark of the divine in me. I do wish I could find out which I am.

But at all events my orthodoxy has fled to the winds. I am Broad, Broader, Broadest! So Broad that I believe everything is good, or has a germ of good in it, and "nothing to be refused, if it be received with thanksgiving." I agree with everybody, and always think it likely everybody's "view" is better than my own. I hold all sorts of heresies and feel myself to have got out into a limitless ocean of the love of God that overflows all things. My theology is complete, if you but grant me an omnipotent and just Creator. I need nothing more.

"God is love," comprises my whole system of ethics. And, as you say, it seems to take it all in. There is certainly a very grave defect in any doctrine that universally makes its holders narrow and uncharitable, and this is always the case with strict, so-called orthodoxy. Whereas, as soon as Christian love comes in, the boundaries widen infinitely. I find that everyone who has travelled this highway of holiness for any length of time, has invariably cut loose from their old moorings. I bring out my heresies to such, expecting reproof, when lo! I find sympathy. We are "out on the ocean sailing" that is certain. And if it is the ocean of God's love, as I believe, it is grand.

But, enough! Now, what will you do with it all?

—To a Friend, The Cedars, August 8, 1876

217. Emotional Guidance

My one trouble at present is that I do not see how anyone is to know certainly the will of God in regard to what we ought to do. In the past I have experienced too much in this respect, and have seen too much of the experience of others, ever to be able again to believe in anybody's basically emotional guidance. It is all very well when you can believe that the impressions on your mind are the voice of the Good Shepherd. But a little knowledge of Christian experience makes this impossible. And I hardly know a sadder sight than to see so many poor honest souls who firmly believe that they at least do know the mind of the Lord and who each feel sure that all the others are mistaken.

I have seen so much of this among Friends that I am heart sick about it. As to trusting to any such guidance myself, it simply is impossible. If nothing else would have convinced me of its fallacy, my experiences with Sarah

F. Smiley would have been enough. She is so sure she is led in every step, poor soul, and you and I are so sure she is not! But the Bible does promise a certain guidance, and I cannot reconcile the facts with these promises. But perhaps it is all a part of our spiritual babyhood. The question is a very practical one however, and I am often at a great loss as to my own course!

Yes, Wm. Hilles is suffering from religious depression. He thinks he was never converted, and is not now! And he is only another example of the sad shipwreck of placing too great dependence upon and certainty in this emotional guidance. He was so sure he was being led, and that he knew the voice of the Lord! I warned him over and over against such an assumption of infallibility, (for it really amounts to that), but he could not understand me. And now in his inevitable disappointment, he has been driven into despair. But I do not speak of this to anyone. It just makes one's heart ache just to be with him.

—To a Friend, The Cedars, September 11, 1876

218. Guidance and the Word

You can rejoice in His will through everything, and can rest satisfied with that which He permits, even though the reason is withheld from you. I am sure that if we could see the ends of things as God does, we would arrange them as He does. He knows where the paths lead; we see only the first few steps, and to follow our own guidance would be often fatal. But our faith must be the most childlike sort to realize this always, and I find it necessary continually to go back to "Thus saith the Lord," in order to convince myself that such a blessed relief from care and anxiety is really the divine arrangement. One word of His will outweighs all the accumulated proofs that seem so unanswerable to our shortsighted vision on the opposite side; and with such declarations as we find in Matt. 6:25, 34 for instance, I feel as if we were armed against all possible assaults of doubts or questionings.

Therefore, dear friend, rest in the assurance that your good Shepherd has ordered all your way for you, strange as it may have seemed. And praise Him for it all.

—To Priscilla Mounsey, The Cedars, Haddonfield, N.J., September 16, 1876

219. God Must Be True

As to my own personal faith, I can only say that if praying for light and truth is of any account whatever, I must believe that God is teaching me. For a whole year now I have been especially praying very definitely and with childlike faith that I might know the truth. If in spite of this I have been led into grievous error, then there is no help for it, and I shall just have to bear it and get along with it the best way I can, for praying will not probably change what praying has brought about.

Knowing the dangers of such an awful shock as I have received in uprooting one's faith, I made a special point of this prayer, and I would not like to think that it had been so utterly ignored as to allow me to fall into the fearful dangers you depict. If God has failed me in my extremity of this past year, I could never go to Him again with any hope of being heard! For I know I have been honest and full of faith about it, and I can appeal to my Lord that He must know that if I have been misled, it has been with my hand in His and my eyes fixed on His face. But I do not intend to let in any such fearful doubts as this, no matter who among my dearest earthly friends may be alarmed and distressed about me. God must be true, though every man should be thereby proved to be a liar; and while I do not for a moment think I have got hold of all truth, I dare not think He has permitted me to believe a direct lie, after all my special and earnest prayers on this very point.

—To Anna, The Cedars, September 3, 1876

220. Delighting in His Will

I believe that this life is only the beginning of our new life, our babyhood as it were, and that to limit our development to it, would be like limiting the child's development to the nursery. I believe God has revealed himself to us as our Brother, as well as Saviour, in the Lord Jesus Christ, and that it was a glimpse of how we are to be made at one with Him. To me Christ is a personal Saviour, not in any sense of appeasing the wrath of God, but as God Himself pouring out His yearning love and pity. I rest in the love of God, and delight in His will. I have no anxieties about a single thing in Heaven or in earth. I am satisfied with my allotment in every particular, because it is all the will of my God. I have so completely handed over the care of myself into His hands that I have no further concern about myself, and am willing to be anything it pleases Him to make me.

In fact I have so little interest in myself that I scarcely ever even think of it. I do not doubt that He who has begun the good work will finish it, and

I am content to leave it with Him without interference. I am very happy, and I try to be good.

—To Anna, The Cedars, September 3, 1876

221. Seeing from God's Side

Nothing could separate me from you! Don't you know that? If I get to be such an awful heretic that you become afraid of me, you will have to say in plain words, "Hannah, I don't want to have anything more to do with you," for no mere hints will do any good. No indeed, I am going to stick to you for life even should we continue forever to look out of different sides of the car.

The truth is I have gotten so completely over on God's side of everything, or rather on what seems to me to be God's side, that I perhaps love too much looking at the human side. Our Father is bound to manage us somehow, and He will, and He is so grand and good that He will be sure to do it right, in spite of us. I began about two years ago to pray that I might look at things from God's side, and it certainly seems to me as if I did. I never could express in human words the things that I have seen as to His glorious nature and character, if I may dare to use the latter word. "Since God is God, and right is right, then right the day must win," Faber says and he adds, "to doubt would be disloyalty, to falter would be sin."

—To Anna, September 29, 1876

222. Bitter, Crushing Disappointment

Nothing but these views of God could have kept me from utter shipwreck in the storm of the past year. No human being can ever know what an awful storm it has been! No one knows as we do the single-hearted devotion of our souls, and no one, therefore, can conceive of the bitter crushing disappointment. The old faith of my early Christian life would have been swept away like a wisp of sand. I do not expect anyone ever to understand what it has been and is. As Robert says no human being has ever yet said a single word to us that met the difficulty, and I do not believe it ever could be said. Only Jesus Christ can speak to our condition, and to me I believe He has spoken, revealing the Father, in whose bosom He dwells.

I do not speak of the outward suffering though that was dreadful. But of the inward. Robert was so comforted and reassured by the Framingham meeting, that he has ceased to be very depressed by the outward aspects of the trouble. But I tell you what has happened to us; we have suddenly grown old, very old. I find that the feelings, and views, and interests of old age are the only ones I can understand, and it is the same with Robert. We are just old people, and that is all there is of it. Think of me as a grand-mother aged 90 and you will understand perhaps. Well darling friend I love you. Interfere just as much as you please and I will love you better for it.

—To Anna, September 29, 1876

223. Anywhere with Jesus

Your letter was great, and has helped me to take the right view of all that has so troubled me in the past. Yes, devotion to the Lord, even though it may be in connection with what to our limited vision looks like fanaticism, is a thousand times better than the wisest and most proper course that lacks this one point of devotion. I have tried both kinds, and I know experimentally.

And I shouldn't wonder if it were really true, as you suggest, that the Lord is finding out, by means of these very extravagances, "who will cling to Him and prefer His love and smiles to the honor and esteem of all the world beside." I do praise Him that I can say now from the very bottom of my heart that I do, and that "anywhere with Jesus" is, in a far deeper sense than ever before, the language of my heart. I see plainly that this "anywhere" may involve loss of reputation, and of all else that one values, but "with Jesus" makes up for it all.

My life is revolutionized. The very hope even of the realized presence of my Lord has transformed everything; and what it will be when he fully reveals Himself I cannot even dream! Abandonment to Him has become an exquisite joy, and to please Him is the summit of my grandest imaginings. But as yet I have had only faint glimpses or touches as it were of His life giving presence. Quickenings of life, I can call it, and nothing else. I am fasting, and praying, and trusting, with my whole soul absorbed in this one intense longing.

—To Carrie, February 13, 1877

224. Neither Doubt Nor Question

My friend in Harrisburg sends me my own tracts which she has marked as my teachers, and I am ashamed not to learn their lessons. So that I dare neither doubt nor question, nor agonize, nor grow impatient at the long delay; but am just shut up to 1 John 5:14, 15, and am compelled in total weakness to say continually, "It is mine; I do receive." I seem to say it without faith and without feeling; but what else can I do? I know the baptism of the Holy Ghost is God's will for me, and I know He hears my prayer for it, therefore, I must know that I have the petition which I desired of Him. And here I must stand, dear Carrie, until the fullness comes. Meanwhile I am learning very blessed lessons and am being humbled in a way that is very necessary for me I am sure. And I praise God for it all with a more intense gratitude than anyone can know.

As for Robert, just as I expected, he has got back his old experience without any trouble. Yesterday morning I urged him to make the same decision I had had to make. To me it came in this way, that either I must believe in this conscious union with Christ and the conscious baptism of the Spirit as being of God, or I must give up all faith in God whatever. And of course I could make but one decision. And I knew it was very much the same with Robert, for in rejecting what he himself had experienced, he could not help turning his back on all religion. I think he saw this plainly yesterday morning, and saw that he must make a definite decision of his will about it.

Then in the evening Mrs. Beck, who seems to have been sent with a special message to Robert, spent the night here, and while she was praying for him he received again his old conscious baptism. It was like floods of life, he says, pouring through him and it has made him very happy. But why is it, I wonder, that he always goes in so much more easily and quickly than I, although the stirring up always begins with me? I must be very wrong somehow. But the Lord has got me in hand and is going to make me all right now, and I will not be impatient.

—To Carrie, February 13, 1877

225. We Need a Person

Your interesting letter from Salt Lake came yesterday. It is all a puzzle the moment we get outside of the religion of a personal Jesus, and I don't wonder at any vagary. We need a person to believe in, or our religion amounts to but little. I find this seeking for the baptism of the Spirit has brought me back to a personal Saviour. Jesus has become again the center of all my religion, and that not by reasoning but by an internal attraction of soul. I believe it is true that the Spirit takes of the things of Christ and shows them unto us.

—To Robert, 1877

226. Standing on the Bible

The mystery is so unfathomable, that I utterly refuse to look into it. I have taken my stand on the Bible, and if that leads me wrong, then I will go wrong, and not care. I will not pry into the works of my watch. That is the watchmaker's business, and if He can't manage them and make them work, it is not likely I can, so I do not intend to worry over them.

If the Bible is true, then it is true, and we can swing out loose upon its promises and its declarations. If it is not true, then nothing makes any difference, for there is no truth anywhere that we can get at. So I choose to sit on my Bible on top of that greased pole, and dangle my feet in the air, and disregard everything else. I have taken John 14:12–27 as expressing my special need and longing, and since they are our Lord's own words, said with His own lips, I think He will know how to fulfil them to me, let my ignorance be what it may. And I know that when they are fulfilled, I shall be perfectly satisfied.

And so will you. Do give up this introverting process, and seek for the manifestation of Christ to your soul. It is our only hope.

—To [?], June 20, 1877

227. Faith, the Stairway to Possession

I delight in Mahan's book. I never mind egotism a bit, for it is the only way one can get at people's real selves and that is what I most enjoy. I am always interested when people talk about "I," and "me" and "my," even if it is only "my rheumatism" or "my servants," or "my children;" and how much more when it is "my experience" and "my victories," and "my joy." Besides, the subject of Mahan's book is one that especially interests me just now.

You ask where I am spiritually—hungering and thirsting still but expecting the filling every day. It would take me too long to go into the details of my experience, besides being very egotistical. But the Lord has taught me some grand lessons lately, and I do believe He is making me a better woman. Of one thing I am convinced beyond a shadow of doubt, and that is that there is yet left in the church the gift of the Holy Ghost to be received definitely and consciously, and that all who do not receive it are but half-equipped.

Faith is grand, but faith is only the stairway to possession, and a church that sits down contentedly on the stairway, will not very soon reach the grand lookout tower. I have sat on the stairway long enough!

—To Anna, The Cedars, Haddonfield, N.J., June 25, 1877

Eliza Gibbons came here the other day and actually compelled me to say I would go with her to Milford, Del. to hold some meetings in a Presbyterian Church. I did all I could to get off, but it was of no use, she would not take "no" for a denial, and so tomorrow I have got to go. I expect to come back on 6th. day. I thought perhaps I could get off on account of the Presbyterian synod objecting so to women, but the minister says he will "whistle" at the synod if only he can get me!
—To Daughter Mary, January 8, 1878

228. Tongue of Fire

I am sure you understand why I do not write oftener. It is not from a lack of desire, but from a literal lack of time. And I think you will understand it when I tell you that in addition to my extensive correspondence, I am writing a book, and also am editor of a paper. The book is my "Bible Lessons," and the paper is "Our Union," the organ of our Woman's National Temperance Union. I had no business taking this editorship on top of everything else, but did it to oblige the ladies of the Union, and to give the influence of my name to the cause, which is one very near my heart. Besides all this, I am continually forced into public work by the urgent entreaties that come to me from all over our country. But I am in excellent health and able to do a great deal more than most people.

I sent you some tracts on the experience of a minister, who after many years of active Christian work, received the conscious baptism of the Spirit, and has led such a wonderful life ever since. Did they reach you? The baptism of the Spirit, dear Priscie, is a most blessed and definite reality, and it is for you. Do not give up seeking it, I beg of you, until you receive it. If you should be anywhere near Sarah Smiley, while she is in your country, get her to tell you about it. Her own experience is wonderful. This was the secret of the power of the early Friends, and it is from lack of this that Friends now pine and languish.

I do believe that if you could receive this glorious gift, the Lord would make you a mighty power. Do seek it. The promise is to you, and the Lord wants you to have it. Let your faith claim it as yours even now. But remember, dear Priscie, that it will be conscious and very definite and oh! unspeakably blessed; and you must not be satisfied with anything short of it. Try to get a book called *The Tongue of Fire* by Arthur. It will tell you all about it.
—To Priscie, January 26, 1878, 1315 Filbert St., Philadelphia, Pa.

229. Out of Self, Into Christ

And yet, dear friend, I have felt inclined to give you a word of admonition too, in noticing the recurrence again of your old trouble of self-analysis and self-reflection. Your inward dryness and barrenness which so often trouble you, are simply after all moods of feeling that may arise from a thousand surrounding causes of health, or weather, or good or bad news of outward things; and they have no more to do with the real attitude of your soul toward God, than a headache does, or a fit of indigestion. The pivot of your whole life lies in your will, and when that is steadfastly set toward God, any accompaniments of feeling or no feeling are of no account whatever. God is the same, and it is His love that is our peace and our security, and not ours.

If you could only learn the lesson of absolute self-forgetfulness, it would save you a great deal of trial. Out of self and into Christ are the two essential steps always, and the last cannot be fully taken without the first. For just so far as we dwell in self, we are not dwelling in Christ, and just to that degree, therefore, all goes wrong. I have learned this lesson through many hard conflicts with the enemy on this one special point. Self-examination seems to be such a truly spiritual exercise of the soul, that we can hardly be convinced of the injury and harm it does to us. But never, never, do we find anything of comfort or help in self; and whenever I yield to the temptation to examine myself I am always plunged into utter despair, until I take my eyes off of self and look straight at the Lord and see a little of His love for me, poor and vile as I am.

I have suffered so much from this, that I have at last given it up forever. Do the same, dear friend, and let the record of it in your letter to me be the last such record ever written or spoken by you. Please do.

—To a Friend, April 10, 1878, 317 Madison Ave., Baltimore

230. Taking the Sting Out of Trouble

I have just had a visit from a lawyer's wife, a Mrs. Browne, who seems to have gotten a great blessing this winter from my "Bible Readings." She is from Harrisburg originally and says that Rachel Briggs has always been considered a little crazy. But what a favor that her craziness takes a form that makes her happy. I think, darling husband, that you are wrong to feel about William Hilles like this. His insanity was purely a result of disease and no worse than many another Christian has had, and it made no difference whatever, I am sure, in his future life. Perhaps it even worked out a far more exceeding weight of glory for him. I believe it did, and so will your trouble, and eternity is the thing, not this life.

I wish you could bow your neck submissively to the yoke the Lord has put upon you and not question His dealings. It would take the sting out of your troubles at once. The dear Lord was as much behind all that took place in your case as He was in Job's case, and I am sure His purposes are as full of love. Do trust Him utterly about it all.

—To Robert, April 16, 1878

231. A Venture of Faith

Faith is the stairway that leads to the manifestation, but it is not the manifestation itself, and to settle down to a pure life of faith alone without the Divine response is to sit down on the stairway, and never reach the place to which the stairway was meant to lead. This I have done in common with hundreds of others, and as a consequence our souls have not experienced that conscious indwelling of the abiding Comforter which is plainly promised in the Bible, and which some Christians have most blessedly realized. I had however got contented with this way of living, and had settled it in my own mind, that this conscious experience was not for me, that it was a matter of temperament, or of health, and that I was called to a walk of faith alone.

But the deep down inward sense of lack always remained after all, but I would not notice it, thinking it must be temptation. Last spring however the Lord by a series of most remarkable providences stirred me up again to a most intense hunger and thirst after this blessing, and I have spent the year in almost one unceasing prayer. And now at the end I am brought in utter helplessness to the point of by faith claiming that I have the petition I have desired of Him, although I have no signs of His presence. It seems a desperate venture of faith, but it must be that His word is true, and that He that asketh receiveth. I am asking for that which I know is according to His will, therefore I receive it! It is mine!

—Journal, March 1878

232. The Passion of My Heart

The effect of the exercises of my heart during the past year has been to empty me far more of self than ever before, and to subdue my will more completely. I am all the Lord's in an infinitely deeper sense than I have ever been before, and I love His will with a far greater intensity. I believe I can truly say it is the passion of my heart! And my own heart cry now is to be made like Christ perfectly and to obey Him utterly! May I learn more and more of it now and follow the blessed inward voice of the Spirit!

> Be faithful to thy unseen Guide,
> Love Him as He loves thee;
> Time and obedience are enough,
> And thou a saint shalt be!
> Then keep thy conscience sensitive,
> No inward token miss;
> And go where grace entices thee,
> Perfection lies in this.

—Journal, March 1878

233. Homely Old Ways

As to "ups and downs," beloved, don't you know that I am one of the kind who never have any. My path seems to lie along a sort of dead level arrangement, that is very comfortable, but not at all glorious. My whole experience seems to be hopelessly commonplace always, except when I am around fanatics, if they are fanatics. And even then the glamour of the fanaticism will not get into my life, do what I may. I see its heights, but cannot scale them, and have to trudge on in the homely old ways, like a poor stupid ox. I cannot even get any inward voices and never could.

I remember when Anna Richards was in the depths of her mysticism, I tried hard to walk in the same paths, but in vain. Scruples would not come although I tried to cultivate them assiduously. I even wooed a sugar scoop "concern," and caps and handkerchiefs, but it was all of no use. And just so it seems to be now. With the exception of that affair of novel reading I do not find myself "called" into anything, nor out of anything.

—To Anna, The Cedars, May 15,1878

234. The Fortress of His Will

Even my Christian work comes to me in commonplace ways, and with none of the romance of Quaker "concerns." I expect the poetry of mysticism is not for me, and I have got to plod on in the prose of commonplace life always. Ah well, amen to this, if it is the dear Lord's will. And I have one romance that never palls—this sweet, beloved, lovely will. No life is without its moments of bliss that is in the fortress of this wonderful grand will. And it is always a fresh joy to me. Do let one of your lessons be on this subject, for Christians desperately need to be taught about it. I will send you a grand hymn as your text.

My sister Sarah [Sally] W. Nicholson has had a severe attack of bilious dysentery and is in bed yet with it, but better. She has suffered a great deal, and fears it will leave her more or less of an invalid all summer. I wish she could get hold of faith healing, but it seems to elude her grasp. What mysteries there are connected with that subject. Some experience such sudden and wonderful cures, and then others apparently with similar faith see no results. I confess I am puzzled and can only explain it on the theory of God's sovereignty in an arena which He does not mean shall be touched even by faith.

—To Anna, The Cedars, May 15, 1878

235. Rationalistic Literalism

As to the "two witnesses," I simply do not know anything and have no theories. I am afraid of too much literalness, having had a dose of it myself in my early Christian experience. I even heard the Rev. Jasper Jones of Richmond Va. prove from the literal words of Scripture that the sun moves around the earth and that the earth is square! It gave me enough of literalism for awhile. My enthusiastic expectation of Christ's speedy coming was disappointed about fifteen years ago, and my present expectations are very mild.

There is a grave difficulty in the way of your plan of giving God the benefit of the doubt. I happen to know at this present moment some cases where this has led to the most frightful fanaticism. It is a safe enough rule for those whose "leadings" go around in a little well-known circle. But get outside of this, and the dangers are immense. You know all sorts of heresies and fanaticisms run towards me like water down a hill for some reason, and I am just now fairly aghast! And the worst of it is that the most fanatical always appear to be the most spiritual. I have got the problem to solve, for the Lord brings it to me. Pray that I may solve it according to His mind.

—To Anna, The Cedars, May 15, 1878

236. Giving Up This Bothersome Self

My darling daughter I enclose $2.00. Be sure to keep an account, for I don't want you to get careless about money; it makes so much trouble later on in life. Alice is down in the nursery today, well again and eating a dinner of broiled spring chicken. John Thomas has just been in here talking. He says Tom Whitall doesn't want to go back to Haverford, but wants to go to some other college. I wonder if Uncle Jim will let him.

I am afraid Tom is tempted to be morbid and analyzes himself and his symptoms too much. Be careful, darling daughter, never to get into that habit. Hand your whole self with all your interests, both inner and outer, over to the Lord's care and then don't pay attention to them or think about them anymore. Self-examination of one's physical symptoms or spiritual symptoms is about as disastrous as anything. Forget self, deny self, put self to death, have nothing to do with it, and let the Lord manage it throughout. That is one of the meanings of consecration. It means that we give up this bothersome self into the care of Another who alone knows how to manage it.

Farewell, precious, your own most loving mother H. W. S.

—To Daughter Mary, May 12, 1878

237. My Father's Arms

I am continually thrown in with the deepest-dyed mystics who claim to know God's will perfectly, but I question whether they really do. Yet it is such a vital question, that I long to know the answer not only for myself but also for others.

I have not got what I wanted yet! By faith I claim that I have the baptism of the Spirit and it really does seem to me that if the Bible is true I must have it. But I am just the same as ever, and find no change whatever in my inward experience; and therefore I feel sure there must be something wrong. Perhaps it is not knowing the inner Voice.

But one thing I know, and that is that I am all the Lord's, and love to be, and that His will is infinitely and unspeakably sweet to me. It grows lovelier all the time, and I wonder how anyone can fear it or rebel against it. And like a poor little child who has lost its way, I creep into the dear arms of my Father and just ask Him to carry me, since I cannot understand His directions. He does all things well, and I can leave myself with Him.

—To Anna, Atlantic City, N.J., May 20, 1878

238. Passiveness of Obedience and Life

The right way to live is to commit yourself and all your interests to the

Lord and leave the management of everything to Him. But I do not know whether I can explain it so you will understand it. I will try, however.

The idea of the Bible is that we must give up our own life and let Christ live in us. "I am crucified with Christ, nevertheless I live, yet not I, but Christ liveth in me." "He that loseth his life shall find it," etc., etc. This means that we must yield ourselves up to Christ as instruments are yielded up to a workman, to be used by Him, and as instruments are of use only in the hands of the workman so we must be in the hands of Christ. But there is this difference between the instruments and us, they are passive involuntarily, we are passive of choice and willingly; and theirs is the passiveness of death, while ours is the passiveness of obedience and life. I mean just this that we give ourselves up to Christ, and He takes us and works, so to speak, for us. He "works in us to will and to do of His good pleasure."

—To Daughter [Mary], Atlantic City, May 25, 1878

239. Careful for Nothing

Our will carries along all the rest of our nature. If we control our will ourselves, then we live; if we surrender it to Christ and let Him control it, then He lives in us. And when we do this, He really does take possession and really does begin to work within us. This is the point where faith comes in. It may seem to us that if we give up managing for ourselves, everything will fall apart; but it is not true. The Lord tells us to be careful for nothing, because He means to take care of everything we commit to Him, and all He wants is that we should really trust Him.

Suppose, for instance, I come up to help you pack. You will leave the packing to me, and then you will trust me to do it and you won't worry about it yourself at all. If you worry, it will be very foolish and will not do any good nor help one bit, and I would feel insulted. All you have to do is to trust me, and then do anything I tell you to do. And the packing will get done, because I do it, and I know how. Do you see it?

—To Daughter, Atlantic City, May 25, 1878

240. Changed Into His Image

In our Christian life it is just like that. If you were capable of doing all the packing yourself, I would not come to do it for you. In the same way, if we could manage our own lives, the Lord wouldn't have to manage them for us. But we can't, and therefore He will, if we will let Him. "And He said,

My grace is sufficient for thee for my strength is made perfect in weakness. Most gladly therefore will I rather glory in my infirmities that the power of Christ may rest upon me. Therefore I take pleasure in infirmities, in reproaches, in necessities, in persecutions, in distresses for Christ's sake for when I am weak, then am I strong."

As to self-examination, it is far better to examine Christ, for by looking at Him we are changed into His image. For "we all with open face beholding as in a glass the glory of the Lord, are changed into the same image from glory to glory, even as by the spirit of the Lord." We are to grow like the lilies grow, without any concern about our own growing, just planted in the grace or love of God, and basking in the sunshine of His presence. "Consider the lilies, how they grow."

—To Daughter, Atlantic City, May 25, 1878

241. He Will Make a Way

Our service for Him has to be as much a matter of trust as any other part of our lives; and if we are really trusting about it, we won't be troubled with whatever happens. We are nothing but instruments, and it makes no difference to the instrument how it is used, or whether it is used at all. And in order to have perfect rest and comfort in our work we must fully realize this. If the Lord wants you to do anything, He will make the way for it, and nothing can hinder Him but your own unwillingness. Just commit your work totally to Him, and then trust Him to manage it, and be satisfied with the way He leads you.

I believe I can truly say that I never worry a moment about my work either before it is done or afterward. I am only the Lord's instrument, and He may use me or not, just as He pleases, and for whatever purposes. It really does not make the slightest difference to me, if only I know that I am doing His will. Why should it? I only want to please Him, and if He is being best pleased by having me here, or there, or hanging me up somewhere without using me, then I am still pleased.

Stop choosing for yourself; be satisfied to let the Lord choose for you. And if He seems to open doors and then closes them, still be content, for He only does it because it is best.

—To Priscie, May 27, 1878

242. Hiding in the Will of God

The secret of giving ourselves entirely to the Lord lies in considering it a real transaction that does actually result in transferring ourselves over to His keeping. After that never admit a thought that it is not done, nor keep on asking yourself questions about whether you will be able to say, "Your will be done," but just meet everything by saying it right away as a matter of course. If we do this, we will take care of trouble right from the start. I have formed the habit of saying at once to everything that comes up, "Yes, Lord, Yes." I know that at the bottom I do want His will done, and I will not listen to anything else.

Read my chapter on "Difficulties Concerning the Will" in *The Christian's Secret*. It just meets this point.

—To Daughter Mary, 1878

243. An Impregnable Fortress

I wanted to write to you and express my sympathy, and to tell you what unspeakable calm comes into any trial or suffering, whenever we are finally able to hide it in the lovely will of God. I know you have learned a great deal about this, and perhaps know more than I do. But even if so, you will not mind being reminded of it, for it is a lesson that one has to learn daily in the pressure of some heavy cares or sorrows.

I have often been compelled to say the blessed words, "Your will be done, Your will be done" over and over a thousand times almost before the sweetness has come. But at last, as surely as God is God, His will has encircled me and mine like the walls of an impregnable fortress, and my soul has sunk into complete repose!

—To Mrs. Gurney, May 29, 1878

244. By the Thorn Road

But to do this, one thing is essential, we must look resolutely and absolutely away from all secondary causes. We never can say, "Your will be done" to secondary causes, for they generally arise from human sins or human mistakes. And if we look at them, we will soon be in despair. But there are no secondary causes in the universe, dear friend. Everything ultimately is God's instrument, accomplishing His purpose, and all is ordered in infinite wisdom and love. Men and women may seem to control affairs or to disarrange them, but behind all the seething and tossing of human affairs, God sits as a Refiner with fire, and not a sparrow even falls without Him! What infinite comfort is here!

But why do I write to you like this? I wonder if it can be that you especially need it just now. I am sure you will be glad to know that the pathway of trial has been turned into a pathway of light and blessing to my soul. The dear Lord has been so good to me that I can only look back and praise Him, and look forward and trust Him. And I have learned that it is indeed true that "by the thorn road and none other is the mount of vision won." The road may be mysterious, but the end is blessed. Therefore, dear friend, we will accept whatever our Father sends with submissive spirits, will we not, and make His dear will the bed where we can rest our weary and aching hearts.

> Upon God's bed I'll lay me down
> As child upon its mother's breast
> No silken couch nor softest
> Could ever give me such sweet rest.

—To Mrs. Gurney, May 29, 1878

245. Simple Faith

I am so glad, darling, that you are beginning to understand about the life of trust. It is not, as Mamie Brown thinks, only for advanced Christians. In fact young people can often live it more easily than grown-up people, because their faith is more simple, and they do not reason so much. The great secret is to be really simple.

I had such a good illustration in bringing Beauty over today. We had only love and care for her in our hearts, and would not have let her get hurt for anything. I have no doubt Maria would have got hurt herself a great deal sooner than to have let Beauty get hurt. And yet poor Beauty could not trust us and kept trying to take care of herself and made frantic efforts to jump out of the window, which would have been her ruin. And I expect she thought, if she thought at all, that we were very cruel to keep her from it.

I could not but think as I looked at her, how exactly like Christians she was.

—To Daughter, Cedars, May 31, 1878

246. Entire Surrender, Perfect Trust

Our plan is to go to the Adirondacks on the 17th. Robert and the rest will go on and get the camp ready. This is our plan. But do not in the least depend on us for we never know what we will do beforehand.

—To Sarah, The Cedars, June 30 1878

Yesterday there was a steady rain all day long, and the mosquitoes, apparently from the whole universe, were driven into our tent to feast on me!! Smoke from a "smudge" would drive them away, but then smoke hurt my eyes so dreadfully that I could only endure it a certain length of time. Last night there was an awful storm. I expected every minute that the tent would blow over and that we would all be driven out into the pathless forest, homeless exiles and outcasts. But it was grand too, and since we did get through safely, I am not sorry for the experience.

So much for outward. The inward has been crowded into a corner in this intensely physical life. Perhaps it is as well for the ground to lie fallow for a while. But I find myself wondering how farmers and people who live outdoor lives can be particularly spiritual. Mystics they certainly cannot be. But I question after all whether so much mystical concern is as pleasing to the Lord as a more natural childlike life that takes no more care for its spiritual growth than the lily does.

The only necessary points in such a life would be entire surrender and perfect trust, and these can be reached without much introversion, if there is only simplicity enough. What a fundamental thing consecration is though. How impossible it is to go on in peace a single moment when there is the slightest bit reserve in it. And how blessed it is that it is like that! I am unspeakably thankful that our Lord is of purer eyes than to behold iniquity, and that he does desire and demand truth in the inward parts.

I think my longing to be pure and good down to the very bottom, is greater now than even my desire after any kind of spiritual manifestations, and I am sure of a pure heart being the will of the Lord, even if manifestations should not be. What a grand salvation it is that proposes to make us the friends of God and like Him. It seems to me that we would not shrink from any discipline which may be necessary to accomplish it, if we but kept in view the glorious end!

—To Anna, Birch Point Camp, Long Lake, Hamilton Co., N.Y., July 27, 1878

247. Ruts, Prejudices, and Old-Time Customs

It is very plain to me that you have a special gift for ministering to young women and for personal dealing with them. And I really believe it is a more effectual line of service than ordinary preaching in meeting. It seems as though the Lord were leading you a little out of this ordinary line, and I don't want you to be afraid to follow His leadings.

Would it be so very dreadful for you to speak in your meetings with a Bible in your hands? It is getting to be quite a common thing among Friends here, and seems to work very well. And somebody has got to be a pioneer over there. Still in any such movement the Lord's voice must be very clearly discerned, and if He wants you to step out in this He will show you plainly. I believe, myself, that Friends have got to get out of their old ruts in order to be in a condition to receive the Lord's full blessing. Such blessing seems to come here only to those meetings where they let the Holy Spirit have free course without any limitations of prejudice or old time customs.

Have you heard how your friend Helen Balkwell has had to give up some of her prejudices? In one of the Western meetings she felt it her duty to sing! And had to get up and tell the Friends, (it was at a Quarterly meeting) about her former prejudices against it, and how she now felt that she must do it herself! David Updegraff was sitting beside her in the gallery, and he said it was evidently a very great cross for her to take up, but that sweet peace was her reward afterwards. I believe she has had to do it several times. She received the blessing of full salvation, or death to sin, during one of the Western Yearly Meetings, and it was after this that this feeling about singing occurred. I suppose it was a test of her consecration and to break down her prejudices. I believe she has been very successful in holding Holiness meetings ever since, and has had a great deal of definite work.

—To Priscie, "The Island Camp," Long Lake Hamilton Co., N.Y., August 2, 1878

248. Have You Got It?

I would like to say a few words in reference to the subject you asked me to write on for Friend's Review. The Scriptures certainly say very little about there being two experiences in the Christian life. For the most part the Christian is evidently spoken of and looked upon as one who has actual possession of all the fullness of Christ's salvation. I think the only exception to this is in Romans 7.

The necessity for two experiences therefore arises from the fact that Christians generally have not obtained possession of this fullness. All could have it when they are first converted, but all do not, and if they are ever going to receive it at all it must be through the steps of a second experience.

The way to meet the arguments of those who say there is only one expe-rience, is to ask them whether they individually and experimentally are enjoying the fullness of the gospel, whether they have habitual victory and uninterrupted peace. If they can answer in the affirmative, then it is evident they must have received the blessing at some time, and if they say it was at conversion, all right, let it be so.

But ask them then what are those Christians to do who don't possess this fullness, whose peace is not uninterrupted, and whose victories are alter-nated with defeats? Are they never to experience these things because they failed to get possession of them at first? If they say such people are not Christians, then confront them with the fact that the majority of the church are in precisely this condition and that the Bible plainly recognizes people who are very far from having constant victory, as being nevertheless the children of God and on their road to Heaven.

The experimental argument is the only one that will meet these opposers. "Have you got it? If not, how are you going to get it; or if you have it, how am I to get it?"

—To Miss Beck, August 25, 1878

249. A Second Blessing

The case of the children of Israel is precisely that they were to have gone into the land when they first left Egypt. It was God's plan for them to do so, and nowhere in all that He had said about it beforehand had He even so much as hinted at any interval between the two things. His "I will bring them out," was always immediately followed by, "and I will bring them in." It should not have been necessary for them to have had two crossings over water, two dippings into baptism, as it were. And yet as a fact these two experiences were necessary, and a long interval elapsed between them, which interval was spent in the wilderness. They were neither in Egypt nor in the Promised Land, but wandering in that which answers I think to the 7th. of Romans, the wilderness experience of the Christian.

They were God's people all the while, and He was with them; but nev-ertheless he always afterward spoke of this period as the "time of provoca-tion;" and He distinctly says that they could not enter in because of unbelief. The cases are precisely parallel. And if the children of Israel, while wandering in the wilderness, had insisted that they must be in the promised land because that was God's plan for them, and because He had not said anything about their coming a second time to the borders of the land, they would have been just about as wise as the persons you allude to.

The truth is we have got to deal with facts, and the fact is that the majority of Christians do need and must have a second experience before they can know the fullness of God's salvation or realize the complete deliverance He has provided.

I am happy to hear that you have at last entered into this second rest. It is hardly worthwhile for anyone to tell those of us who have taken these two steps, that there is but one. We know better; and our own experience is far more convincing to us than a thousand theories. The two experiences in my own life have been equally marked, the first being not one which was more striking than the last.

—To Miss Beck, August 25, 1878

250. The Vision of the Mystic Land or the Veil of Common Sense

I had no chance, when we met so hurriedly, either to hear or to tell anything new. But I don't know that I had anything new to tell even if there had been enough time. My whole inner life is usually too meager to be worth living. Such views of the perfect bliss to be found in the will of God, and such a passion of love for it! I can never describe it.

My soul just gloated over the texts that asserted God's ownership of me and His demands upon me. It seemed unspeakably blessed that He would have me all for His own—body, soul, and spirit; and I felt as if I must cry out to the universe to come and taste of the exquisite beauty of His will. Then the vision of the mystic land vanished; but the blessedness of the Divine will remained, and my soul is struggling for new words to express it. How can I make the world know it? How can I tell even the church?

I say the vision of the mystic land vanished. But perhaps I should say the veil of common sense, and a clear judgment, and a consideration of the proprieties covered my eyes, and I could not see. But it left me aching and bereft. And I must see that land again, and enter into it, or I cannot be happy. Now, beloved, would you say that mysticism, and the near presence of the Lord, even with fanaticism, was better than a safe, and correct, and proper common sense walk at a distance from Him? Which would you choose? Would you rather be near to God in a "sugar scoop" bonnet and cap and handkerchief, sitting in the gallery of an Orange Street meeting, than far off from Him dressed as others dress, and walking in the ways others walk?

You will say this is not the alternative. I know it. But I ask, if it were the alternative, which would you choose?

—To Anna, September 26, 1878

251. An Undertone of Gladness

You must teach consecration, and must be definite about it too, and sometimes this is a mighty hard row to hoe. I cannot express how thankful I am for the relentless pressure my dear Methodist friends put me under years ago on this matter of consecration. It was a terrible wrenching to my ideas at the time, but it has lasted, and since then the will of God has truly become the very passion of my heart! The simple thought of it fills my life with romance at any moment, and always it gives me a secret undertone of gladness beneath everything else in life. I feel as if I needed a new vocabulary to express the joy of it! I must read Godet. I cannot give any opinion on his views of Christ until I have considered the subject more fully.

I am not at all shocked at what you tell me about them; and it would be just like our God to take our place really and actually, and share our lot even in its limitations. I think I would have done it if I were in His place. Don't think that is irreverent. I only meant that whatever I see in man's noblest moods, is, I am sure, surpassed by God. He must be better than the creatures He has made. And then He could easily afford to become man, since He was God. I am watching Beaconsfield with the deepest interest. I hate the English for undertaking to protect Turkey, it is so mercenary and selfish. But if the Lord is behind it all, one can only wonder and wait. But it does not seem to me that the church is ready yet for the Lord's return. The vessels of the virgins are not filled with oil. But they are filling them and the cry for more realized communion, of which I speak, is one sign of this. I wonder if we can hasten His coming by helping to fill these vessels and to prepare the Bride?

Anna, when once the soul has begun to know God, old prejudices must go! And before the two grand facts of His justice and His love, all the old creeds and notions vanish like clouds before sunshine. He is a glorious God, with nothing to mar His perfections! Praises be to His Name!

—To Mrs. Shipley, 1878

252. The Inward Voice

Inwardly I am learning many precious lessons, chiefly, I think at present, in the line of knowing the inward Voice, and following it without reserve. There is a great awakening on this subject in the hearts of many Christians, and, strange to say, I cannot find anything printed about it anywhere, not even among Friends' books or tracts. I attended a convention not long ago, where the subject was brought forward prominently, and I wanted to send some Friends' writings on the subject to a few of the leaders of the meeting to show them that it was not a new discovery but was unable to find a single thing.

Have you ever paid special attention to this subject, or what do you know about it experimentally? It seems to me that it is a most wonderful privilege, and, if it is really true, how infinite the loss of all those whose eyes are blind to it. For myself, I find that the sweetness of a life of obedience to this inward Voice is greater than I can be express, even though it may lead into some hard pathways. Isaac Pennington says, "the yoke leads to the rest, nay, the yoke is the rest," and I find this is to be true. There is no rest anywhere half so sweet as the rest I feel when under this blessed yoke. Tell me your experience about it.

I am so glad you can work with more of an abandonment of trust than you once did. Always remember, dear friend, that "one sows, and another reaps," and that the one who sows is not likely to gather the harvest also. The "results" are as much due to the sower as to the reaper, but it is the reaper alone who sees them garnered.

—To Miss Beck, December 5, 1878

253. Only Go on Loving Me

All right! I'll ask no questions, and think no thoughts. Neither do I wonder. The only surprise has been that you ever cared to come at all. And I confess Mrs. Miles was rather more than even I could swallow whole. But I must see and know all sorts, and this often leads me into disreputable company, into which I have no desire my friends should follow me. Love me, beloved, but do not endorse me. The Lord does not lead me in the ordinary paths, and as I dare do nothing but follow Him wherever it may be, I want all my friends to "clear their skirts" of me at once and forever. Only go on loving me through it all, as I would you, if you should join St. Clements or become a Plymouth sister!

The effect of our prayers on Sally has been that her faith grows exceedingly, and that she seems on the verge of a complete healing. The Lord had secrets of faith to reveal to His people I am sure, which only a few are prepared as yet to receive. But I do want to be one of these few, and I won't interpose any conscious hindrances upon whatever or however He teaches me.

—To Anna, February 19, 1879

254. Inexorable Love

I am working out in my mind and heart the problem of character and character-building, and I find it terribly challenging. So much that is uncontrollable by us goes into the formation of our character, and even often unconscious to us; and we are helpless before it. If it were not for God, the knowledge of this would be unbearable. But with a God to rest on, how glorious it is. And to know that His love is strong enough to be inexorable is all we need for absolute rest. I often want to pity and spare myself; I could not help it. But He never will, never for a single moment; and therefore I am utterly at ease, and don't have a care. "Consider the lilies how they grow," and grow like them.

And what is of any account compared to being good. Aren't you glad that you gained that victory over your judgmental spirit? I really do want to see that thing completely removed from your nature, and I know it can be; and perhaps it is. Is it?

—To Anna, April 28, 1879

255. God in the Smallest Details

I have had a visit by one of the most deeply taught Christians I have ever met. She had the most delightful experience as to guidance that I ever heard of, so perfectly simple and natural and so sure. She says she knows the Lord's voice, and has no questioning. And I learned more from her in respect to this than I ever learned from anyone else. She "acknowledges God in all her ways," and consequently He "directs her paths" in each of the matters in which she thus acknowledges Him. It fills life with an added and unspeakable delight to live it, in all its smallest details, in the actually realized presence and guidance of God. The difference between this and life without it is not in principle, but only in the carrying out of the old principles into smaller details. It is to bring God just as much into the domestic and ordinary details of life as a minister among Friends for instance brings Him into their meetings; so that the same solemnity and sweetness will be upon our spirits in our daily duties as in our distinctly religious work; and the same guidance that leads us in one will lead us in the other.

Do you get the idea? How does it sound to you? I have always felt that there ought to be no separation between our religious life and our natural life, that God intended them to be one and the same, just as a bird's life is. And I am sure the divorce between the two has come from some other source than the divine. Isn't it an uprising of self which must have a kingdom of its own to reign in, from which God is, partially at least, excluded? I think the Lord is teaching me something about this, and I trust to be able so to commit myself to Him so that He will reign supreme as the God of every action. But I shall have more to tell you about this someday perhaps.

—To a Friend, Hancock St., Germantown, Pa., May 18, 1879

256. The Learning Experience

It seems somehow as though I have never been allowed to learn lessons in any way but by an actual experience of the whole process. Things that others have learned from their parents or friends without going through the processes themselves, have come to me only as the result of an actual working out of the whole subject from its initial steps upward. Before I could be a believer I had to go down into absolute heathenism; before I could learn the broadness of God's love, I had to embrace the narrowest Calvinism; before I had a sight of dependence on God, I realized the extremes of self dependence.

And so also here, before I could know true spirituality I must go through the forms. This no doubt has been God's order for me, and I can see the wisdom of it, in this at least, that the lessons so learned can be taught with a clearness and power that nothing else could give. It was just so about war, and about women's preaching; I only understood them after an experience of revolt from the traditional views in which I had been trained.

—To a Friend, Hancock St., Germantown, Pa., May 18, 1879

257. Hearing and Obeying the Word

How near it brings the other world to have one we love go into it! And how insignificant it makes the things of this world! Of what use are all the care and work and worry to make and keep things straight in this world?

Sometimes I feel as if I must shake myself free of it all and just stretch my soul out after the unseen realities. But it is better rather to make the earthly cares a heavenly discipline and mount on them to heights of development which only such training can give.

I had such a lovely "opening" as George Fox calls it on two verses the other day. It was in Luke 11:27, 28. Someone was saying how blessed was the mother who bore our Lord, and He answered, "Yea, rather, blessed are those that hear the word of God and keep it." The lesson taught me was this, that no circumstances, however blessed, were at all to be compared to the blessedness of hearing and obeying the word of God, not even that wondrous blessedness of being the mother of our Lord Himself!

And then it came to me as a great comfort that while to be His mother was a blessing which only one woman out of all the millions could have, the greater blessedness of hearing and obeying is free to all, rich or poor, Jews or Gentile, old or young. And I have thanked God for it ever since.

—To a Friend, Hancock St., Germantown, Pa., May 18, 1879

258. Two Grand Secrets of His Kingdom

In the palace or at the washtub, in meetings or in home life, everywhere and always this greatest of all blessings, His guidance is available, and nothing can hinder our receiving it if we ourselves are but willing. I wish I could express in words just how wonderful this all is. But the Lord doubtless is teaching you, as He is me, that after all to hear and to obey are the two grand secrets of His kingdom. And I am learning more and more how to hear, which is an unspeakable joy to me.

I see that God Himself is continually speaking to every one of us, if only we have the ears to hear; and I am finding great blessing in continually acknowledging his voice in everything that comes to me. I mean literally everything, so that no moment or act of my life is left outside of His direct and personal guidance. I do not think, dear Priscie, that Sarah Satterthwaite's experience is one only for a few. I believe the difference between her and others is only that she has ears to hear the Voice which speaks to others as well as to her and as much. I think you may know the same blessed guidance.

—To Priscie, Hancock St., Germantown, Pa., June 20, 1879

259. He Knows and I Will Be Content

The Second Coming was pressed a good deal and Sarah is very full of it yet. Somehow it all seems very spectacular and after the flesh to me. And it does not tend to spirituality say what they may. What with their seven judgments, and their two resurrections, and their rebuilding of Babylon, and their two Witnesses, and their time and times and half a time, there is such a complicated arrangement of affairs altogether, that one's best comprehension can hardly unravel it. And since Christ has come to me in my heart I cannot care so much for His outward coming.

If this outward Coming were to usher in at once a reign of peace and joy I would long for it unspeakably; but according to the students it is to introduce first seven years of unparalleled tribulation and anguish, and I cannot long for that. Still He knows, and I shall be content; only somehow, I have the feeling that I will ask to be allowed to stay down on the earth during this tribulation to help the poor souls bear it. How can we enjoy ourselves up "in the air" when we know that our going has taken away the last restraint upon wickedness, and that we have left the poor world to an unbridled carnival of sin? But what would Dr. Brooks think of me?

—To Anna, Clifton Springs, July 8, 1879

260. But "I Do Fly"

I would not argue much on religious subjects with Marie Bigelow if I were you. In such arguments the unbelieving one always gets the better of it, because the region of spiritual life is unknown to them and they cannot understand its language. It is like a bird trying to make a mole understand its mode of life and its joys of existence. The only thing you can do effectively is to testify to the reality of spiritual things, just as the bird would say to all arguments against it. "But then I do fly, and there is the end of it."

—To Daughter Mary, July 31, 1879

261. Ministering at Ocean Grove, N.J. (Methodist Holiness Camp Meeting)

I could not get a minute in which to write to you yesterday. It was meetings and enquirers all day long. Somehow I seem like a magnet to attract souls in trouble as soon as I speak. I guess the mother element is very strong in me, for I find my heart yearning over my audiences as a kind of mother hen over her brood, wanting to gather them under her wings; and that I expect draws them. I spoke from the stand yesterday morning to a large audience, and the Lord helped me. Dear frightened Elder Stokes was comforted, and Brother Adams gave me the fullest kind of endorsement. One funny thing happened, that dear crazy Brother Thomas in the afternoon went to a little meeting and said that he thought there must have been something wrong in my sermon because he found that everybody without a single exception spoke well of it! In the afternoon I led a conversational meeting in the Tabernacle, for asking and answering questions. Elder Stokes endorsed this meeting fully called it a "Methodist class meeting led by a Quaker."

This is really a most delightful place; cool invigorating air, a circle of charming and interesting people, lovely meetings all the time, capital preaching, and every convenience of city and country and seashore life combined. I do not wonder that Esther Nicholson calls it "Paradise Regained." What a grand soul she is. Here she boards in a tiny little room in a second-rate boarding house at $8.00 a week in order to save money to give away. And dresses like a guy besides. She sends her warm love to you, and says she wants to have you here for three days entirely under her control, and then she is sure she will send you away in love with Ocean Grove.

Farewell dearest! It will not be long now before we meet.

—To Robert, Ocean Grove, August 9, 1879

262. "Following Fully"

But now for my experience. I had first a real heart searching time as to the inward voice, and came to a more complete surrender to it than ever. And then all of a sudden as I was riding alone in the cars the Lord revealed Himself as if He were close beside me. It was not a vision, nor any physical sensation, but just a sense, a knowledge of His presence. It seemed so real that I almost involuntarily put out my hand to clasp His. And I whispered to myself, "Oh how lovely! Oh if it would only last!" Immediately the words came with conviction "I will never leave you nor forsake you." I believed them, and from that moment He has been consciously with me.

He is with me now. His arm is round about me, I am resting on His bosom! It seems to me the fulfillment of that verse, "At that day you will know that I am in the Father, and you in me, and I in you." I know it. Praise His Name! I suppose this is only what you have always had, but it is new to me, and is unspeakably precious. No physical manifestation whatever has accompanied this, but it is better than any physical manifestation would be unaccompanied by it, and I seem to feel somehow that He will give me what is right. Since He is so close at hand, He cannot help it.

But this is I feel only the beginning. My great hunger now is to know His voice. I feel that I must know it! And yet this confusion of voice is so great that I can only now and then distinguish His. But since He is so close He will surely make me know it somehow, and I can only wait. But "following fully" means something I find! It means literally the loss of all things, both inward and outward.

—To Sisters, Hancock St., Germantown, Pa., August 14, 1879

263. The Leadership of the Spirit

I have attended three of our summer conferences, and have had such a press of work in connection with them that every moment has been full. I sent you the little book issued by Dr. Cullis at his conference, which will give you a little idea of the sort of meeting it was. There were some wonderful results there, and many, many hungry souls found richest blessing. And the Lord gave me more power to help than ever I had before I think, besides leading my own soul into a place of nearness to Himself that is far sweeter and more blessed than any I have ever known before.

You remember I told you in my last letter of my greatly increased light on the subject of walking in the Spirit. This light has grown brighter continually, and I have learned to know His voice as I never had thought it possible I could, and have been led along most blessed and wonderful pathways. There has come to me a consciousness of His presence with me that is so real that it often leads me involuntarily to put out my hand as if I could actually clasp His, and day and night I feel His arm around me, and my head is on His breast! You can imagine how much this blessed experience has increased my love for His sweet will, and yet I feel as if no one could know how unspeakably precious this will is to me. No words can express it!

And this is such a marvelous transformation that I can only say, "It is the Lord's doing and is marvelous in our eyes!" A transformation I mean from what the natural man ever could of itself feel concerning the Divine will. I remember so well the days of my rebellion against it, and am filled with praises to the grace that has so transformed me. It has come too, strange to say, by the way of the cross, verifying those lines of Faber's: God's will is sweetest to him when It triumphs at his loss.

264. "Just to Mind"

The Lord has called for some very close surrenders of self and self-will, and in the surrender has come the revelation of the sweetness. That is, we must die that we may live—the old Quaker doctrine too much lost sight of now. Yes, dear friend, you are right, we do need the "ancient virtue," for Quakerism, if it doesn't have the baptism, it is nothing. And my heart is fairly burning sometimes to call in trumpet tones to the sleeping church, and awake it to its original power.

But what can we do? One thing the Lord has laid upon three of us, my brother James, Dr. Rhoads and myself, which I will tell you confidentially, as they do not want it talked about. We meet once a week to wait on the Lord for an outpouring of the Spirit upon the Philadelphia Yearly Meeting! It seems presumptuous for only three to ask, but the Lord seems to have led us to it, and it is nothing to Him to work by many or by few. Do unite your prayers with ours. As Dr. Rhodes says, there is literally no hope for Philadelphia Yearly Meeting except an outpouring of the Spirit. All ways, and plans, and methods are hopeless. And no performances of man's getting up can ever accomplish any real Divine work.

It is only necessary for an instrument to be perfectly pliable and ready and the Master can use it. I am learning more and more of this for myself, and realize such a blessed rest from all responsibility, except just the one responsibility of obedience. As a dear little Christian said one morning in her time of prayer "Dear Lord, I thank you that I have nothing to do all day today but just to mind;" so I feel that I have nothing to do all the rest of my life but "just to mind." And this is so simple.

—To a Friend, "Oak Lawn," Hancock St., Germantown, Pa., August 17, 1879

265. Chunder Sen

I have read Chunder Sen, and do feel just like sailing for India to see him. What a grand revelation that man has had! It stirred me to the very depths. Oh, beloved, how it shames us who have such a blaze of light all our lives long! Where did we take the fatal turning that has led us so far astray? Did this woman sin, or her parents, that she was born blind? I thank God however that the light has come at last; and like Chunder Sen I say that the "residue of my independence has been swallowed up by the all-conquering all-absorbing grace of God, and I am sold forever!" How wonderful that word, "No independence" is! It cuts down to the root of everything; and yet is so full of life, Divine life, that it seems to bring the soul out into the grandest place of liberty. It seems just like one of God's coincidences that I had been learning the very lessons in regard to this which Chunder Sen's announces. I know the "I am" he knew. And God has said to me "I am your church and doctrine; I am your creed and your immortality, your earth, your Heaven, your food, your raiment, your treasure here and in Heaven. Believe in Me." To me it is a life, a free, independent, Divine life, back of all forms, an absolute, universal life, that can fit into any form, or can exist without form. It would be true then that circumcision availeth nothing, nor uncircumcision. That is, one might enter into the form or might remain without, just as led by the Spirit at the time. I cannot but think this is the deeper insight into the truth; and the more I look to the Lord about it, the clearer are my convictions. Well, I must follow the light, my light, that which is given to me, even though it separates me from all whom I love! And sometimes I think it may.

—To Anna, "Oak Lawn," Hancock St., Germantown, Pa., September 11, 1879

266. Broad as the Universe

But I think, beloved, you have misunderstood my position somewhat. I never thought of such a thing as saying that the believers in the Bible were in their A.B.C.'s. I have not a question about the truth of the Bible. I bow in absolute submission to the authority of the Bible, but even among those who do this there are honest differences of opinion as to the interpretation of the Bible; and I feel as though I have been led into deeper views of its spirituality than I once held. I accept the same words I used to accept, but they mean a very different thing to me now. Do you remember that saying of one of the Pilgrim Fathers, I think, when they were about to start for America "I am persuaded that much light of truth is yet to break forth from God's word, which as yet we have not reached."

This covers my ground. It is out of the Bible itself, "spiritually discerned," as I believe, that I have learned all the truth which so rejoices my heart. I acknowledge that. I am "Broad," but I believe the religion of Jesus Christ is as broad as the universe, and all I hold, I hold in utter loyalty to

Him as my Lord and my God. My "broadness" is original, not out of books or from teachers.

—To Anna, "Oak Lawn," Hancock St., Germantown, Pa., September 11, 1879

267. Counting on God

And now, beloved, I want to ask you one question, Is God to be really counted on as a God is present with us? With all your orthodoxy, neither you nor Sarah F. Smiley seem to me to count on God.

I have counted on Him. I came to Him years ago definitely and honestly to know the truth. I am not such a fool as to want to hold any error; and the one prayer I have prayed more than any other has been that I might have the mind of Christ, meaning not only His nature, but chiefly I think His intellectual views of things. I wanted the truth as it was in Him, for He is the truth.

Following and accompanying this prayer have come the enlargement, and deepening, and spiritualizing of view that so trouble Sarah. Am I to reckon on God and believe He has answered my prayer, or am I to think He has utterly disregarded it, and has left me a prey to delusions and errors?

I confess, beloved, that I have not come to understand my Bible that way. I believe God when He says, if any man lack wisdom and ask for it in faith he shall have it. I knew I lacked. I had not one ray of confidence in my power of search to find it out; I had to do it fresh up from the bottom in this, as in all my other views. It seems as though the Lord has had to put to death all my traditional views one after another, only to give them back to me fresh from and in Himself. I am amazed sometimes to find out what a genuine "early Quaker" I am.

—To Anna, "Oak Lawn," Hancock St., Germantown, Pa., September 11, 1879

268. Knowing God

It was very comforting to know you don't think me such an utter renegade. I cannot imagine how anyone could have got the idea that I discarded the Bible. I suppose it arose from my speaking of the spirit as distinguished from the letter. But I only meant that the spiritual meaning is often so much deeper than appears on the surface, as even to seem almost in contrast. The Bible never was so much to me as now, and the life and sayings of our Lord Himself seem to me heretofore to have been almost a sealed book, so wonderfully full of meaning have they become to me of late. At present I do not want to read anything but the Gospels, and they are glorious!

I have found there is an infinite difference between knowing God, and merely knowing about Him. We recognize this difference when it comes to earthly relations, and are never satisfied in reference to those we admire until we come to the personal acquaintance which brings us to the place of knowing the one we admire. And to know God means I am sure a far more intimate relationship than we generally enjoy. But is it all implied in the oneness for which our Lord prayed?

—To Anna, Hancock St., Germantown, Pa., September 27, 1879

269. At Any Cost

Oh, to be one with God! I have often talked about it, but it seems to me that only lately have I begun to know what it means, if even I do as yet. Only of this am I sure: self must die, before this oneness can be realized. And that is good. Who wants to keep even the least mite of the old hateful self life if there is any way of getting rid of it? Let self be crucified then, by any process, at any cost, so that only the glorious life of Jesus may be made manifest in our mortal flesh! For such a destiny, who would hesitate at the cost?

I know I have given myself utterly to God without any reserve. I know I want nothing but His will. I know I mean to follow Him fully as fast as He gives me light, therefore, I know I belong to Him body, soul, and spirit with all my spiritual capacities and all my natural powers. And being wholly His, He alone must put me to use. I will, therefore, acknowledge Him in everything exterior and interior, and my faith will grasp the fact that He is working in me to will and to do of His good pleasure, no matter how it may seem. Definitely and forever I consent now to die to any self life I am aware of.

From now on, it will be not I but Christ; no more I in the willing, no more I in the doing. I will not yield to my self life either by word or thought. I will not see or know anything but Christ living in me. God is in fact, and shall be in my acknowledgement, all and in all. In Him henceforth I will consciously live, and move, and have my being.

In utter dependence upon God alone to make this a personal definite reality to me, I leave myself in His Hands today.

—To Anna, Hancock St., Germantown, Pa., September 27, 1879

270. Getting Home to God

I must tell you of the wonderful vision God has given me of Himself. Not an emotion, but a knowledge, a sort of real seeing. It seems to me somehow as if I had gotten home to God. As if I had been taking refuge in all sorts of things until now, but had at last been driven out of them all and had found myself in God. I wish I could tell you about it. It is as if I had got to the bottom of things somehow, back into the very beginnings of them all and had found it was God. "For of Him and to Him and by Him are all things." I have discovered the truth of this, that it is a fact. He is really all in all, the beginning and the end of everything; the King in His own universe, the one only and omnipotent Creator!

I have never known an omnipotent God before. I have only known a bounded, limited, helpless God; and I have never therefore been able really to reckon on Him as a positive presence and power. I have feared enemies and dreaded precipices. But I see now that no enemies can for a moment withstand such a God; and one can't fall down any precipices when one is already at the foot of them. Read Ps. 139 and you will get the idea, that is if your eyes have been opened to see it. "Beset" by God, only think of it! It is grand, dear Carrie, thus to find God in everything, and to be able down at the bottom of everything, and behind everything to rest in God. Faber says, "God only is the creature's home," and it is like getting home to get to Him.

—To Carrie, 1315 Filbert St., October 16, 1879

271. The Bottom of Things

I only wish I had the time and ability to tell you of the grand discoveries the Lord has made to me of Himself this summer. Not emotional discoveries; I never felt myself further from emotion; but conviction, consciousness, reality, intuition, an inward sense that goes deeper than belief, that is in fact knowledge. It seems to me as if all my life before this I had been knowing about God, but now have come to a place of knowing Him Himself, a personal acquaintance as it were.

But I cannot tell it. It is like a getting home somehow. It is as if I had got at last to the bottom of things, to the place of foundations, where I know by a sense beyond all knowledge how God is really the beginning and the end of everything; the King in His own universe; the one only omnipotent Creator! I have never really known an omnipotent God before.

He has been a bounded, limited, helpless God, and therefore He could not be trusted utterly and alone; He needed helps to His omnipotence to make it real, or availing. But now I see that "of Him, and to Him, and through Him are all things," and my soul rests with an absolute settlement in His arms of omnipotence. "Even the devils are subject unto Him."

Oh beloved, it is such a comfort to get down to the very foundations of things, past the place where precipices can be feared, or doubts be dreaded. To know God is to have every question forever answered, every longing stilled! But I cannot write it; I must wait until we meet and can talk it all over, if the Lord permits.

—To Anna, 1315 Filbert St., Philadelphia, Pa., October 17, 1879

272. You Bid Us; We Obey

Have you seen the "Praise Meeting of the Birds"? I want to send you my portion out of it.

> And the birds which migrate praise You,
> For guiding us aright
> When, at Your summons given,
> We take our mystic flight.
>
> Urged by a vague strange longing
> We flee from storm and cold;
> O'er mountains, seas, and forests,
> Our onward course we hold.
>
> We know not why we wander,
> You bid us; we obey,
> And through the pathless azure
> Follow the appointed way.
>
> We trust You; and Your answer
> Smiles in the summer sun,
> That warms us into vigor
> When the far goal is won.
>
> Ah! if we stayed to question,
> To prove, to understand,
> Winter and death would seize us
> In the forbidden land.

—To Anna, 1879

273. The Utmost Verge of Light

We are enjoying ourselves exceedingly. The meetings are splendid, and of all sorts, so that everybody can be suited. Last night a man preached whose spiritual power is wonderful, and he just seemed to sway that audience of thousands of people as if it had been one man. He preached on reality, and I felt as if no one could ever again endure any shams in religion of any sort. Then he made everybody who wanted to be real through and through hold up their hands, and afterwards kneel down all over the ground and ask God to make us real.

His name is Benjamin Adams, and there is one thing he said years ago which has never left me. It was this that he "always kept his obedience up to the outmost verge of his light." This is the secret of a true life I am sure.

—To Mary, 1879, Ocean Grove, N.J.

274. Careless, Confident, Single-Hearted

To be right oneself is so much more important to us than to try to set others right. First pluck out your own beam, before beginning on another's mote. So, darling Carrie, do not let your desire to see Sarah F. Smiley set right upset your own spirit and make it hard for you to get right yourself. I know you are one of those grand candid souls who have the inward impulse to speak out when things need correction. And I would not change you for anything, but I don't want you, darling, to be too generous in this direction, and hurt your own soul because of it. It is easy to do this, unless one is consciously led by the Spirit in every step; and I feel myself to be as yet too little acquainted with the sweet inward Voice to undertake much of it.

So, "Then why do you lecture me?" I hear you ask. Ah, Carrie, you are my parish, as I am yours. I love you. You and I have a dear inherited right of help from one another, and must never let it slip. I wish I could tell you the unspeakable inward ease of soul that comes to me from my utter surrender to God. It seems as if I really might be a little baby in the Father's arms with not a care in all the universe. Two lines I met the other day in a poem on Adam in Eden just express my feelings:

> Careless, and confident, and single-hearted,
> Trusted in God, and turned himself to sleep.
> That is just what I do.

—To Carrie, 1879

275. Growing Content

I don't have time to speak of my own experience except just to say that God is all in all to me in these days as never before. And Christ is God, the Alpha and Omega, the present, living personal, omnipotent God, in whom my soul rests with an absolute content. I have realized lately what it means to be the Lord's garden and to be kept by Him as a vineyard. "Ye flowerets of the field," Siddartha said, "Who turn your tender faces to the sun, What secret know ye that ye grow content?"

It seems to me that I have found out the secret, and that I am growing content.

—To a Friend, February 2, 1880

Ray is ill with Scarlet Fever and Mary with diphtheria. Of course we are in quarantine. And our Saturday meetings must be given up for the present.

> Upon God's will I lay me down
> As child upon its mother's breast,
> No silken couch or softest bed
> Could ever give me such sweet rest.

—To Anna, February 5, 1880

276. Ripe for Heaven

Our darling Ray has died. She must be very happy today, and I am so glad for her that I do not let myself grieve. She had a very sensitive nature, very much given to introspection, and I often thought was destined to a life of suffering. I am thankful to have her safe in Heaven.

As to myself, you know I never did care much how I fared if only my children could be happy; and what greater joy could I have secured for her than what she has entered upon now? She looks lovely; there is the sweetest smile on her face, as though just at the last she had had a glimpse of the opening blessedness. Perhaps she saw her Grandma Whitall. It does seem lovely for them to have died so near together.

I am quietly resting in God, content with His sweet will; and am seeking to learn the lessons He means to teach. As far as I can read it, for me it means only a more utter abandonment than ever to the interior life of divine union and a more faithful obedience to the voice of the Spirit. What it means for Robert I do not know, and am afraid to meddle. I believe it is better to leave him with God. I know how you all sympathize with me, but I hope you can also understand something of a mother's unselfish joy over her child's consummated happiness.

Ray and I had some lovely talks while she was sick. She was ripe for Heaven.

—To Carrie, February 9, 1880

277. The Mother Cries—Content

The enclosed card will tell its own story! Our dear mother died of an attack of Pneumonia, after only a few days of very little suffering. Our little Ray was taken with Scarlet Fever the day of her funeral and died at the end of four days, also without any severe suffering. It seemed lovely, within a week of one another, for the grandma and grandchild to go home. After Ray's death her little face was radiant with a heavenly smile as though she might have had a glimpse of the opening glories just as she passed away. I cannot help feeling that she saw her dear grandma.

Ray has been like an angel this last year, though indeed I actually do not remember ever having to punish her and scarcely to reprove her. She said to me one day last summer in her bright childish way, "Mother, it never used to seem as if I could really understand what trusting Jesus meant. But now I have just got a 'grip' of it, and it is so nice." And it was 'nice' to her, for I think I never knew anyone who made it more practical.

When I first realized that she was ill I began at once to say, "Your will be done," over and over; and the Lord has kept me quietly hidden in the impregnable fortress of His love and care; and has given me such a sense of Ray's present happiness, and her eternal deliverance from all future care, or sorrow, or sin, that my gladness for her swallows up my grief for myself. A mother's love is always contented if her children are happy, no matter how she may fare herself; and I am content now.

Do you remember those lines of E. B. Browning's on a child's grave at Florence? They seem as if they might have been written for me.

> Meanwhile, the mother cries, content!
> Our love was well divided;
> Its sweetness following where she went,
> Its anguish stayed where I did.
>
> Well done of God, to halve the lot,
> And give her all the sweetness;
> To us the empty room and cot,

To her the Heaven's completeness.

Oh, dear friend, what a fortress the sweet will of God is! The arrows do not touch the soul that is hidden there! I can tell this with tenfold power and emphasis now, for I have proved it to be so wonderfully true.

Logan and Alice were away at Boarding School when Ray died. Their father went to them & told them, but did not bring them home on account of the infection. They have borne it beautifully and Alice writes today, "Last night Jesus filled my heart with such incomparable joy that instead of crying, I smiled myself to sleep. It all flashed over me how happy Ray was. I want to go to Heaven myself, and Ray was almost a part of me; so as I would be happy if I were there, therefore I am happy for her."

Mary was ill with diphtheria in another room when Ray died, and is not yet out of bed, though convalescing nicely. We are all resting quietly in the sweet beloved will of God.

—To a Friend, February 12, 1880

278. God's Choice Is Perfect

I want to tell you about my Ray's departure for her lovely home in Heaven. You ask whether I prayed for her life with strong groanings. No, indeed a thousand times, no! Could I have been so selfish when God was giving her a chance to reach the blessed Home in such a short and easy way towards which the rest of us are travelling with slow and weary feet? Could I have had the heart to hold her back? No, dear friend, my love for my darling child was too strong for that. I only asked that the journey might be short and easy, and that nothing we were doing to prolong life might be successful if it was His will to take her. For I know that God's choice for each one of us is always a perfect choice, and that His choice for my Ray must be as much better than my choice, as He is wiser, and truer, and more loving than me.

I miss my darling unspeakably. But I never did care much how I fared if only my children were happy; and why should I care now, when a happiness infinitely beyond any my tenderest love could have compassed, has come to my child through the free grace of God? And when, as you say, I flutter down to earth, the thought of the sweetness that has come to my Ray, and the knowledge of the sweetness of God's will for me, keep me in unbroken peace.

—To Mrs. Gurney, 4653 Germantown Ave., Philadelphia, Pa., March 10, 1880

279. Inclusive Rest

Ray was a very spiritual child, and had been wonderfully ripening for the last year, though so full of childish merriment that we scarcely noticed it at the time. But we all did notice how entirely without a fault she was, an unbroken and unclouded Ray of sunshine from one end of the year to the other. Her little "Journal" is full of wonderful things for a child like her to say, and reveals a depth of simple practical trust in God and an earnestness of purpose that convince us now that she was ripe for Heaven.

Her little face was radiant after death, fairly illumined with a surprised happy smile, as though, just at the last minute, she might have caught a glimpse of the opening glory. You cannot think what blessed secrets of her new life that smile has taught me.

And now I have three in Heaven and three on earth, and for the first three all my anxieties are ended. Surely it must be an especial kindness of my God's that three of my children are spared the care, and sorrow, and sin of this life!

And can your heart yet say, "Well done of God to halve the lot"? Or do surges and waves of intolerable sorrow sometimes sweep over you still? I will not let those surges sweep over me. When I see them coming, I run and hide in the fortress of God's will, and there I am safe.

I often think of you with deepest interest, and long to hear of your complete victory.

—To Mrs. Gurney, 4653 Germantown Ave., Philadelphia, Pa., March 10, 1880

280. Steps of Faith, Steps of Obedience

Did the sanctification Dougan Clark taught say one might enjoy the delicious quiet of a retired life with an easy conscience? For if it did it would certainly have suited me, I am growing so lazy. I often feel nowadays as though I should give up all public work soon. It is so repugnant to me. Do you think it is old age?

And yet I know my power for effectual work increases, and I know I tell deeper and grander truths than ever. And the doors open increasingly on every hand. I do not understand it. But I am content to leave it and wait. I have got to God, and He can fix all things straight, and I do not even need to know how He is going to do it. It is such a rest; just what our Lord said, rest to one's soul, and there can be no deeper nor more all inclusive rest than that.

I will send you my reply to John Y. Hoover soon. I intend to print it, and so be, understood once for all. I believe narrowness is rather more intolerable to me than any other form of mistake among Christians. It is so unChristlike.

As to the way to retain what we have obtained, the only way is obedience. You may perhaps obtain it by a flying leap, but to keep it something other than flying leaps is necessary. We are not kangaroos in the divine life, but snails rather, and any swerving, even the slightest, delays our progress seriously. "Steps of faith" will not carry us everywhere; "steps of obedience" also are absolutely necessary. and the preaching which exalts the first at the expense of the last, must always in the long run prove a failure. First the blade, then the ear, then the full corn in the ear. This is always God's way in any work that is to abide. Only mushroom growths come up in a night full statured. But it is an endless subject, and I cannot fully develop it here.

—To Anna, May 12, 1880

281. God's Wideness

I would write to Joel Bean if I had time, for I feel a great spirit of unity with him, and can truly sympathize in his terror of David Updegrapf. But, as you say, if they could only both be broad enough to tolerate one another, or even more, to see the needs for one another, how grand it would be. I am unspeakably thankful to have been brought out into a little of God's wideness, which embraces all honest reaching out towards Himself. He has spoken to us at sundry times and in divers manners, and it is no wonder if we speak in the same diverse fashion to Him.

Did I ever tell you what Jukes says that some who call themselves "brethren" do it because they have none of the toleration of fathers towards the young and the weak, but are full of the arrogant intolerance of the older brother who cannot endure the childish doings of the little ones? I know all about that intolerance, for I once was full of it. But now I see that those who are the furthest along the way will always be the most tolerant, or at least ought to be, just as shepherds are tolerant of their flocks.

—To Anna, 4653 Main St., Germantown, Pa., March 14, 1880

282. The Cross Is the Teacher

I do not in the least renounce any of my old views of sanctification; I only step on them to higher things. It is true that by the definite steps David Updegrapf teaches, the soul is brought into a place of harmony with God that might in one sense be called heart purity or death to sin. But this is only the beginning. After that comes all the growth and development, and God's crucifying processes which accomplish in fact that which has been claimed by faith.

In a letter I have just received from Andrew Jukes he says, "Some speak and act as if they thought that advance in the knowledge of the truth could be acquired by effort, and by our searching this, or willing that. But, unless I mistake, all real growth in knowledge is just a revelation which comes, not be effort, but by and in our accepting meekly the varied experiences we are called to pass through, every one of which in one way or another makes us learn our own helplessness and the help and grace and power of Him who manifests Himself to us in our tribulation. Thus the cross is the great teacher, not the mere doctrine of the cross, but the actual crossing of our will which is indeed the crossing of ourselves."

—To Anna, 4653 Main St., Germantown, Pa., March 14, 1880

283. Helping Not Hindering

No one here approves of Joel Bean's course in leaving his seat in meeting although many of us feel that he had more than enough provocation. But no matter what the provocation, we must receive one another as Christ has received us, and we must permit the exercise of the "diversities of gifts" while keeping the "unity of the spirit," or we shall cause "schism in the body." But I cannot go into this now.

I am preparing an article for Friends Review on the subject which I will send you. It covers the ground of my endorsement of the "Salvation Army." They are doing a work and reaching a class in a way I could not possibly accomplish, and I feel that as far as I can, I must help and not hinder them. Mark 9:38–41 contains the principle upon which I desire always to act. "Because he followeth not us" is not a reason for rejection in the light of Christ's teaching, it seems to me. The truth is my "broadness" embraces every soul that is reaching out after God and every instrumentality that helps any to find Him, no matter how different it may be from my own views or ways. But thank you all the same for your words of counsel. I always love to have them.

—To a Friend, 4653 Germantown Ave., Philadelphia, Pa., May 24, 1880

284. Divergence and Peculiarities

As you say, culture and tastes and interests, all are so widely divergent that nothing but the Lord's own grace could, I am sure, preserve harmony. And even with outward harmony preserved, there would still be inward chafing of spirit except where one has gained victory over this sort of thing.

And it is here you seem to have failed somewhat, if I read your letter correctly. Your inner rest and calm have been ruffled, even though you have not allowed any outward expression of it. Of course this shouldn't be; there is a victory, in Christ, even for this. And perhaps if I tell you how my greatest triumphs have come in this respect it may throw some light on your own problem.

I have had a great deal to do with difficult people, and I soon found I would be in condemnation all the time unless the Lord had taught me the art of associating with them harmoniously, and true to His promise, to make a way in every temptation. He taught me the lesson to settle down to the peculiarities of people as I would to the heaviness of lead and to be no more provoked at these peculiarities than I would be at the manifestation of the weight of lead.

Also He showed me that I should "receive others as He had received me," for He knew my frame and remembered that I was dust. Since then as soon as I find anything disagreeable in the make up of people, I accept it as part of them, and do not expect anything else; and commit it to the Lord asking Him to make the trial and discipline it brings just the medicine I need at that time. In this way incompatible people have become my chief means of grace, and many a time I have turned them into chariots, or rather the Lord had, which have carried me to places of triumph over self that I could have reached in no other way.

—To a Friend, Estes Park, Colorado, August 18, 1880

285. As Christ Accepts Us

The chafing thing about other people generally is that you think you have a right to expect something different from them, and when they don't do it, you chafe. But if we accept them as they are, just as Christ accepts us, remembering that they are dust and that we are too, all chafing vanishes. At least it has worked out that way in my experience. Of course it is all the Lord's work, but I am detailing here the process by which He accomplishes this work for me. And I am sure He will do the same for you, if not in this way, then in some other. Only be very simple and childlike in your trust about it, and never be satisfied short of complete victory.

Nothing that has been said about the Yosemite is too enthusiastic. The lessons of the summer to me have been only a deeper one of trust. The God who can create and sustain such marvelous works of nature can surely care for me without any anxiety on my part, and I have no more worry about my care than the mountains or the grass have. The texts that filled my mind most were two, "His greatness is unsearchable," and "His mercies are over all His works." And these two together seem to be all the soul can need for itself and for all the world beside. So great, and so loving, and so just, surely we can trust Him without a fear!

—To a Friend, Estes Park, Colorado, August 18, 1880

286. The Confidence of a Baby

I do believe the true secret of soul rest has been revealed to you at last! It is just to take Christ as our all in all, resting our whole souls in Him and in His care with the utter confidence of a baby, and accepting all life as it comes to us, as directly from His dear Hands.

I am so glad for you. And now I do not see any reason why you should ever again fall back into the restlessness. In fact, I think it will be only because of rebellion or unbelief, if it should ever happen again; and I do not believe the Lord will let you fall into these sins, for any length of time at least. I know in my own case, whenever I feel the least symptom of unrest, I at once can trace it either to rebellion or unbelief, and then I know I must give it up without a moment's delay.

—To a Friend, Estes Park, Colorado, August 22, 1880

287. Rest to Our Souls

It is a great thing to find out that unrest is a sin and proceeds from sin. We are so apt to think it inevitable, and even perhaps meritorious in some mysterious way. And of course while these thoughts lurk in our mind we cannot get the victory over it. But to learn that it is sin, that it is a turning away from Christ, a rebellion against His perfect will, this gives us courage to flee from it in horror.

When the old temptations therefore return to you, dear friend, take them to Christ as you would any other sin, and never for one moment permit yourself to indulge them. Isn't it wonderful that Christians should take so long to find out what the Bible proclaims in the plainest of language—that if we come to Christ we shall find rest for our souls? If we don't have rest then, it is because we have not come to Him. There is no middle ground. If we come, we have rest; if we don't have rest, we have not come.

I am always brought up short by this. I dare not continue in unrest a moment, because I know it means that I am turning away from Christ. But no doubt the Lord is teaching you all this and much more that I cannot stop to tell you now; and I am unspeakably thankful that the full light has dawned on you at last.

—To a Friend, Estes Park, Colorado, August 22, 1880

288. Failure Somewhere

But just here a question comes, which I have in vain tried to answer. Why is it that Friends, who were especially raised up by the Lord to teach this truth, seem to fail so to make it clear, and their members generally have to learn it from other sources? What is the matter with Quaker preaching, that it seems generally to be so ineffectual? Why for instance has it been necessary for your lessons to come from outside, when your heart is so staunch towards the church of your birth? And it was the same way with me, and in fact with nearly everyone I know, except in the West where they have adopted the Methodist ways, and seem in consequence to see direct fruits to their labors.

I wish someone could find the answer to this question. I long to see Quakerism the foremost in the great battle field, and it seems to me their "call" meant this. But somewhere there is a failure. Where is it? If I were a Quaker Preacher and had the usual want of result to my preaching, I could not rest a minute until I tried at least to discover the cause. More and more am I convinced that Quakerism was in its first founding pure, unadulterated Christianity. Every advanced truth that the Lord teaches me, I find is only a return to pure Quakerism, and I think those grand old forefathers of ours were among the world's best and noblest. Sometimes I fairly burn to proclaim the wonderful facts concerning them and their teachings in such a way as to electrify the church. I almost think it could be done again as it was at first, if God would only raise up the leader. But perhaps this is not what He means; perhaps they have had their day, except as a small but faithful body of witnesses to spiritual truth.

—To a Friend, Estes Park, Colorado, August 22, 1880

289. The Inner Way

The knowledge that God became incarnate in order to save the human beings He had made seems to cover the whole ground of my need so completely that I do not see anything to worry about. I am not what you would call "pious," but I have plenty of faith. Of course God will attend to me, root and branch, for He is God, and I am His creature. And as to any inner life, the "mystics" I have met have so scalded my heart that I seem somehow to have conceived a sort of horror of mystical reflection. I feel as if it was all self-evolved and very dangerous. But we must have a chance to talk this out, for it is a most momentous question.

Anyhow, at present, I am "taking it easy" and trusting my Father to manage it all. In one light, I am doing just what is always preached as the highest type of piety, looking away from self and seeing only Christ, being so absorbed in God's greatness and love as to have no thoughts of self. But somehow it does not seem to be a high type of piety in me. Well, I cannot settle it, but God can, and if He wants me to understand about it, He will teach me, and I do not mean to worry.

—To Sister, Home, September 2, 1880

In her lifelong drive to test out spiritual experience for herself, Hannah met all kinds of exotic spirituality which she discovered led to all kinds of fanaticisms because they were centered in subjective guidance led by purely emotional impulses. Out of all of this she learned to turn more and more to the clear truths of Scripture, the advice of trusted Christians and her own common-sense reasoning to discern God's direction for her life.

290. Driven to Believe

You have gotten my idea exactly about the garden and the Gardener. I am sure the Scripture teaches us that that is the relation we hold to God, and as I cannot possibly take care of myself either inwardly or outwardly, I am driven to believe that He will. There does seem sometimes a difficulty about abandoning the care of one's interior life; as though we ought to help in some way in it. But when we can't help, when we always fail every time we try, when we are weaker and weaker all the time, what is a body to do, but abandon it all to God? And it is what the Bible teaches us to do. Just get the Concordance and look up the passages on gardens, and trees, and flowers, and grass etc., and see how wonderful the parallel is. The only thing we have to do is to yield and obey.

And I have had a revelation about guidance that seems to make obedience a far simpler thing. It has come to me through seeing the fatally sad mistakes made by so many. It is this that the voice of God comes through our judgment, and not through our impressions. Our impressions may coincide with our judgments or they may not, but it is through the latter alone that God's voice comes. And when people go by impressions in opposition to their judgments, they are turning from the true voice of God, to follow the false voices of self, or of evil spirits, or of morbid consciences, or of some evil influence from other people.

—To Sister, September 13, 1880

291. Guided by Judgments Not Impressions

I have had a great deal of light on all the lines of fanaticism lately and see clearly the point of departure at last. It lies in accepting the "leadings" of seducing spirits as the voice of God. Up to now most of us have ignored the teaching in the Scriptures about our conflict in heavenly places with the "wicked spirits" there, and as a result, they have had a chance to work on unnoticed and unresisted. Hence the delusions into which so many have fallen.

—To [?], 1880

The Bible says that He will guide the meek in judgment, and it doesn't say He will guide them in impressions or feelings. I believe this going by impressions always leads either into fanaticism with many or into inanity as with others, while the people who are led by God through their judgments make very few mistakes. Think of this, and tell me your views.

—To Sister, September 13, 1880

292. Nothing Less Can Satisfy

Those lines about the flowerets are from *The Light of Asia,* page 121. I believe the Lord has taught me the flowerets' secret, and I too am growing content. How can it be otherwise when once the soul knows God? Just to say, "God is," seems enough to me now to answer every thought of need.

Every dispensation the Lord permits to come upon me seems to be meant only to settle me deeper and deeper in God. I find it true, as Faber says

> God only is the creature's home,
> Though rough and straight the road,
> And nothing less can satisfy
> The love that longs for God.

How thankful I am that He will not permit anything else to satisfy! I think I see in the undertone of dissatisfaction that runs through your letters, that He is bringing you to the place where He Himself, and not work for Him, nor friends, nor success, nor anything else can satisfy you. All the writers on the advancing life say that a renunciation of all the activities of the soul must come before God can be all in all. I mean an inward renunciation, not necessarily outward. We must be "content" to grow as God pleases, even if on an Alpine height in an unseen crevice. For it is for His pleasure we were and are created!

—To [?], 1880

293. God Is on Your Side

You ask where conversion comes in this view of mine. Just where it does in the other at the moment of belief, only it is belief in a different sort of God altogether. I go to a sinner now and say, "Poor soul, God loves you; God is your Father; He is on your side. He came down to this world in a human body, just to take your lot upon Him and to bear your sins and sorrows. He met your enemy and conquered him, so that you need not fear him any more. He is not angry with you.

He took your sins upon Him and made your cause His own. He is reconciled to you. He declared that He forgave you when He was on earth, and He declares it still in the Record He left behind Him. He says if you will only trust Him He will get you out of all your troubles. He will beget His own spiritual life in you, and make you a partaker of the Divine nature. You shall be born of the spirit, and be filled with the spirit, and so shall love holiness and hate sin just as much and as really as you now love sin and hate holiness. He will save you now from your sins, and some day will take you to live with Him in never ending joy."

The sinner begins to believe this, and the moment he believes it, God begins to work. The sinner is born again. It is beautifully simple.

—To Anna, January 21, 1881, 4653 Germantown Ave., Philadelphia, Pa.

294. The Voice of Love

And if the sinner asks for proof, at once I would say, "Haven't you felt the strivings and drawings of His love in your heart? Haven't you known moments of holy longing and of bitter grief at your failures? Haven't you had heavenly visions come to you sometimes when God gave you a glimpse of what a life with Him might be? These were the Spirit's work, and are the voice of love and yearning from the Shepherd who is seeking to save you. Yield to these, and let Him save you."

He believes, he yields, he turns, he trusts, he begins to follow. In this approach, the moment of conversion may be definite, as definite as in any other conversion. I believe just as definite work may be done on this plan as on any other, and that it will be far more real, and unspeakably more God-honoring. And as to character, it makes the grandest sort of Christlikeness. Of course God meets people on other planes if that is the best they know, and does all He can for them with such false views of Himself, but oh! how unspeakably thankful I am to have grown out of it.

I wish I had time to write to Joel and tell him how much I enjoyed his views. I entirely agree with him as to the superficiality of much of religion. It cannot very well be anything but superficial, if it is a correct doctrinal belief and not a regenerated life that is the point aimed at, and considered of the first importance. My soul hungers for realities. For the "kingdom of God is not in word but in power."

—To Anna, January 21, 1881, 4653 Germantown Avenue, Philadelphia, Pa.

295. Private Sacraments

A writer on the spiritual life, whom I have been reading with great profit lately, says that the providential duties which come to us in the circumstances of life in which God has placed us are "private sacraments" to each one of us, and are often our chief or even sole way of becoming saints; but that in order to get the blessing out of them that is intended for us we must, in performing them, inwardly unite our wills to God, and do them solely for His glory. An "interior spirit," he says, glorifies everything.

I am so glad of that revelation that came to you about "Be careful for nothing." To see that as a positive command emancipates the soul! Tell your brother Samuel that I have had to learn as an actual experience that "he that believeth maketh not haste." I have found that hurry, anxiety, precipitancy, impetuosity and all kindred dispositions are fatal to any real interior growth. God is slow, and we must be slow, slow and very still in spirit, if we would be like God. I am sorry we did not meet.

Robert has not been very well lately and on consulting a physician he found he had some disease of the heart which will require care and a freedom from all unnecessary exertion. But he does not suffer, and we feel very safe in our Father's hands. I rather think he is indulging a secret hope that he may not live many years, but we do not look ahead. Probably this weakness may account for the very great disinclination to exertion which has seemed to grow upon him of late years.

296. Inner Stillness

I do not think you are "taking things easy" exactly, only there does seem to be some line of holding you fast to shore somewhere. There does not seem to be the real inner abandonment that is necessary if the soul is to know complete union with God. But this last letter comforts me about you more than the other did. And slowness of movement is no disadvantage in the more advanced stages of spiritual growth. Faber says God is always slow when He is doing a deep and lasting work. I wish you had Faber's *Growth in Holiness* to read a little of it as a part of your devotions. I find him very helpful. Here is a sentence for you out of it.

Until we feel the presence of God habitually and can revert to Him easily, it is astonishing with what readiness other subjects can preoccupy and engross us; and it is just this which we cannot afford to let them do. Newspapers keep not a few back from perfection.

Inward stillness is essential to knowing God. You and I have got to get still somehow, darling Carrie. But only God can do it. But we can put ourselves in the attitude of soul for it.

I expect to go to Bellefonte, Pa. Saturday to spend a week holding meetings.
—To Carrie, February 2, 1881

297. The Winter of the Soul

Fenelon says, "True humility consists in a deep view of our utter unworthiness, and in an absolute abandonment to God, without the slightest doubt that He will do the greatest things in us." That's good, isn't it?

I find this winter of the soul through which I am passing a dreary place, except for my faith in the Divine Gardener, who is, I trust, preparing the ground for an abundant harvest. I changed the word "am sure" to "trust" because it is only by faith that I know it, and "am sure" seemed to imply a more absolute knowledge. Mrs. Caldwell said when I was there that no soul could get into the deepest things without going through this winter, but I wonder if now and then one is not carried over on a wave of glory? Weren't you?

—To Sarah, March 7, 1881

298. Into a Large Place

Did I ever send you a tract called the "Winter of the Soul" by Madame Guyon? It seems to me it must be just what I am going through. Fenelon describes it in his 24th chapter, "Naked Faith." He says, "When our foundation is not upon any imagination, feeling, pleasure or extraordinary illumination; when we rest upon God only in pure and naked faith."

Now it is a dreadful crucifixion to be in this state; and all the more so because it does not seem that that's the way it ought to be. But all the spiritual writers say it is a necessary stage in the growing interior life, and I expect they know. Often it seems to me I cannot have anything but what I call a "recollection." I believe God is and that He is a rewarder of them that diligently seek Him, and I put myself in His presence by faith and then wait. My mind is in chaos, my heart is desolate, but my will holds steadfastly to God. It seems as if this would be forever, and as if nothing different could ever come to me; but I choose to exercise a steady faith that God will deliver me out of all this into a large place sometime.

But, Carrie, even if it should be forever, still the end would be worth it! To think of being made, even after an eternity of suffering, one with God! Why the very thought sets my soul on fire! And since I have seen so clearly that this, and not safety from punishment alone, is the salvation God offers us, all my views of the Bible seem to be undergoing a change. Our old way of explaining things seems so crude and on the surface somehow. The inner sense is opening to me now and it is as much grander and deeper as can be imagined. But I am well convinced that no one can see this inner sense until it is opened to them. But then it is like daylight after midnight.

—To Carrie, March 12, 1881

299. Dying to Self

And now, my beloved friend, I want to tell you of what I think the Lord would have you do before entering upon your proposed work for Him.

And it is just simply this: to abandon self to His keeping, and accept His will in place of all self's desires. Your troubles all come from too great a care for self. And in a work of the kind before you, there will be so much to hurt self and cause it to suffer, that unless you can have it put to death first, you will have a hard time of it I fear.

I mean by dying to self that you must get to the place where you will not care what happens to self. Where you can be misunderstood, and misinterpreted, and maligned, and insulted, and trampled upon, and be content with it all. You may say this is impossible; but is it not just what we are commanded to do; "For even hereunto were ye called: that ye should follow His steps, who when He was reviled, reviled not again; when He suffered He threatened not; but committed Himself to Him that judgeth righteously." We are literally to walk in Christ's steps, "as He walked," and this leaves no room for the self life.

Now, dear friend, I think if you will make a definite surrender of this inner self, let it all go into God's care and determine from that point on to pay no more attention to its claims than if it did not exist, but to let the Lord alone care for them, you will have a wonderful deliverance.

—To a Friend, May 11, 1881

300. Christlikeness

It was a time of wonderful illumination; and one lesson I learned more fully than ever before was this that the divine life in the soul consists far more in principles than in emotions, and that consequently to be Christlike in character is of infinitely more importance than to have the most ecstatic feelings and revelations. Now this is a great comfort to those of us who do not have much emotion. For principles we can have, and a Christlike character we can cultivate, while we are powerless in the direction of producing emotions. Does not this thought look reasonable to you? Of course the character of Christ consisted of principles, and if we are to be one with Him, it must be one in principle rather than one in emotion. In fact we do not know what His emotions are, but He has told us of His principles. And I have found that the most emotional people are often the most unChristlike in character, and that a clear calm judgment is impossible where there is much emotion. Let us be content then, dear Priscie, with what the Lord gives us; and care for nothing but to become more and more Christlike every day.

—To Priscie, In camp on Arapahoe Pass, The Continental Divide between Middle and North Parks, Rocky Mountains, Colorado, July 18, 1881

301. The Dear, Plain, Simple Old Bible

I declare, Sally, I am about at wits end. Harris [a commune leader in California] has put out a new book called *The Holy City* which a lady at Worcester lent me. It reads to me like the wildest lunacy. But I sent it to Mrs. Caldwell [a friend and New Thought teacher] to get her opinion, and she writes back that it was perfectly delightful to her, and that just to hold it in her hands for a few minutes rested her like a baby! She said she had had enough experiences on the same line to understand most of it, and that she felt it to be very advanced truth! Very advanced indeed it must be, for I could not make sense even out of a good deal of it, and what sense I did make was just a series of wild visions or dreams which simply cannot be true. And yet Harris in his senses prints them and Mrs. Caldwell, in her senses, and plenty more people too, believe them! I confess it stumps me completely.

I know there are lots of experiences ahead of me, and when people say they have experienced things, what can a body say? I wonder whether there can be any truth in it? But you must see the book, and then you can sympathize with my wonder, and not until then. I am going to send for it, just as a literary curiosity, and to let you all see what wild things people can believe.

—To Sister, Camas, Idaho, July 28, 1881

302. Settle Back on Christ

The effect on me is to make me settle back on Christ and on His teaching as the only rest. Among all the voices, each saying a different thing, what a comfort it is to have His dear authoritative voice saying, "I know, listen to me; I will tell you the whole truth. I speak only what the Father tells me to say. I am the truth, believe me, follow me." I feel as if this was the greatest rest, and I have taken to reading His words with real avidity. I am going to pin my faith on to Him, and let all the other voices go. I mean on to His written word, something I can be sure of.

As to inward voices, I am convinced there is no certainty there. And as to emotions and visions, I have lost every particle of confidence in them. Mrs. "Moses" sees visions continually, and has Christ present with her in bodily form every few days and talks with Him and He tells her she is all right! And as to Harris, his visions are endless. But the dear plain simple old Bible is not visionary or emotional. It deals with facts about God, and I am just going to believe those facts and there have it. And among other things Christ said, "Ask and ye shall receive." He must have known, so that is what I mean to do.

—To Sister, Camas, Idaho, July 28, 1881

303. From Death to Life

I see your difficulty in regard to that pessimistic view of human nature, and I don't agree with it anymore than you do. That was the old-fashioned theology, which no one in those days who tried to be religious at all dreamed of disputing. That was not the point in the book that attracted me. It was the profound philosophy of its teaching concerning the death of the selfish life in us. The clue you has missed is this, that we are created human beings but are called to become divine beings. It is a question of moving out of a lower form of being into a higher. It is as if the choice were deliberately put before a monkey whether he would like to become a man. He is good enough as a monkey perhaps, but if he is to develop into a man he must consent to let the monkey nature die and must receive the man nature in its place. He must lose his own lower life in order to find his own higher life.

Can't you understand this? We are good enough perhaps as human beings, (though this has never been my experience), but we want to be more than human, we want to become "partakers of the Divine nature," and the only way out of one life into another must be by the way of death and resurrection. "Except a corn of wheat fall into the ground and die it abideth alone." This is in the very nature of things. Out of the death of the lower always springs the resurrection of the higher. Out of the death of babyhood springs the glory of manhood. The two lives cannot exist together. Because life is an interior principle, and not a system of outward action; and if I persist in being a monkey I cannot be a man, let me ape a man's manners as much as I may.

Fenelon's whole teaching is to show us how to let the lower life die, and the higher life take its place. Doesn't this give you the clue? And doesn't it also answer your question as to what the "Higher Life" so called is? It is the divine life lived out practically, to put it in short. I'll send you my *Christian's Secret*, which if Miss Dike will care to read it, contains my "views" on the subject. Perhaps you had better read it yourself, since I don't believe you ever did.

—To Daughter Mary, October 9, 1881

304. Perpetual Liberty

Your letter from Lawrence is just at hand, and I am delighted with it. It has the true ring of faith and surrender in nearly every word. And I confess I would far rather have the story you tell me than one of a great manifestation or overpowering emotion. The way the Lord is leading you is far better for character building than the emotional way, and character is the only really stable thing after all.

In answer to your question as to whether the baptism of the Spirit always makes working for the Lord easy, I can only give you my own experience. Working for the Lord became easy for me, not by any conscious baptism, but by really giving up any concern for self. I abandoned myself to God's care, and consented down at the very bottom to be a fool or anything else He pleased; to be thought intrusive for instance, to be considered conceited, to be blamed as forward, or as ignorant, or as presuming, to be in short the offscouring of the earth, and to have my name cast out as evil, if faithfulness to Him seemed to require it. I consented to be misunderstood and misrepresented; and I have had and do have all the time plenty of this, but I do not mind it in the least. It is the Lord's affair, not mine, for I belong to Him, not to myself.

It is only this utter letting go of self, darling, that makes things easy. No doubt a strong emotion would make you forget self for awhile and so would make things easy, but when the emotion passed the old torment would come back. But if you will let the Holy Ghost so baptize you as to immerse you into the death of the self life as a principle and not as an emotion, you will get a perpetual liberty. You can help this, darling, by continually riding rough shod over yourself, by continually acting with an utter regardlessness of self. For instance, you can consent to bear "seeming to thrust in," you can disregard the dislike you have of "putting yourself forward"; you can say, "Yes, Lord, I will even be willing to seem poking, and forward, and intrusive for your sake."

That will be principle, dear child, and will strengthen thy soul far more than any emotion.

—To Child, October 11, 1881

305. "A New Creature"

I am so glad you have gotten that idea about the divine life flowing up in us here and now. That is the secret of things. Paul says, "Neither circumcision availeth anything nor uncircumcision," of course not for they are all outward and do not touch the life. What then does avail? Paul answers "but a new creature." And that new creature is the divine nature implanted in us or begotten in us by the Spirit of God begotten by God, therefore a partaker of God's nature necessarily.

Of course we are still human and the Bible recognizes this, and recognizes the needs of our human nature. For instance Christ made wine just to please the people, and in one place we are told to go to a feast if we feel like it. And He Himself seemed to need human love and human companionship. He noticed whether he was kissed and felt lonely without His disciples. So of course we are meant to enjoy human things, only always see to it that they help in the development of the divine life in us.

That sermon was simply horrible! That minister knew nothing whatever about God, and could not have had the faintest conception even of what true religion really is. I would not go to hear him again. You had far better stay at home and hold Quaker meeting with yourself, or read one of the Scotch sermons. But I think that you are too firmly grounded in the divine reality to be hurt by such falsities as that.

—To Daughter Mary, January 1, 1882

306. The Loneliness of the Heart for God

And now to try and explain that point about being satisfied by faith. It is a difficult thing to put into words. And first I would say that of course whenever there is a something satisfying something always comes in to spoil it. Either there is death, or there is separation, or there is a change of feeling on one side or the other, or something, and the heart is driven out of its human resting place into God alone. Sometimes God permits a little taste of a satisfying love to a human being, but I do not believe it ever lasts long. I do not mean that the love may not last, but separation comes in some way, and the perfect satisfaction is taken out of it.

Your loneliness is not only because you are unmarried and have no very close human ties; it is the loneliness of a heart made for God but which has not yet reached its full satisfaction in Him. Human love might satisfy you for awhile, but it would not last.

> God only is the creature's home
> Though rough and straight the road
> Yet nothing else can satisfy
> The soul thus made for God.

If only you can see this and settle down to it, it will help you very much. You will give up, as I have, any expectation of finding satisfaction in the creature, and will no longer suffer with disappointment at not finding it. And this will deliver you from the worst part of the suffering of loneliness. You will accept it a God-given blessing meant only to drive you to Himself. Your loneliness is only different in kind but not in fact from the loneliness of every human heart apart from God. Your circumstances are lonely, but your loneliness of spirit does not come from these, it is the loneliness of humanity.

—To Priscilla, 4653 Germantown Avenue, Philadelphia, Pa., January 8, 1882

307. Evidence of Things Not Seen

Nothing but God can satisfy this loneliness of humanity. No change of circumstances, not even the dearest earthly ties, not my continued presence even, could really satisfy the hungry depths of your soul for any length of time. I am speaking out of the depths of my own experience when I say this, and you may believe me.

But now the question is how to bring one's self to be satisfied in God when there is no feeling. And I do not know what else to say but that it must be by faith. I see the difficulty you speak of, and I confess it does seem an odd sort of thing to do, to become satisfied by saying one is satisfied, when one is not. But is it not just what faith is described to be "calling those things which be not as though they were."

And what else can we do? In my own case I just determined I would be satisfied with God alone. I gave up seeking after any feeling of satisfaction, and consented to go through all the rest of my life with no feeling whatever, if this should be God's will. I said, "Lord, you are enough for me, just yourself, without any of your gifts or your blessings. I have you, and I am content. I will be content, I choose to be content, I am content." I said this by faith. I still have to say it by faith often. I have to do so this very evening, for I am not very well, and feel, what I expect thou would call "low." But it makes no difference how I feel. He is just the same, and he is with me, and I am His, and I am satisfied.

—To Priscilla, 4653 Germantown Avenue, Philadelphia, Pa., January 8, 1882

308. Glad and Thankful

It is like this. A child has set its heart on something which the mother does not see fit to give; but nothing else will satisfy the child and it is restless and unhappy. After awhile however better counsels prevail, and the child gives up its wishes and consents to be satisfied by faith, because it chooses to be, but soon it begins to feel really satisfied, and ends by being glad and thankful. This I think explains the philosophy of it. Our Father does not see best to give us just the feeling we want. We think nothing else can satisfy us but we know He knows best so we give up and choose to be satisfied with what He gives, or rather with Himself.

At first this has to be simply by faith, but it will at last get to be a real satisfaction. I think the Lord was teaching you that that day on the ship, and that he wants you to say, even if necessary through your tears, "Yes, I am satisfied with God." And I want you, my precious child, always when longings for me come, to turn them straightway into longings for Christ. Make a business of this, dear. Say to Him the things you would say to me, if I were there. It may seem an effort at first, a sort of putting on of something that is not real, but never mind. It is real because it is the choice of your will, and sooner or later the feeling of it will come.

With all my heart I sympathize with your loneliness, for I understand it! And I shall not stop asking the Lord about it until you can tell me He has satisfied you fully.

—To Priscilla, 4653 Germantown Avenue, Philadelphia, Pa., January 8, 1882

309. Self-Glorification

The command is "Do not your alms before men to be seen of them"; that means with the object of being seen of them, for the sake of having glory of men. It is the purpose of the doing that is the question here, and the command only refers to that purpose. It does not mean literally that no one must know of our almsgiving, but that no one must know of it for the sake of our getting glory from them. We do not need a command to tell us that this is a mean motive. And the trouble with human nature is that it is so inclined to glorify self whenever there is the least chance, that we have to keep a pretty strict watch on ourselves not to do it.

All we need in order to show us what a horrid thing self-glorification is, is to get hold of someone who is vain without any good grounds for it. It is like a caterpillar being so vain of his grub life as to keep it in preference to reaching out after the butterfly life. When we see that our destiny is to be one with God, we cannot care for any earthly glory. But until we do see this fully, I don't suppose we can help caring a little, and I would not condemn it very severely.

It is only a "stage." When people are in love they do not care for any praise but the praise of their lover, or at least only as the praise of others will please that one. And the philosophy of Christ always touches the highest heights of love, and of self abnegation or rather self effacement for the sake of that love. You will understand it someday.

—To Daughter Mary, January 10, 1882

310. Learning to Know God

Your letter sent just after reaching home made me very happy. All you told me of the last part of your voyage, and of your experiences was lovely. It showed so plainly how wonderfully the Lord is teaching you. That you had that feeling of the impossibility of being frightened although it seemed as if you ought to be, is one of the strongest proofs possible of your having learned the "secret of the Lord." It was certainly very different from what you experienced when you first came over here! You are learning to know God, and it is this that makes fear and anxiety seem impossible to you.

It is no effort for the soul to trust who knows God; the effort would be all the other way. Of course I mean fully know Him when I say this. For in a partial knowing, while there will be grand deliverances, there may be also times of relapse into the temptation to fear. And do not be discouraged if these temptations come to you sometimes. I think you know how to meet them, now that you have given up the liberty to indulge in them.

You ask why I did not make you give up your fears sooner. I didn't think of it; and I suppose the Holy Spirit did not bring it to my mind any sooner, because you would not have been ready for it. I think our Divine Teacher sends us our lessons at the right time always.

—To Priscilla, 4653 Germantown Avenue, Philadelphia, Pa., January 14, 1882

311. A More Abundant Life

You ask whether you ought to express desires for anything God does not give. I always feel a "check" myself from expressing such things, because they really are not true, for if God does not give it I do not want it. I would be afraid to have anything He thought best for me not to have. And therefore I would advise you not to say such things. They all help the soul to be discontented with what it has, and God's lesson to us is always one of contentment. I am sure our words and our expressions do affect our inner life. We overcome by the blood of the Lamb and the word of our testimony. Let us always say then the thing our wills are choosing as best.

Yes, that verse in Is. 42:6 is a blessed one, and was certainly like an "engrafted word" to you. Do not for a moment doubt it. How much proof you are constantly having that the Holy Spirit is filling you and abiding in you. Do notice these proofs, and let them confirm your faith. Perhaps I can see them even more plainly than you can, and so I want to remind you.

I feel a very great drawing to England, much greater I am sure because of the tie between you and me, and it does seem to me that sometime I shall be with you there, though as you say it does not look likely now. I am afraid Robert would never consent to my going while he lives; he is so afraid of a revival of the scandal. But if the Lord wants me to go He will make a way, and unless He wants it I would not for all the world go, nor would you want me to. Oh how wonderful it is to rest in His perfect and lovely will! In the 12th chapter which we have tomorrow, Sunday, read verses 23–26. They contain my idea of development—the death of one life in order for the development of a higher one. And on every plane this is a necessity, even when it comes to motives. If a higher motive is to be developed the lower motive must die. We are always dying that we may live. And death always introduces a more abundant life.

—To Priscilla, 4653 Germantown Avenue, Philadelphia, Pa., January 14, 1882

312. The Mushroom and the Oak

That revelation of yours was a foretaste of what one day will be your life. It was a glimpse into the "heavenly places" which are your destined home. Don't be discouraged because it seems to have vanished for a time. Leave it and wait. Another one will come to you. It is the butterfly beginning to stir in the cocoon, and feeling itself cramped in its old quarters, and having an instinct after its resurrection life. Many such openings, and many struggles will come, before the full deliverance comes. And this is all right and in the Divine order. Remember the story I told you of the butterfly which had its cocoon clipped by ignorant kindness, and which in consequence never had any strength in its wings and therefore could not live in the new life. All of God's best and most lasting works are slow. Compare the mushroom and the oak. Then too, hothouse growth always spoils a plant in the end, though it seems to make it flourish for a time.

Trust the Divine Gardener with your growth, darling daughter, and do not worry yourself about it. Of course the time will come when it will not be a fleeting glimpse, but a continual vision; but that will be as your character becomes like Him. Only characters that are like each other can "see" each other in the only true sense of seeing. And as you becomes Christlike, you will "see" Christ. "Blessed are the pure in heart for they shall see God." Of course; for no other could possibly have any comprehension of Him. Do you catch this thought? Are there more people whom you cannot possibly comprehend; pure selfishness for instance, no woman it seems to me can comprehend that. We have got to be selfish in order to comprehend selfishness; and so with unselfishness, and everything else.

—To Daughter Mary, January 19, 1882

313. Failure, Forgiveness, Forgetting

The main point is this, that discouragement because of a failure is always a greater fault than the failure itself. It is all right to see the failure, if there has been one, but the moment it is seen it must be confessed and left with the Lord and forgotten. If, for instance, you did fail, you ought to have taken it right to the Lord, and left it there and thought no more about it. Even your discouragement seems to me to be a sign that Satan saw thy fixed purpose was to be faithful and obedient, therefore, he put forth all his power to turn you back. He would not have troubled you so much, if you had not been filled with a true spirit of devotion to the Lord. For I do not believe that you were unfaithful that morning. You prayed, and I feel that that was as true a keeping of your promise, as what you felt you should have done originally would have been. The only way to baffle Satan at such times is to do as I say, confess, be forgiven, and forget the whole thing.

Give up all future self-reflective acts. By this I mean all thinking over either your successes or your failures. The moment the action is passed, forget it, and pass on to the next. It is the rule of my life never to think over any past action. This saves me all temptations to self-elation and all temptations to discouragement, and enables me to live continually in the present moment with God. Fenelon says, "Make it a rule to put an end, at the close of every action, to all reflections upon it, whether of joy or sorrow. When we are no longer embarrassed by these restless reflections of self, we begin to enjoy true liberty. False wisdom, on the other hand, always on the watch, ever occupied with self, constantly jealous of its own perfection, suffers severely whenever it is permitted to perceive the smallest speck of imperfection in self. The chagrin we feel at our own defects is often a greater fault than the original defect itself. It is the outcome of a despairing self-love."

Nothing so decidedly aids solid spiritual progress as when one is able to view one's own failures without being disturbed or discouraged. You will find by experience how much more your progress will be helped by a simple, peaceful turning to God than by all your chagrin and spite at the faults that exist in you. Only be faithful in turning quietly to God alone, the moment you perceive what you have done; do not stop to argue with yourself; you can gain nothing from that quarter, and will only make things worse, while the simplest look towards God will calm your heart and deliver you.

—To Priscilla, 4653 Germantown Avenue, Philadadelphia, Pa., January 22, 1882

314. Neither Male Nor Female

I thought you might like to see these reports of my first speech on Woman's suffrage. I am thoroughly roused on the subject for I have had so many cases of grievous oppression of men over their wives lately that my blood boils with indignation. And before you are married I want to have your position as the equal of your husband settled on a legal basis.

The moment one looks into the subject at all it seems utterly incomprehensible how we women could have endured it as patiently as we have. Literally and truly up to within a very few years women have been simply slaves. And some women say they like it! Ugh! It is one of the worst vices of slavery that its victims are contented with their lot! Nothing but the vote will set us at liberty; but that will, for then we shall be not only women, but human beings as well. Now we are nothing but women.

In my speech I said I had come to the advocacy of this reform by the way of the Gospel, that Christ came to break every yoke and set free all that were bound; and that I wanted to follow in His steps and share in His work. I said that the gospel did not arbitrarily upset the existing order of things, but it put a land mine under every wrong and oppression that finally would blow them up. And that therefore women were made free by the working out of the principles of Christ who had declared there is neither male nor female in Him. They made fun of me in one of these slips, but of course all reformers must expect that.

—To Daughter Mary, January 29, 1882

315. God Is Enough

Nothing can really comfort any soul but God. Just God Himself. All you tell me of your longings only make me say to myself more and more emphatically, "It is God my precious child needs, God Himself, and not His gifts—God as her indwelling life." I do not mean by this anything you do not already possess, but only that which you do possess shall be received, and rested in, and enjoyed. When children have set their hearts upon any special thing they cannot be contented without that very thing, no matter how much else they may have that is delightful and valuable. They want the moon, and nothing else has any charm.

And this is just our way about spiritual things: we fix our hearts on some special "blessing" or "experience," and will not be content without it, although we have far more than enough for perfect content, if we would only think so. I know this from a long and weary experience. Now I am satisfied with God. I choose to be. And whatever else I may have or may not have, I am always going to be content for I shall always have God.

Now, darling, you have God, and that must be enough for you. You must be content. It is wrong for you to allow yourself to indulge longings which cannot be fulfilled. You must turn at once from all such thoughts and utterly refuse to give them entrance. Just as I utterly refuse to let myself indulge in grief for my children who have left me, so must you refuse to indulge in grief because of being separated from me. It is really disobedience, darling, to indulge in grief. If a mother is compelled to deprive her child of any pleasure or to forbid her any joy, it grieves her to have that child indulge in continual complaint over the loss.

—To Priscilla, January 28, 1882

316. The Faith Cure

We really have been stirred up on this faith healing question lately. You may have heard me speak about Saidee's brother Tom as having broken down from overwork several years ago. For four years now he has been doing everything possible to recover his health, but all in vain. His last venture was a voyage to the Cape of Good Hope, but he came back worse than he went.

When Dr. Cullis was here a week or two ago, Tom felt drawn to try the faith cure, as everything else had failed, and Dr. Cullis prayed with him twice and told him to say he was healed. He began to say it, and, poor fellow, he had a hard battle, for a whole week there was no sign of any improvement. His mother and I were immersed in the deepest sympathy with him, and we all had to fight for our faith together. It was a great strain on me, because I am not yet fully convinced about faith healing being available for everybody at any time. But my heart ached so for dear Tom and his father and mother that I had to help them with all the faith I could muster.

After a week, however, Tom began to improve, and there has been a most wonderful change in him in every way, and he is full of praise to the Lord. It has, of course, made a great stir among all our circle here, for Tom was always a great favorite. He has gone on to Boston now to spend a little time with Dr. Cullis to have his faith strengthened, and perhaps to help the Dr. a little in his faith work.

If he really does get entirely well I believe I will have to give up and adopt Dr. Cullis' view of the subject. He says Matt. 8:17 teaches clearly that Christ bore our sicknesses just as much as He bore our sins, and that we may be delivered from the one by faith precisely as we are delivered from the other! If this is true, it would revolutionize the church! I am not convinced yet that it is true, but I confess that passage looks wonderfully like it. I will mail you some little books about it. Ask your sister Charlotte and your cousin Mary Agnes to compare Matt. 8:17 with James 5:14, 15 and see whether they get any light on the subject for themselves.

It would be glorious, would it not, if Christians universally could dispense with all human doctors and be cured by the Great Physician alone, and could show the world a continual miracle of healing? Dr. Cullis thinks all disease is from the devil, and is a direct attack from him upon God's children, just like temptation to sin is, and must therefore be met in the same way. There is a good deal of Scripture that seems to support his view. But I do not know.

—To Priscilla, May 7, 1882

317. Enthusiasm About God

What an unspeakable rest it is to know that after all God is always attending to His business. I do not know what would become of me, if I did not know this. As Paul says, "I know Him whom I have trusted" and therefore "I am persuaded" that He has the whole matter in hand both for me and my children, and for you and yours, and for all His creatures, and that He is attending to it just right. Before I knew Him, I had my grave doubts about this. But now! Ah, one cannot doubt a God like ours, when once He becomes known! But I am not in a pulpit, so will draw in. Only, Anna, somehow I always become enthusiastic when I begin to talk about God!

I am still pondering over that matter of the Spirit, and also about the "Signs." Thanks for all your suggestions; they are very helpful. Let me have them whenever you can, please. I do not want to be one-sided. I do not think I ignore emotional guidance. I believe it is one of the voices, but can never be depended on without the harmony of the other voices. I wish you could be immersed into a real fanatical element long enough to "sense" it out. It is the exact counterpart of the true, as far as I can discern, and where the point of difference comes in I cannot for the life of me discover. But I wait. God will teach sometime.

And meanwhile I must rap every spirit that comes to me over its head and find out whether it has any common sense, before I can surrender myself to its guidance. And I believe you do too, in spite of all your mystic nature.

—To Anna, May 24, 1882

318. The Healing Question

I went up to that invalid friend's who has been trusting for faith healing for so long. We had a little Bible class in her sick room. She does not seem any better. And yet she sticks to the testimony that she is healed, since that is what Dr. Cullis told her she must do. It does not seem right to me somehow.

The fact is this faith healing matter grows more and more perplexing all the time. You remember that funny friend of mine Elisabeth Nicholson, who went with us to the prayer meeting about President Garfield? She is not particularly consecrated, except in quite an ordinary fashion; she does not believe in the "Higher Life" at all, and she is very much afraid of fanaticism. And yet the other day she wrote me as follows "The 31st. of May, sitting waiting for the dinner bell to ring, I talked to the Lord like this, "Lord, you know the muscles of my back are weak, and cause me much pain. You know I have inherited this through two generations; that I have been very indifferent about healing, making it an excuse for not visiting or doing anything I did not want to. But now, if it will honor you and if it will give me more strength to work for you, Lord Jesus, then I ask thee to heal me instantaneously." It was done! From that moment I have not had a pain; nor even the soreness which often made me shift my position. It no longer seems like me, but somebody else! I have done my hardest work since then without pain."

Now what are we to think when such saints as some I know can't get healed with all their praying and all their trusting? There is a secret somewhere that we have not fathomed yet, I am convinced. Meanwhile, I would advise every sick person to try this way of prayer and faith anyhow. It cannot hurt, and it may be a grand success. My nephew Tom Whitall is not well yet. He thought he was for a few days, and was very jubilant over it, but his trouble all came back, and he has been having a hard conflict. Now he has gone to a water cure to fight it out. My heart just aches for him. I wish I understood!

—To Priscilla, June 16, 1882

319. God's Lesson for Me

Here we are in the heart of the Rocky Mountains, nearly 8000 feet above the sea, with canyons, and waterfalls, and lakes and snowy peaks all around us. To get here we had to take a dreary ride across the mighty Colorado plain for hundreds of miles through heat and dust that was almost intolerable. But on last Friday evening we reached Denver at the foot of the mountains, and found there lovely mountain airs and glorious mountain views, and felt repaid for all our discomforts.

The children are overjoyed, and I am happy for them. But for myself, I have a strange feeling of being out of my right place, which sobers everything for me. And yet this feeling must be a mistake, for certainly it was all the Lord's doing that things went as they did just at the last, and that I came out here instead of going across the ocean to you. So I do not pay any attention to this "feeling," and simply accept the sober sense of things as being God's lesson for me for this summer, and try to do my duty in the place where I find myself. There is a wonderful rest in just doing the next, right thing just as it comes whatever one's circumstances may be. It is so simple and easy to get at, and so sure to be what God wants. One thing I know He wants is for me to take an absolute rest, and I am trying to do it thoroughly.

—To Priscilla, Idaho Springs, Colorado, July 3, 1882

320. God Unveiled in Christ

The memories of the grand cliffs and mountain peaks will always be a delight to me. And always an inspiration. Also, making God seem so real and so mighty. And all around us are the snow capped mountains and green valleys, and rocky canyons, with views of such grandeur and beauty that I could not describe them, even if I had time, which I have not, for our young party keep me busy with their excursions of one sort or another, and with the consequent sewings and mendings that result from all this. Our party consists of Robert and myself, the three children, and Saidee Whitall, and we are bound for Colorado first, and then California and the Yosemite, if all goes well.

But our journeyings are not of any special interest to you, and a guide book will tell you about the country better than I could. The stages of our mutual journeyings through the interior country of the spiritual life are of far greater interest to us both, I think. And yet even here I find a change. Somehow experiences have lost their charm for me, and it almost seems a waste of time to talk of them. God only is the theme that arouses my enthusiasm. Not my experiences of God, but God as He is in Himself, His character, His mind, His ways. But especially His character, what He really is in Himself, for upon this point, it seems to me, all else turns.

Give me a good God, and my soul is at rest, whether He makes me any promises or not. It is the character of my friend that settles the question of my trust in him and of my safety in his care. And this is true of God also. All that I care for consequently is to become acquainted with God. And for this I must go to Christ. Only in the face of Jesus Christ is God revealed as He is. All other revelations are but partial, and are therefore, in so far as they are partial, untrue. But in Christ He has unveiled Himself. And oh, what a revelation! What love, what tenderness, what goodness! Touched with a feeling of our infirmities; tempted in all points as we are; a God just like ourselves, we made in His image and He in ours! Ah! who could do anything but trust Him?

—To Priscilla, Colorado Springs, Colorado, July 14, 1882

321. The Bible, Safety from Deception

Our perplexities increase instead of diminishing as our children grow up, do they not, Carrie? It is so hard to know just how to manage grown up children. But I comfort myself that my Heavenly Father has them in hand just the same as He has had us, and that He will see to it that they have the right discipline in spite of our mistakes with them.

Oh, Carrie, what should we do without God! I feel just like a cheated child who has been deceived by false voices and pretended friends and who flies to the mother's arms and listens to her soothing voice, and is at rest. So my soul rests in God. All else deceives and betrays me, but he remains faithful; and as soon as my soul touches Him in any perplexity or fear, I am at rest. But it is God alone, the bare God, if I may so express it, who gives me this rest. Not my experiences of Him, not His manifestations of Himself, not His promises, but just God, God as He is in Himself, and as He is revealed in the Bible.

I seem more and more shut up to this. All "experiences" and "leadings" and "baptisms" seem so unreliable to me. I am like a person who has seen the wires that pull the puppets and who cannot therefore be interested in the puppets any more. I find that spiritualists have all the "baptisms" and "leadings" and "manifestations" that Christians have, with precisely similar symptoms. The same "thrills," the same "waves" or currents of life, the same spiritual uplifts, the same interior illuminations; they even see similar visions of Christ, and hear similar interior voices. And, as Mrs. Beck says, the true and the false are so much alike, that taken in themselves, it is utterly impossible to distinguish between them. I mean of course all these emotional elements.

Thank God, there is a place of assurance and safety from deception and that is in the Bible, and in the life and words of Christ. If we pin our faith on to Him we cannot mistake, for He was God. I rest here; I can rest nowhere else.

—To Carrie, Yosemite Valley, California, July 31, 1882

322. Faith and Works

First of all, that book. How odd it is that that very book should have been the one that last summer lead me into an acquaintanceship with Christ that has so far surpassed any other I have ever had as to seem like a new era in my life! Never has He been so real to us as since then, never so divine, never so trustworthy, and never so altogether lovely. It seemed somehow as though the reading of that book took away a veil from before my eyes which had hid the real Christ, and had made Him only a sort of a myth to me.

I saw in Him then such a complete answer to agnosticism that I have been amazed ever since at the possibility of any soul with access to the New

Testament remaining for an hour in such a delusion. And He has been to me such a revelation of God as no words of mine could ever tell to human soul!

The "Spirit of the life" is the only really valuable thing after all. How true the old Friends were when they used to tell us that it was not what we believed but how we lived that was the real test of salvation, and how little we understood them! The missing link in their teaching was just that which we could have supplied if they would have listened to us, the faith in God's love and forgiveness, and the knowledge of our sonship in Christ. Put the two together, and we have a perfect whole; for just as faith without works is dead, so are works without faith dead also, and neither can spare the other.

I can say a hearty amen to every word of your letter; what I see is of very little account, but my obedience or disobedience to it is vital. Someone says, "A string of opinions is no more saving faith than a string of beads is prevailing prayer." And as you say, my opinions about God may all be wrong, but if my loyalty to Him is real it will not matter. It seems as if it would be enough just to say, "God is," and, "Be good," and then all would be said. It is the practical things that interest me now, the work that eases pain, and brings comfort, and uplifts humanity. This poor bewildered world with its awful problems of sin and suffering appeals to my soul. I rank myself in its side, and ask for no blessings that are not common to my fellow men.

The Temperance work seems to me the most hopeful of all the present movements for the race. There is no mysticism there. It is down to earth.

—To Anna, Yosemite, California, August 4, 1882

323. Campmeeting

In our hotel I found one of the housekeepers who was a devoted adherent of mine and who told me of a Holiness Camp Meeting in progress in the country outside of the city. I thought I would enjoy going for a few hours, though I supposed I would be a perfect stranger to everyone. But I thought the spirit of the people and their hymns and "experiences" would be a blessing to me.

Just as I neared the ground in the horse cars I asked God to lead me to the right persons, and no sooner had I entered the gate than I saw a Philadelphia lady whom I used to see at meetings there long ago coming to the pump for water! I spoke to her and she recognized me at once, gave me a hearty welcome, and then introduced me to the leaders of the meeting and to all the dear saints right and left. I received a perfect ovation! They had all apparently read my book *The Christian's Secret,* and were full of it, and of the blessing it had been to them "next to their Bibles" the "constant companion of their devotions," the "greatest help of their lives" etc. etc. And they fairly overwhelmed me with their delight at seeing me, dear souls.

They would hear nothing but that I should stay and preach for them in their evening meeting, which I did, under a large tent. It was altogether quite a refreshing experience. But one thing bothered me. They had a meeting for faith healing, and insisted on my going to it to teach them! I could not bear to upset their faith by telling them of the practical difficulties I see in the subject; so, I went and tried to throw myself into the current. I told them I had had no personal experience in regard to it, and so could only speak from hearsay, but that I would give them Dr. Cullis' teaching, and that seemed to satisfy them. But I can tell you my heart ached to hear some poor invalids there declare they were healed, when it was perfectly plain to everyone else that they were not.

I do not know what will be the outcome of all this agitation on the subject of faith healing. In all parts of the church it is being made prominent, and enough wonderful results follow it to excite a continually increasing interest. And yet there are far more failures than successes, and I dread the reaction. For these failures are nearly always with the most devout Christians, and it is an awful strain on their faith.

—To Priscilla, Monterey, California, August 14, 1882

324. It Puzzles Me

You know that invalid lady Mrs. Wood up in Germantown and you may remember my having told you that she was trusting for faith healing? Poor soul, she is not better yet, after declaring ever since February 14th. that she was healed that day. Meanwhile she had a sister-in-law, an old plain conservative Quaker, who had been an invalid for twenty-one years, and had not taken a step all that time. She heard of Mrs. Wood's praying for healing, and wrote to ask her about it, and Mrs. W. wrote back pouring out her whole heart, texts and everything. The woman laid right hold, and the next day after receiving the letter, she petrified her family by walking down stairs and appearing at the dining room door while they were at dinner! They were actually too frightened to offer her a seat, until a child present, who did not know the stupendous nature of the miracle that had taken place, gave her his seat.

Now why should this conservative old Friend, who certainly could not have known much about the way of faith, have been healed, and poor dear Mrs. Wood, who had Dr. Cullis to pray for her, and teaching of all kinds on the subject of faith, fail in it so utterly? I confess it puzzles me. They say that Spurgeon has come out strong on the subject of faith healing. Do find out, and tell me about it, if you can.

—To Priscilla, Monterey, California, August 14, 1882

325. The Harmony of God's Voices

I trust the Lord has fully comforted you by this time. I think I can explain about that voice which seemed to tell you you should have a summer vacation with me. I don't think it would have been possible even had I gone, for my sister had made me promise not to allow anyone to join our party, as she really was not well enough to have anyone else around. It seems to me that this is an illustration of my views concerning the harmony of all God's voices being required before one can be sure any voice is valid.

For instance, no matter how strong your impression might be, if the way did not open, then the impression could not have been God's voice. In the matter of your going to Ireland, the way seems likely to open, and all the voices are in harmony. And if this continues to be the case, then the impression will prove to have been God's voice.

You must never forget that the harmony of all God's voices is the only safe test of any one voice being really His. You will have many impressions probably which will not stand this test, and they must all be discarded as from some other source than God.

—To Priscilla, Monterey, California, August 14, 1882

326. Not Because We Are Good, But Because God Is

I wish I could talk to you about being satisfied by faith, for I am afraid I can't explain it satisfactorily on paper. It is simply this, that we are so sure that God always gives us the very best thing always that we are satisfied, no matter how we feel. As soon as we are really sure that a thing is best, we cannot help being satisfied with it, for who could be anything but satisfied with the best?

For instance I go out to buy a dress. I look at a great many pieces of goods, but am not satisfied with any of them because I do not feel convinced any of them are the best. At last, however, I become convinced that one piece is really the very best and the most suitable, and then I am satisfied at once. All we need is to be convinced that the thing is best. Now we know by faith that just what God gives us each moment is really the best thing we could have, whether it is outward or inward, therefore we are satisfied. And if our faith is strong enough we shall feel satisfied. You have to keep saying it by faith because you are not yet quite fully convinced that you have the very best. But I am convinced of this down to the very bottom, therefore, I do not have to say it by faith; I am satisfied. I would not have anything different for all the world, unless God should arrange it differently. And this is not at all because I am so good, but because I have found out how good God is.

I do not think I can make it any plainer. And I cannot see where anyone could find any objection. The suggestion that being satisfied in this way by faith might make one lazy is answered by the fact that the Holy Spirit is always present to check or stir up the trusting soul, and there is no danger of laziness where His power is yielded to and obeyed. A satisfied soul will be an obedient soul always I am sure. It may make us lazy on the line of "creaturely activity," for all our restless strivings and agonizings will be over, and our souls will dwell in "peaceable habitations" continually; but this is not laziness. Do you see it?

—To Priscilla, September 20, 1882

327. With All Your Heart

I had quite an "opening" this morning in meeting on the text, "The Lord taketh pleasure in His people." I was thinking of you and of Logan and Alys, and of the intense pleasure I take in you when you are happy and good. I thought of how I enjoy your letters where you tell of your happiness, and of how sometimes the tears of joy fairly will come when some point or proof of your goodness comes to my attention.

And I seemed to have an insight into the heart of God towards us, and of the pleasure He takes in us when we are happy and good. If you did not tell us of your happiness we could not take half as much pleasure in it, and the God, in whose image we are made must like also to have us tell Him how happy we are. Of course He knows it, but He likes to hear it, just as we like to hear our loved ones say the things which we already know are in their hearts. Then I went on with the verse, "He will beautify the meek with Salvation," and I thought of how I love to see you look nice and to dress you beautifully, and then realized how God was just the same towards us and enjoys making us beautiful with spiritual graces.

Keep claiming your promise whenever it comes into your mind, and soon, darling, all other love will fade into insignificance compared to the depth and reality of your love for God. It has with me. No one is of any account beside Him! But perhaps it is the disappointments of life that have helped to bring me here; and you will need to know more of these. And yet He is able to make all grace, and consequently this grace, abound towards you, even without any disappointments. At any rate your position in regard to it is right, to trust Him to enable you to obey His command, "Thou shalt love the Lord thy God with all thy heart." It will come somehow I am sure.

—To Daughter Mary, September 24, 1882

328. Believing Is Seeing

I am so interested to hear about your using the Bible in Friends meeting. It does seem clear that the Lord is calling you to do it, and it really looks too as if He was "opening the way," since nobody has reproved you for it. I do not believe you will ever have to force it on unwilling congregations. That I think is seldom God's way. He goes before His own sheep when He puts them forth. I was so glad to see that you believe that He manages it just exactly right, and must be satisfied with what comes. If doors open and results follow, be satisfied; if doors fail to open and you see no results, be satisfied still. If you are received with kindness, be satisfied; if you are snubbed, be satisfied. Say with Paul about it all from beginning to end, "I have learned in whatsoever state I am, therewith to be content." I dare say some things may not be quite what you like, but be satisfied even if they are not.

With regard to that verse quoted by Minnie, it distinctly says, "More present to faith's vision keen," and that is just what I mean that faith is so strong as to be really better than sight. In earthly things we say, "Seeing is believing," but in heavenly things, "Believing is seeing." I cannot be more present to you than Christ, because He is with you and I am not. You may think of me more, but you certainly cannot think of me as present with you! As to your love for me being more conscious to you than your love for Him, I guess that is natural at this stage of existence for you. It will all come right I think. Only keep turning to Him with loving obedience.

—To Daughter Mary, September 24, 1882

329. The Christian's Secret

Your sympathy and love is more to me than all the plaudits of the greatest crowds. It is so wonderful that we can think alike on these great questions for the uplift of humanity. There is no friendship so precious as that between a mother and daughter, as the daughter grows up into the mother's maturity. And I am filled with thankfulness for my daughter!

We are having a grand time. The whole city is stirred, and the women are being emancipated. One thing delights me. Our platform is as broad as humanity; we take in everybody, no matter what their "views," or church relationships. And yet we are more decidedly Christian than any other convention or conference I ever heard of. It is such a testimony to the reality of the religion which embraces all humanity.

Every day, from eleven to twelve, right in the midst of our business meeting we have an hour for a devotional meeting when we tell the story of the life of faith to the crowds who have come in to witness our proceedings. I spoke to them yesterday on "Knowing God" for ourselves and then showing Him to others. And I was followed by a great many short words of testimony as to the blessedness of it, ever so many of them saying that they had learned the secret from my book *The Christian's Secret*.

It is perfectly wonderful how that book has gone over this whole country. Wherever I go I am met with stories of its value and blessing. So many people even here have told me that it is "next to their Bibles." I would rather have written that book that has brought comfort and joy to so many sad and weary hearts than be the Queen of England. The faces are shining with peace and they tell me that it has all come through that book. There was one dear hump backed girl here who was made a hump back by having a chair pulled unexpectedly from her. She had a life of misery and rebellion until my book came, and now her face is like sunshine.

—To Daughter Mary, Women's National Christian Temperance Union Ninth Annual Convention, Louisville, Ky., Oct. 25, 1882

330. God's Order: Fact, Faith, Feeling

You asked another question which I wanted to answer at once, but didn't have the opportunity. It was about the reason why you should feel the presence of the Lord so much less when speaking to some people rather than to others. The whole reason is in you, yourself. It is the fear of man that comes in in the first case and takes your eyes unconsciously off the Lord and fixes them on man, and of course then the sense of His presence is lost. Not His presence itself, but only the sense of it. And the only way to treat such a thing is with silent contempt.

Say to yourself, "The Lord is here just as much as He ever is with me, but I am such a dunce as to be looking at the people instead of at Him, and so I do not see or feel His presence so much. But it is all right, and I just mean to think only of Him." Crucify your feelings at such times; it is a perfect chance. And never judge by your own feelings whether a meeting has been a success. One's own feelings are most misleading things.

I often find that my most successful work is done just when I feel the coldest and most dead. And many other workers have told me the same. You see we mean to get something done in other people's hearts, and it is the truth that does that, not our feelings. Friends, judging by their feelings, often think they have a grand good meeting when not another human being thinks so at all! Ignore your feelings altogether, and look out for the work done.

How strange it is that feelings will crop up all along the line as stumbling blocks. And how absolutely necessary it is to ignore them at every point. I gave a talk the other day on the three Fs. in religion; God's order and man's order. The first being Fact, Faith, Feeling; the last being Feeling, Faith, Fact. And it applies everywhere; to this matter of feeling His presence as much as to anything else. If we take God's order about it there is never any difficulty. If we take man's order there is difficulty all the time.

—To Priscilla, On the cars returning home from Louisville, October 31, 1882

331. Spiritual Laws

Yes indeed, I will pray for Florence. It seems to me she might try the faith cure, for I suppose no other means are of much account and I know that a very great many people are being healed by faith in these days. It seems to me it is like this, that our faith lays hold of spiritual forces which are superior to natural forces and which therefore can overpower them. It is not that God's mind is changed, but that we become able to avail ourselves of powers that He has put at our disposal in the spiritual realm. I expect His real will for us is health always, but if we disobey natural laws His will is thwarted, and it is only by bringing in spiritual laws that we can overcome the evil tendencies caused by sin, either our own sins of ignorance or our ancestors' sins.

I am afraid I am not very clear. But just as a wire does not create the electric current but only draws it down in certain directions so our faith does not create health but only draws the vitality of the spiritual realm down into our vessel. It is wonderful what faith will do. And if F. could be cured in that way it would be lovely. At least I hope she will pray about it. Tom's case is a great encouragement.

—To Daughter Mary, November 1, 1882

332. My Parish

I wish I could tell you in one sentence about our Women's Christian Temperance Convention at Louisville, for I don't have time for more, and yet I want you all to share the enthusiasm and the inspiration it brought. It was a deeply spiritual time, which is always my part of the interest, and consecration and faith were the prominent thoughts and lessons.

I of course cannot make Temperance speeches, and I do not care for the details of the business. But my special line of work is the spiritual part, and there never was a grander field. I am Superintendent of the Evangelistic and Bible Reading work, and this gives me direct influence over 60,000 Christian women, and indirect influence over all their congregations; and the Lord blesses me in it wonderfully. But if I were 1,000 women instead of only one, I could not fill up the needs of my position, as you may well know. And oh, how my heart goes out to women. I am so thankful the Lord has given me my parish among them.

And actually, Anna, it begins to seem almost to me as if the Bible was written more for women than for men. At any rate we need it most. What a wonderful book this Bible is! Every day I live it becomes more and more precious to me. Christians do not half know it, that is the trouble, and I believe one large part of my mission is to get them to study it more systematically and carefully.

—To Anna, November 5, 1882

333. Recognition

Recognition is my great word just now. All things are provided and are even already given, only recognize that you have them, and you have. This is Scripture, and it is also divine common sense. "All things are yours"; He "hath blessed us with all spiritual blessings in Christ." Believe and you shall receive. "Come and ye shall find." Of course, because it is all here already, and all ours.

Oh, what we have missed all these years from not having had eyes that could see! At least, what I have missed. I have hungered so for things that all the time I possessed if I had only known it. Somehow my two summers out in the wilds of nature, with no meetings and no religious influences, only God and His works, have been more helpful in my interior life than any other thing I have ever known. They have brought me face to face with God, and I have seen Him. Not in a vision, as so many think is the only way of seeing, but as one sees a truth, that is comprehends it. And in the seeing I have found, what I never expected to find, more emotional joy than I have ever known before. The fact is our God is so wonderfully good, and lovely, and blessed in every way, that the mere fact of belonging to Him is enough for an unspeakable fullness of joy!

—To Anna, November 24, 1882

334. Daily Dying, Daily Yielding

At Mrs. Keen's meeting Tuesday Andrew Keen spoke beautifully about this. He said we were apt to make such a foolish mistake about spiritual joy, in thinking about it as a thing separate from that which causes it, as though it were a lump of something, a sort of concrete, complete in itself, and independent of causes. He said we did not act this foolishly on the earthly plane, that there we were always happy or joyful because of something; our joy always had a source in something good or pleasant. I was delighted to have him express my mind so clearly. It is just what I have been learning; and I am now no longer concerned about having spiritual joy as a thing by itself, which I confess I used to be.

In looking over one of your letters, I see that you say that yielding to God and death to sin amount to the same thing, and I entirely agree with that. It just means consecration and trust. The "dying daily" means the "daily yielding." Not that we take anything back in order to yield it up again but we just keep yielding. And so about dying to sin daily. We die to it as it is presented. I see as I read your letter about it over again that you have seen the idea clearly. The Lord is teaching you and you are having "openings" of truth just as I do. It all comes by recognizing His voice and listening to it, "hearkening" the Bible would say. How can God talk with souls that do not recognize His voice when He does speak? In the nature of things it is impossible.

—To Anna, November 24, 1882

335. Acquainted With God

It is God's plan to have us ask for what we want, and I am sure there are many things we might have for the asking, which we do not get because we do not ask. It is part of the family training, and brings us into communion with God, just as the child telling the parent what it wants makes a oneness of feeling and communion between them. Don't you know how I have always said to you, "Ask me for what you want; let me know, and let's talk about it." It would not be half so good if we had not this kind of communication.

If I just provided what I thought best, and you just accepted it and said nothing, what would you know about me on that particular plan? I by my superior wisdom might know you, but you could never know me. And the object of all our life in this stage is to make us acquainted with God. Consequently He makes things largely dependent upon our communication with Him, and gives when we ask, things that otherwise we would not have. It is best for us not to have them when we do not ask, because we have to be taught our need of asking.

Of course all truly filial asking has "Thy will be done" in it, just as your asking of me has in a measure. I say in a measure to the latter, because you cannot be sure of my wisdom always, but of God's we can. Therefore I feel free to ask Him for everything I want, for I am sure He will not give it if it is not best. But you know you have to be careful what you ask us for, because we do not always have the sense to say, "No."

Now I am sure Christ came to heal bodies as well as souls, and I want you and Florence to ask Him. I expect all your bad health is the result of the disobedience to some hygienic law, and so you must ask for wisdom to understand those laws, and then when you know them you must obey them.

—To Daughter, December 4, 1882

336. Laws of the Kingdom

Of course praying is not of the slightest use while any of God's laws relating to the subject prayed for are being violated. What you had better ask for Florence is that she may have some convictions on the question of health. Tell her she might just as well expect to have prayer keep her hand from being burned if she were to hold it in the fire as to be kept well while violating the laws that regulate her health.

The trouble is ignorance. We are just like babies with fire. They do not know that it is an inevitable law of fire to burn, and they are very surprised and hurt when they put their fingers in the pretty flame. You are right about doing being a kind of praying. It certainly is the highest type of communion and the kind the Lord values the most. One of His very little noticed words is, "Not every one that saith unto me, Lord, Lord, shall enter into the kingdom of Heaven; but he that doeth the will of my Father which is in Heaven."

There is common sense in this. For in the nature of things I cannot enter into the kingdom of Heaven in regard to any matter, health or anything else, unless I obey the laws of that kingdom. And in praying my idea is that by means of it we are brought into harmony with those laws as we get to understand them. Praying does open people's "top eyes," slowly perhaps but surely. And I believe if F. prays definitely for health, she will begin to have convictions.

—To Daughter Mary, December 8, 1882

337. Amen to Sorrow

I am afraid the scolding I sent you in my last letter sounded unsympathetic, but I didn't mean it that way. I only wanted to show you that you must obey the Lord's command not to let your heart be troubled or afraid. There is absolutely no other way to meet your problems. And I am so sure that this way will bring you a glorious victory that I felt as if I must press you into it with all the influence and all the authority my love could give.

I am sure that you must not always be looking ahead. I am sure you must live just one day at a time, taking no thought of any kind for tomorrow. It is a glorious chance for you to abandon yourself unreservedly to the love and will of your Lord. And I believe if you will do this, it will be the doorway for you into a far deeper relationship with the Lord than you have ever known yet. Nothing brings the soul into such oneness with Him as a surrender of something that is difficult. What Faber says is profoundly true, that

> God's will is sweetest to us, when
> It triumphs at our cost.

It does not seem at first as if it could be sweet, but when we have really submitted, it always becomes sweet. Someone wrote to me the other day, "I conquered my sorrow by submitting to it," and I could say, "amen" to this. I have conquered many a sorrow in the same way. And I want you to do it with this sorrow you are fearing. Just say, "Your will be done" to the very worst form of it, and then leave all the future with Him.

—To Priscilla, December 18, 1882

338. On God's Altar

There is no other way for you but to surrender utterly and to cast all your care on the Lord, and leave it there. You must not think of it or brood over it, but must dismiss it from your mind altogether, except whatever degree is necessary for proper self-care. By this time the Doctor has probably given his decision, and you know your fate. I cannot help hoping that your fears have all been dissipated and that you have found out there is nothing seriously wrong.

But if not, and your worst fears are confirmed, then you must bow your neck to the yoke and must accept your life as the very best thing that could have come to you. If it is a tumor, then a tumor is God's best gift to you. I don't write like this because I can't sympathize with all your dread and shrinking, but because I can and do sympathize intensely, and because I know so well what a hard trial it will be. I say it all because I know there is no other way for you to find peace and victory.

You can only conquer your trial by submitting to it. But if you will submit, it will become your joy and crown of rejoicing. Oh darling, please submit! Lay yourself as a living sacrifice upon God's altar. Say "Yes" to Him about it all. "Yes, Lord, Yes. Your will, not mine. Your good and perfect will! I am content to suffer; I am content to be laid aside, I am content to be an invalid all my life, if it is your sweet will."

I do not believe that you can exercise any kind of faith for healing until first there is this utter unconditional surrender. How my heart aches for you! And yet I can only say, "Your will be done." He knows best. He will give my child what is best for her I am sure, although it may not look best to either her or myself. I trust Him.

—To Priscilla, December 31, 1882

339. A Life Not a Performance

You ask about prayer. I believe as we come into a more real relationship with the Lord our association with Him becomes a life, and ceases to be a performance; and while prayer is really more continuous than ever, it certainly seems to have less stir and fuss about it, and to require far less formality. It seems to me it is the difference between paying visits to a friend and being at home with that friend. We used to visit God, and of course then it was important to pay long and frequent visits. But now we are so at home that to doubt Him seems more foolish and nonsensical than it ever did before.

I quite agree with Irene Beard that you and I do have feelings after all of a certain sort. For instance we are glad that God is our God and Saviour, and feel at rest in His care, and we are lighthearted about the matters we have committed to Him. Now all this is feeling, although it is not just the kind we have been used to thinking was the right kind. But we never could make people understand it, and I think the safest way still is to ignore our feelings in the matter of religion, and speak only of our faith.

Or rather, speak of the facts, for it is neither feelings nor faith that are the important things after all, but only the facts which the feelings or the faith are to lay hold of. I think I must write an article on this subject of facts. I believe if in all matters we would just come down to the simple facts, the bottom facts we might call them, we would be saved a vast amount of trouble. Does God love us or not? Is He caring for us? Will He neglect us? Is His will good? Do we want it or not? These questions honestly answered will cut through the knot of most of our difficulties I am sure.

—To Priscilla, 1882

340. Perfectly "Regardless"

There is but one course open to you, whatever your condition may be, and that is the course of entire surrender and perfect and utter trust. I have said enough about this at various times to make it perfectly familiar to you, and here I can only add to it all my warm entreaties that you will not hesitate a moment, but will keep this attitude constantly, come what may. If you become an invalid, then invalidism is the best and highest thing in all the universe for you, and you may well be "satisfied" with it; for we are always satisfied with the best.

I would certainly ask for healing if I were you. Ask the Lord to teach you about it. Ask Him to give you faith. But I do not think I would try to work myself up to faith about it. That sort of faith fails so often. But as I said before, no sort of faith will heal you, I think, unless there is a full surrender first to have a tumor and be an invalid if that is God's will for you. Less experienced Christians might be healed without consecration, but I do not believe you could, after knowing so much of the divine life.

You will be interested to know how well Saidee's mother is getting along. She seems to be perfectly "regardless" ever since she made her surrender, and speaks and prays in the Germantown meeting, or anywhere else that she may happen to be, apparently without a thought of fear. It is a marvelous change for her. Oh, how much time would be saved if only everyone would do the same! I have two ladies on hand now who are just entering into a consecrated life, and I just ache to make them see the blessings of being "regardless." I think a good tract might be written on that, don't you?

—To Priscilla, January 10, 1883

341. Secure of Finding God in All

I must quote you Madame Guyon's lines which I have written in my Bible opposite the close of Ecclesiastes and the opening of Canticles. I have them just there because I think they contain the lesson of those two books. Ecclesiastes gives us the utter insufficiency of anything earthly, even the best, to satisfy the heart; and Canticles gives us the all-sufficiency of the Beloved One to satisfy in spite of all circumstances.

> All scenes alike engaging prove
> To souls impressed with sacred love;
> Where'er they dwell, they dwell in Thee,
> In Heaven, in earth, or on the sea.
> To me remains nor place nor time,
> My country is in every clime;
> I can be calm and free from care
> On any shore, since God is there.
> While place we seek, or place we shun
> The soul finds happiness in none;
> But with my God to guide the way
> 'Tis equal joy to go or stay.
> Could I be cast where thou wert not,
> That were indeed a dreadful lot;
> But regions none remote I call,
> Secure of finding God in all!

I do not like to think of you as needing to have "things" pleasant around you when you have God within you. Surely He is enough to content any soul. If He is not enough here, how will it be in the future life when we have only Him Himself? Or at least where His presence is the highest joy? If I were you I would ask for and trust for a contented spirit before anything else. Heb. 13:5 tells us why we should be content. "Let your conversation be without covetousness; and be content with such things as ye have for He hath said, I will never leave thee, nor forsake thee."

That "for" explains the whole matter. And I think perhaps this is the lesson the Lord has meant to teach you by the unsatisfactoriness of your circumstances during these past years. I want you to be able to say, even in the midst of the most untoward things, that you are content with the things you have.

—To a Friend, January 17, 1883, Providence, R.I.

342. The Reasonings of Unbelievers

I suppose I don't need to be worried about you because you are only going through a "stage," and yet I am afraid that you are on a road that will lead you into the sad, and dreary, and unhappy, and unscientific, haven of agnosticism. Is it necessary for you to read Herbert Spencer? It is so hard on this earthly plane to believe in the existence of a heavenly or spiritual world, even under the most favorable influences, that it doesn't seem wise to increase the difficulty by feeding one's mind on the reasonings of materialists or unbelievers. It is as if I should insist on reading books which argued against the science of astronomy, and should fill my mind with everything that would make it hard for me to believe the statements of astronomers. The belief in a personal God is a necessity to all true spiritual life. I do not say a necessity always for right living; but always a necessity for any conscious interior spiritual life.

I have watched the growth and development of agnosticism in your father, and I can assure you, darling, that it would almost break my heart to have my children travel on the same road. And to me it seems one of the most unscientific things possible to doubt the existence of a personal God. As you suggest, the intelligence and will displayed in the universe prove a Being behind them; and the Bible reveals just the Being we would expect Him to be. Therefore, common sense says, "Accept the God who is revealed in Christ as your God and trust yourself to His care."

I am content to say that I do not know Him fully, that in fact I only can know Him in part "through a glass darkly," but I can and do know that He is, and that He is good. And with this I am content. But if I argue from the fact of my ignorance that He does not exist I should be committing a folly

236

equivalent to that of a child refusing to believe in the existence of a man of genius because it could not comprehend his genius.

—To Daughter Mary, January 27, 1883 4653 Germantown Avenue, Philadelphia, Pa.

343. Two Beliefs

You must consider the outcomes of the two beliefs, if you want to understand the subject intelligently. Looking the world over you will find that those who believe in a personal God are the good, and the noble, and the peaceful, and the triumphant souls, while those who do not are the defeated and miserable ones. Take my own case. All in me that is good or noble comes directly from my belief in a personal God. And my greatest strength has come from my persistent holding on to this belief, through days and months of fierce temptations to the contrary. Your father gave in to the doubt, and has lost at last all sense of any perception of God. I held on, and have come at last to a consciousness and knowledge that is simply unassailable. The temptation is in the air, and I do hope you can escape it; but a steadfast holding on to the God in whom you have, in the past trusted, will at last bring you out into a grand place of assurance.

Do, my precious daughter, hold on here. It is a far more dangerous place than you think. I have sent to England for something that will help you. It is Macdonald's *Diary of an Old Soul.* Someone sent Mrs. Dickinson one, and we are fairly devouring it. He knows God, and to have a knowledge such as his is worth any possible conflict to attain.

As to what you had to say about the creation of mothers being the best display of God's character as a mother, of course it is; that to me is the revelation. But it is the revelation of what existed before it was revealed, and therefore of something in God that we can rest on as an attribute of His own. And this is true of all His revelations. What we want is to know His character, and we learn it by the things He does, just as we judge an artist or a poet by his works. But I cannot write more now. I will arrange to go to see you just as soon as I can, precious. I want to save you from all the snares I can, and I have had such an experience of successful battling with doubt that I think I can help you.

—To Daughter Mary, January 27, 1883, 4653 Germantown Avenue, Philadelphia, Pa.

344. I Know Its Fascinations

No, darling daughter, I am not anxious about you really, but I know there is great danger of agnosticism to any thinking nature that starts out on the Spencerian tract or any similar one. And faith alone can save you, my precious child, from a wretched shipwreck of your spiritual nature. I understand all that line of doubt, because I have been near it many a time, and I know its fascinations.

I have had a real burst of enthusiasm for Christ today. I was thinking of the dreadful bondage women are in all the world over, and of how all the emancipation that has ever come to us has come through Christ, and I felt all the enthusiasm for Him a slave would feel for an emancipator, and said to myself, "Let all men deny you, yet I will not." Ah, daughter, we women don't have such a friend as He is in all the universe, and we must be loyal to Him, if no one else is.

Father talks as if you have settled down to agnosticism. He says you have given up the idea of a personal God. I beg you not to talk to him about such things. His unbelief is most contagious. I often have to pray all the time he is talking to me; but afterwards my faith is always rewarded by some grander revelation. That was the way it was this morning. He had been pouring floods of agnosticism upon me, and I had been praying all through it when, after it all, such a vision of Christ came to me as the liberator of women, that my whole heart went out to Him with a perfect burst of love and loyalty. Do not say anything to father about this, but write me a letter telling of your faith, and I will show it to him.

How nice Logan's letters are. He is developing beautifully. But do, precious daughter, try to keep him believing. It would be dreadful to have him an agnostic. I am afraid it would ruin his life.

—To Daughter, February 7, 1883, My 51st birthday!

345. Yielding to His Making

This is your nineteenth birthday, and I am thanking my Heavenly Father for giving me such a lovely gift as a daughter like you. All your life long you have been nothing but a delight to me. And I hardly know anything now in which I would want you to be different. I love you, my precious, with an inexpressable mother-love, and you may always know this wherever or whatever happens. Moreover I am on your side against the whole world, and even against myself, if this last could be possible; which however I do not think is, for your side is my side always I guess!

I will see you so soon that I will not go into any of your "love affairs" now. I only want to send you a little love letter, and a thousand heart kisses, and to tell you that I am content with you. Not that I do not expect you to grow better and better in every way. But I mean for now that I am content with your present stage at your present age. God is making you, and His making is often slow, but it is always sure and I am content to leave it with Him, for I do not think you will hinder Him.

Only, precious, hold your faith in Him steadfast. Do not let any doubts of His existence find the least lodging in your mind. Of course they will come, the very air seems full of them, everything we read seems to suggest them. But the steadfast faith that will hold through everything is I think like the creating will of God. And I know that often it is like the pangs of creation to have the "faith of God," and "call those things which be not as though they were." Is not that a grand definition of faith? It is in Romans 4:17. And it gives the clue I think to our part in the matter of our saving. Read Eph. 1 and see what God's purposes are for all of us, and you will understand my content about you when I see that He is at work making my precious child, and that she is yielding herself to His making.

—To Daughter, February 14, 1883, 4653 Germantown Avenue, Philadadelphia, Pa.

346. Speaking Against God

Don't you feel glad that you gave it all up to the Lord before hearing those assuring words from the Doctor? I hope it will teach you a lesson you will never forget, and that you will never again permit yourself to be anxious and worried over any possible evils. I would feel I had committed a positive sin if I would do it; and I want you to feel the same.

I am sure anxiety is a far greater sin than we usually think. I had an "opening" the other day on the amount of unbelief contained in some of the questions which the soul asks. Look for instance at Ex. 17:7: "Is the Lord among us or not?" This is called in the text "tempting" the Lord. Look also at Psalm 78:19. "Yea, they spake against God; they said, 'Can God furnish a table in this wilderness?'" Their question here was called "speaking against God," and if we think about it we shall see it really was that; for it surely would be speaking against a hostess if her guests should question whether she was able to provide them with enough to eat, when she had invited them to visit her.

I feel sure that questioning God or His ways is only a subtle form of speaking against Him. Nothing but absolute submission and confidence can be tolerated on the part of souls who are brought into union with Christ.

—To Priscilla, February 16, 1883

347. Seeing God Through Me

Your loving praise is very sweet to me, even though I may think you look through eyes made kinder by love than they by rights ought to be. If only you can learn some little sense of what God is from your thoughts of me I shall be more than content. I think I have learned more about the character of God from remembering what my own father and mother were to me than in almost any other way. And I do long to be to my children a little faint picture of what God is. I simply mean what He is in His relations to us, for of course I could not picture Him in any other way.

> O great heart of God! whose loving
> Cannot hindered be, nor crossed;
> Will not weary, will not even
> In our death itself be lost!
> Love divine! of such great loving
> Only mothers know the cost,
> Cost of love, that, past all loving,
> Gave itself to save the lost

I think I understand this.

—To Daughter Mary, March 25, 1883

348. No "Supposes"; Smile into His Face

God's will is good and pleasant; and should worst come to worst I am sure you will find it so, and you will realize consolations you have never dreamed of. You must struggle against the temptation to look forward and worry with all your might, for there is no consolation for future troubles promised. And yet, at times, I have found a wonderful consolation even for the future in saying to myself, "Well, it cannot be as I fear unless it is the will of God.

And if it is His will then I shall be glad to have it." And this has seemed to hide me in a fortress of peace in reference to this dreaded future.

I wish you would form the habit of just saying, "Your will be done," whenever the thought of your tumor occurs to you. Say it, even if it does not seem to convey much meaning to your mind. The meaning will gradually come as the habit is fixed. And dismiss all "supposes" about it at once whenever they come trooping in. There are no "supposes" in the future anyhow, there is nothing but the will of God before us.

I believe the child of God ought never to say, "Why?" or "Wherefore?." It is "speaking against" God. Perhaps you may be tempted sometimes to ask these or similar questions, darling, especially if your health might not be as good in the future as in the past. It would seem to us with our human vision that just now when you have come to the point of entire surrender as to your work, it would be the time for your health to improve instead of to fail, and very naturally you would be tempted to ask, "Why?." But you must not yield to this. You must just meet it with, "Yes, Lord, your will be done."

I have had such a blessed "opening" on God is love. We all know something at least of what love is, and therefore we know something of what God is, for He is love. And every time we feel any love in our own hearts, or see it or hear of it in others, we may say to ourselves, "That is what God is." Don't you see how soon we would get to know God in this way? It has opened up wonderful vistas of blessing to me, for I am sure I know something of love, and therefore I know a little of how altogether lovely God is. And I wonder more and more how any one who had had the least glimpse of His love and His loveliness can have a care or a fear. Do think of this always, that whatever comes to you must be the expression of tenderest love. It could not be otherwise for God is love.

Smile into His face then, dear child, and say, "Yes Lord, your sweet will be done." I think it would please Him.

—To Priscilla, Newport, R.I., July 1, 1883

349. What We Endure More than What We Do

You ask whether there is any danger of your loving your work for Him better than His will for you. I think there is, and I think you must leave off the "for Him" and just say loving the work for the work's sake. For there is where the danger comes in. If you loved the work simply because it was for Him, you would be just as glad not to do it for Him as to do it. To suffer for one we love is often a far more beautiful and meaningful thing than to work for that one. Jukes says the strength of our love is shown far more by what we endure than by what we do. And I believe it is true.

There is no harm in loving the work for the work's sake, for that is God's order, but the harm comes in when we let our love for the work interfere with our love for His will. And this is your danger. If the "for Him" was the prominent thing it would seem to you just as acceptable to suffer as to work. Read carefully my November leaflet on fruitbearing. There has been a great mistake made in this matter of fruit.

One remedy for your "low" times would be to ward off their approach, when you feel them coming, by resolutely turning your attention to something else. I do not think it is good for you to pray and agonize over it, but just simply in the fewest words possible commit it to the Lord and say, "Your will be done," and then go and do something that will make you forget it. Read, or write, or talk to someone, or go out for a walk and pay a visit, anything rather than let yourself think of the subject, even piously. Dismiss it from your mind totally.

I think the thing to say about Robert when anyone asks about him is just this, that he never recovered from the nervous shock of that time in England, and that he is suffering an eclipse of faith from actual nervous collapse. That he cannot go to a meeting without nausea, and that the least return to his old lines of thought makes him really ill. This is all the simple truth. And I believe the secret of all his backsliding lies in his physical condition purely [he was a manic depressive]. I am sure that as soon as he gets rid of his body it will all be right.

—To Priscilla, November 22, 1883, 4 A.M., Thursday, Railroad Depot at Hartford, Conn.

350. Laws of Health

It's no wonder that doctors are provoked at the way Christians ignore the very first laws of health, and because of it bring themselves such misery and make so much trouble for others. I believe myself that the laws of health are as imperative as the moral law and bring as sure a retribution, not so lasting in their consequences, but as sure. And I am so glad you can tell me honestly that you are really taking care of your health.

Our bodies are the Lord's tools with which He does His work, and we have no more right to misuse or neglect them than a workman would have to misuse or neglect the tools belonging to the master carpenter. Always remember this when you are tempted to neglect your health in any way.

I have been thinking that perhaps those waves of depression that seem ✓
to sweep over you, are purely from physical causes, and the result of the
tumor, causing depression and gloom. Now it may be that this is your
whole trouble and that it is not want of faith, but a part of the disease. If
this is the case, then you must not blame yourself, but must simply try to
rest in the Lord through the dark times, and be content to be depressed
and gloomy if that is His will. Only see to it that your will does not give in
to any rebellion or to any worrying. Fenelon says the whole of piety resides
in the will, and I believe he is very near the truth. And your will is right, that
I am sure of, so don't be troubled at your upset emotions.

—To Priscilla, 1883

While at Smith College, Mary Smith fell in love with a young English
Catholic lecturer who was visiting the area—Frank Costelloe. The growing
seriousness of the relationship stirred Hannah's "tiger" motherhood instinct
enough to confront Costelloe on his commitment to equality between the
sexes and the authority only of love.

351. "I" and "Not I" Love

I want to take the opportunity to say a few words to you on the subject of
marriage. As you have doubtless discovered, after my husband, my daugh-
ters mean far more to me than anyone else on earth. I believe motherhood
is more of a passion with me than with most women. And I often think I
must feel just as a lioness feels when her cubs are in danger. Therefore you
will understand I am sure why I write as I am now going to do.

I want to ask you definitely what kind of love you will have for my
daughter if you win her to yourself? I have discovered that husbands have
two sorts of love which I would describe as the "I" love and the "not I"
love, to use an expression that I sometimes use in reference to religion. The
"I" love is a selfish love. It makes everything center around itself, and mea-
sures everything in reference to self. Such a husband says of his wife, "She
must conform to my wishes; she must live my life; she must merge her individuality into mine." Such husbands are very demanding.

In a real oneness both have an equal voice and equal rights; there cannot be a question of authority between them, in the very nature of things.
The decisions must be joint decisions, the authority must be equal. But
you may say, must there be no final appeal? I answer "No" and "Yes." "No"
emphatically as a matter of sexual deference, a thousand times "No." As a

matter of greater wisdom or of greater comprehension of the question at issue, "Yes." And this superiority of judgment is quite as likely to be on the side of the woman as of the man. Each should have authority in their own sphere. If the question is one the man understands best, he must decide it; if the woman, she must. To make authority a matter of sex belongs to the barbaric ages when every question was decided by brute force. Man was the stronger physically, therefore he was the master. Now it is not brute force that rules, but mind and spirit, and these have nothing to do with sexual differentiation.

—To Frank Costelloe, 1883

352. Submission Only in Love

Men talk about two becoming one in marriage. Where this assumption of authority on the part of the man exists, that one means the man only. For there cannot be oneness in reality between a master and a slave, however indulgent the master be.

I never could put into words how deeply I feel on this subject; nor how a woman's whole soul revolts from this position of slavery, when once her eyes are opened to see it. It degrades and humiliates her in her own eyes with an anguish that no words can express. And I am convinced that most of the misery in married life arises from the fact that, unconsciously perhaps, but inevitably, the woman is chafing against the degrading bondage of the tyranny of sexual inequality. In short, I believe in a perfect equality between husband and wife as between man and man, with a "not I" religion on either side. For of course it is not only the husband who should have this unselfish love, but the wife as well.

I know nothing more absolutely unjust in itself nor more productive of misery to the woman than the assumption of the place of authority on the part of men. It reduces women at once in principle to the position of slaves, dependent altogether for their happiness upon the whim of their masters. I consider that any free born woman who consents to marry a man holding this view of his own right of authority over her, enters into pure and simple slavery, and is sure to be sooner or later a miserable woman. It is no matter how kind her master may be, he is still in principle her master and she is in principle a slave, let her chains be as gilded as they may; and this is simply intolerable to a free spirit.

The question as to whether he ever asserts his authority or not is entirely minor to the intolerable fact that that is the position he holds towards his wife, and that such are the relations between them. Any amount of anarchy and confusion would be better than for one soul to be in chains to another soul like this. Whatever submission one may render to the other, must be voluntary and from love, otherwise it is the most degrading bondage. Woman is man's equal, the other half of the human being; and to usurp authority over her is so to dislocate the divine order and to cause loss of harmony in all the relations between the sexes.

—To Frank Costelloe, 1883

353. Anticipation and Achievement

It is the first day of the new year. And I feel a wonderful sense of exhilaration that life is passing so fast, and that soon the summons must come that will set my spirit free from its prison house of flesh. I do not believe anyone ever enjoyed growing old like I do. I am nearly fifty-two and it is a perfect delight to me. Not that I am the least unhappy here, but the joy of the life to come seems to me so superaboundingly glorious that often it seems to me I can hardly wait. To see Him whom my soul loves face to face; who can imagine what that will be!

But I did not begin my letter to go off into a burst of anticipation like this. I only wanted to tell you that your letter and the little forget-me-not book have both reached me, and were both very welcome. The book is full of blessed thoughts, or rather truths. I am trying to cure myself of calling God's truths, "thoughts," for I find our words have a very great effect in influencing our views, and to say thoughts makes it sound as if they were not really facts, but only the notions of some of us.

Someone says we are always straining out after a life that is beyond our present powers, and adds that this a sign of our divine origin and destiny. Don't you think this may be the reason we are always so dissatisfied with every attainment of achievement? And may it not account for your aspirations for your work being so far beyond your realizations? To yourself your work looks small and poor, but to the Master, who sees your heart, it must look far different. Like the widow's mite, if we give all that we have, the Master will say "she hath given more than them all."

—To a Friend, 4653 Germantown Ave., Philadelphia, Pa., January 1, 1884

354. Created for His Pleasure

In our family reading today we came across this, "But He that built all things is God," and it has given me a lovely sort of insight into God's character on a side where we do not often look. I mean the side of loving beautiful things and delighting in making them. For there are the most exquisitely beautiful things in this National Park far more exquisite than man could ever have made; and the knowledge that God has "built" them shows how He loves beauty. Then that verse came to me that says, "For thy pleasure they were and are created," and I thought, "Yes, these things were created for His pleasure, and I also was created for His pleasure." These things are really beautiful, and it is easy to see how he can take pleasure in them. But when we look at ourselves it seems impossible. Therefore I am sure He means to make us into something He can enjoy; and if He is pleased we shall be sure to be. So that I am at rest about myself and about all the world too.

And, darling, your present trials are no doubt a part of the means by which this creative process is being accomplished in you. And I can see how it is accomplishing it too, in the chastening of your spirit and the subduing of your will. So there is something to be thankful for even through it all.

—To Priscilla, July 13, 1884, Mammoth Hot Springs

355. Confident Faith

And now about Lillian. You can do a great deal for her just by being such a rock of goodness yourself that, in her mind, she can always hold to you like an anchor. Don't pay much attention to her varying emotions or excitements. But hold up a steady standard of right, and bring L. to it. And then, darling, do not, whatever else you do, let yourself be worried or anxious. This is a far greater hindrance to helping than anyone yet appreciates. After all, real help is only in the spiritual region, and therefore the spiritual part is the part to keep perfectly right. People often think their anxiety and unhappiness will not hurt people if they refrain from expressing it. But I have found by experience, and I am convinced from philosophy, that the subtle unseen spiritual forces that emanate from our spirits are far more important than the outward tangible influence that we exert consciously.

Therefore you must trust for Lillian. You must hold her to God by the power of your own confident faith; not by your efforts, remember, but by your trust. And perhaps, darling daughter, this may be one of God's ways of bringing you blessings. We can bring cheer and help into the midst of other's sorrow by our cheerful confidence that it will ultimately result in blessing.

Meanwhile, Lillian is not very unhappy. This is a "stage" through which she must pass, I suppose; but she will come out of it when she has developed a little more, and you can do nothing but wait. Be good yourself. That is the principal thing, and keep your nature strong and healthy. Especially avoid being worried or unhappy about L. Do not let yourself lie awake at night to worry about her. Commit her to God, and trust.

I have tried both ways, darling, and I have invariably found that when I trusted about the person who was on my heart I helped them, and when I worried and was unhappy I dragged both them and myself down. All whom I have helped have told me afterwards that it was not half so much what I said or did that helped them, as what I was, my calmness and cheerfulness and hopefulness. It is not saying cheerful and hopeful things that does it but being hopeful and cheerful. And you may help Lillian in this way, for God loves her and has her in His care.

> Love Divine, of such great loving
> Only mothers know the cost,
> Cost of love that, past all loving,
> Gave itself to save the lost.

—To Daughter, November 3, 1884

356. Out of Unbelief and an Avalanche of Doubt

In all your turnings and overturnings, darling, you must never forget the fact of me. With an utterly unbelieving nature, and with avalanches of doubt hurled on me from every side, I have come out into a place of knowledge which is absolutely intuitional to me now. I could as easily think of myself apart from myself as to think of myself apart from God. I believe you will get there too sometime, but I do not want to see you floundering too long.

I must say one word in reply to your suggestion that all motive for work would be gone if we believed everything was working out all right. It is this, that we are in a world which can be made better, and which we individually can help to make better, because we are in a developing world. But when things are developing we do not worry over the different stages, we simply do all we can to help in each stage and then wait in patient confidence for the future developments. If we are making something for instance, its unfinished conditions during the making process don't discourage or distress us if we are only sure what it will be in the end. If we thought they were finalities, they would distress us, but not when we know they are only stages. And the fact that there are stages is really an encouragement to go on working, since the end will surely pay for it all. Then too, for our own sakes, for our own development, our share of the work must be done all the time.

—To Daughter, Baltimore, Maryland, Saturday, November 7, 1884

357. A Vortex of Activity

I am in an Indian Rights Convention. That is the Convention of our National Women's Indian Association. I am the National Treasurer, and the time I have had to get my accounts straight is beyond expression! Someone says figures are possessed of original sin, and it really seems like it. I never imagined I could get into such a bother over a few figures.

We are doing a grand work for our poor Indians, in creating a public sentiment in their favor. For, to this point, our nation has treated them in the most outrageous manner. My visit to the Sioux Indian Reservation this last summer has stirred my soul to its very depths. They are our brothers and sisters, and we must care for them!

It seems as if my life was never so full before. The campaign for Mrs. Hunt in Penna. which I am conducting is very absorbing. I sometimes have a dozen telegrams a day and send as many away, to say nothing of the innumerable letters. We have 67 counties in Pennsylvania and Mrs. Hunt has to speak in each one, and I have to arrange it all; and the difficulties are past belief. Every evening has to be filled up, and the journeys cannot be too long between of course, or she would not get from one place to another in time. And just when everything is arranged nicely, there comes a telegram to say that they cannot have her at a certain place, and then another place has to be chosen. But it is of no use to try to tell of the perplexities of this work. Only I want you to know that I am in a perfect vortex, and that I really cannot get time to write.

—To Priscilla, November 19, 1884

358. Almost Swamped

Frances Willard is here for three or four weeks to write a book. She and Anna Gordon have my room to sleep in because it is so quiet, and they write in the little sewing room. She is charming, as ever, and we enjoy having her very much. But she piles the work on me mountain high! I am almost swamped. She wants me to have what she calls a W.C.T.U. School of the Prophetesses somewhere in the summer, and have all our women who feel called to public work come to me to be taught. And she is actually talking Robert into the notion of building a place for it in some cool mountain spot! He feels rich today because some mining stock he has, has begun to rise. I let them talk! For I have no idea it will come to anything. Although, judging by you, I think I must be a pretty good hand at manufacturing preachers! [laugh squiggle] Only I am afraid the rest will not love me as you do, and therefore I shall not be so successful.

I have hosts of other things on hand too, and never was so busy before in all my life. Literally, I am often unable to get five minutes for anything but my work. The revision of my Bible leaflets requires great care, now that they are to be put into a permanent form, and when I will have time for them I can't see.

—To Priscilla, October 1884

359. Piety in This World

Poor Charles Coffin [a Quaker pastor] was here last night, and, oh Sarah, what trouble he has had and is having. I could tell you all about it if I were with you, but I don't want to put it in writing, except that just as much as he was loved and honored and respected before, his experience is the opposite now. He says no words can tell their sufferings. Then Rendel Harris [Johns Hopkins professor] was here too and he has just sent in his resignation to Johns Hopkins on account of this vivisection fuss; and it is probable that he and Helen will have to take up their march again and find a new home and new work. Then there was Robert, three doctrinaire men, all three quite eminent in the religious world, and all three under a cloud. It did seem rather strange.

I told them the trouble with them was that they had all been righteous overmuch; they had not mixed enough of life as it is in this world into their religion. You and I have had such a spice of "the old Adam" in all our religion that we have never been able to quite turn the corner into the region of super piety. I am sure this has been my salvation many a time. We were made to be human beings here, and when people try to be anything else than the humans God planned for us to be, they generally get into some sort of scrapes.

—To Sarah, March 12, 1885

360. The Strokes of the Chisel

It is dreadful for me to be deprived of my beloved "basin" for so long, especially when I have so much I want to pour into it. I fairly ache for one of our good old fashioned powwows where we have so often settled all our own affairs and everybody else's, with the words at the end of all our talk "Well, I'm sure I don't know." And this is what I say to myself now when I think of you; I literally don't know how to understand your case at all. Why should you have all this to suffer when you already had so much? And why the mind cure has failed with you when it has succeeded with so many others? And why the faith cure has failed too? And why, if you are going to get well, you do not get well faster? I am sure I don't know.

But I suppose all these whys have faded out of your horizon as Willie and the rest of us have. It must be your weakness that causes this indifference to everything. I know sometimes when I am very tired I lose all my interest in everything for a little while. But only for a very little while to be sure; still it helps me to understand.

But oh, Sarah, don't you get tired to death of lying in bed and trying to breathe? Or are you too weak even to know that you are tired? It is dreadful to me to think about all you must be suffering; and sometimes I feel as if I must do something to stop it! But I can only fall back on my one unfailing comfort about all who suffer, that it works out for them "a far more eternal and exceeding weight of glory." I am sure it does this whether the people who suffer are conscious of the process or not.

It is like the strokes of the chisel that hew out the statue; each stroke tells for something I am sure. So you, with so many strokes, must be undergoing a marvelously beautifying process, that will develop you someday into a "vessel unto honor" far beyond what you can guess. I have always believed that in the next stage of our existence you would outrank both Mary or me many times; and I am surer than ever of this now.

—To Sister, March 15, 1885

When it was evident that Hannah's efforts to break up the relationship between Mary and Frank Costelloe were failing, Robert and Hannah decided to take Mary to England for a year to be near her friend under their supervision. They had hopes that his Catholicism would still interrupt her apparent free-fall into marriage. It didn't.

After Mary's first child, daughter Ray, was born, the Smiths moved to England to be near her. They never resided in the United States again. Robert whiled away his time in minor projects and meditating in a large treehouse he had built for himself at their estate south of London named Friday's Hill. Hannah kept busy in numerous social causes, but mainly in the temperance and women's suffrage movements. She was instrumental in bringing the American and British movements together into an international movement. She also continued her writing and preached in Quaker and other churches in England.

361. Detachment from Our Idols

It took me all day yesterday to get through the pile of letters that had accumulated during my two days' absence. And today I have had to revise the leaflet on "Chariots" for a tract, for everybody is calling for it. I wonder what I will think in Heaven of all this writing that keeps me so busy here. Do you suppose I will "hold it in derision," as the Bible says God does some things.

Well, beloved, since you can keep everything private, I will send you the list of questions we have sent Mr. Costelloe, that you may see how matters are going there. Mary is in love with him, and there is no denying it. But there is still a hope that she may see his Catholicism to be an insuperable barrier. But this hope is very faint, and in my soul the detachment has come. She has been too much of an idol to me and I suppose a detachment was necessary.

I could be in the depths, but I will not, for God is my joy and my expectation is in Him alone. I suppose it is necessary that this life should lose all its charms in one way or another, and this is a most effectual way for me. Return the questions as soon as read please, as I want to have them at hand when his replies come. No, England will not be a bed of roses, but of thorns. But it has got to be, for if we did not go over there he would come here and that would be worse. Oh Sarah, children are "dear" in more senses than one.

—To Sister, March 20, 1885

362. Love's Pain of Loss

In short, if he were not Catholic and if he lived in America, we would feel that our daughter had secured a prize. She does not, however, mind either of these drawbacks and rejoices, in fact, in the thought of living in the midst of all the grand political and benevolent movements which interest her lover, and which are to be found in London as nowhere else. So we have settled down to it as to the inevitable, and are content to sacrifice our own hopes of having our child always near us, to her decision for her life, since all her happiness seems bound up in it. In fact we do not feel that we dare to interfere any further. And I have so fully committed it all to the Lord from the very beginning, that I must believe it is of His ordering or at least of His permission, for her best welfare, whether it result in joy or sorrow.

Whether the reason for all this lay in the fact of our too great love for this precious and lovely daughter, or whether she herself may have been in greater danger than we knew from the agnostic spirit of the age, I do not know. I can only say from my heart of hearts that the Lord knows what is best for her and for us, and will order her life aright, and that His will is my choice for my darling child. I suppose we shall see her married before we return home, and perhaps then bring her and her husband home with us to visit her home friends. But do not speak of this until I write you that it is settled.

What it will mean for me to have this precious daughter living in England, I dare not contemplate! But I must leave this until it comes, when I am sure He will give me the strength I need. But I can understand how somber all your life is without the sunshine of your Anna. I often wonder why in the Divine plan it was not made easier for us to be separated from or to lose those we love. And I think that it is arranged as it is just so that we may have the discipline of the suffering.

Can we escape the fact that suffering and sorrow are a part of God's plan? In the faith cure people seem to think that they have discovered a newer gospel, but I cannot see it. I am asking for light, and when I see it clearly, whatever it may be, I shall be sure to let you know. As far as I can understand the mind cure [Christian Science], it is only the science by which the faith cure works, at least as Mary Thomas teaches it. She says it is simply doing on the plane of physical health what we did on the plane of sin when we reckoned ourselves dead to it and alive only to God. If the atonement covers sickness as well as sin this would all be true; but does it? Do let me have any thoughts that come to you about it.

—To Anna, Steamer "Eider," July 1, 1885

363. Canon Farrar

Today is Sunday, and we went to hear Canon Farrar who preached in St. Margaret's Chapel right by Westminster Abby. It was a wonderful sermon on the revision of the Bible, and dealt forcibly with all timid holding onto old errors for fear of upsetting the cause of religion by an acceptance of the proved truth. He said, "What do you want, that which the prophets really said, or that which you have always been used to thinking they said?" Then he fairly thundered against those who bolstered themselves up in wrong things by taking texts and ignoring principles.

It was a very broad sermon, but to my mind a very orthodox one, and calculated to reach the witness in all thoughtful minds. Then he showed the folly and blindness of the rejection of the Bible in the face of all it has accomplished for the nations that have received it, and in face of its marvelous adaptation to humanity under all its varied conditions. I know you would all have enjoyed it.

—To Family and Friends, July 4, 1885, Henrietta St., Vere St., London

364. The Master's Will Before the Master's Work

I have been longing to write to you to tell you where I think you are wrong about your work. You evidently love the work more than you love God's will, and in this case it is plain that your first thought in it is not service to God but a gratification of your own activities.

Suppose a soldier who had been ordered to guard a post would be unhappy because he liked the active fighting better, would it not be plain either that he did not trust the general's wisdom in placing him there, or else that he preferred his own gratification to the will of the general? If the Lord sets you to guard a lonely post in perfect stillness from all active work, you ought to be just as content as to be in the midst of the active warfare. It is no virtue to love the Master's work better than the Master's will.

But in fact, under such circumstances, I do not think it is the Master's work we love, but our own work. I think you must surrender your love of work to the Lord, and must say "Yes" to a life of absolute inactivity. Work is in danger of becoming your idol. Work is your bondage evidently, and you have to give up your will and choice in it to be "loosed" from it. Perhaps this is the lesson of your trial.

—To Priscilla, July 16, 1886, 40 Grosvenor Road, London

One of the most unique aspects of the Higher-Life Movement in England was the conferences for the promotion of holiness held on the beautiful Broadlands estate of Lord and Lady Mount-Temple in Romsey. Mount-Temple was the illegitimate son of Lord Palmerston, one-time British prime minister. Broadlands is currently the home of the Lord Mountbatten's descendants and the Lord Mountbatten Museum. It was here, in 1874, that some of the earliest English holiness conferences were held and continued annually for about ten years until Lord Mount-Temple's death. The attendants at the meetings ranged all the way from canons of the Church of England to members of the Salvation Army and all the way from Amanda Smith, the black holiness evangelist to George Macdonald, the renowned Victorian writer. The Mount-Temples were ardent supporters of the Smiths, who were frequent guests at their Hampshire estate and their townhouse in London.

365. George Macdonald and Broadlands

George Macdonald, Mr. Corbett, and I were the three who had the most unity. It has been a sort of dream of my life to be somewhere where I could sit at the feet of these two teachers; and I was really thankful to have it brought about so delightfully. I enjoyed it to the full. One evening I arranged with Lord and Lady Mount-Temple that Macdonald should have an hour all to himself, just after afternoon tea, when he could talk to us right out of his heart with no one to interrupt; and I told him just to let himself go and say whatever came into his head. He began by reading the following poem, which he said he "found" once. I knew he meant found in his own brain. He called it "A Talk With St. Peter."

> Oh Peter, wherefore doest thou doubt?
> In truth the scud flew fast about,
> But He was there, whose walking foot
> Could make the wandering hills take root,
> And He had said, 'Come down to me,'
> Else had thy foot not touched the sea!par!
> Christ could not call thee to thy grave!
> Was it the boat that made thee brave?
> Easy for thee, who wast not there,
> To think thou, more than I, could'st dare!
> It hardly fits thee thus to mock,
> Secure as thou wast that railway shock!
> Who said'st this morn, 'Wife, we must go,
> The plague will soon be here, I know!'
> Who, when thy child slept, not to death,
> Said'st 'noting now is worth a breath!'
> True, true, great fisherman! I stand
> Rebuked by waves seen from the land!
> Even the lashing of the spray,

The buzzing fears of any day,
Rouse anxious doubt lest I should find
God neither in the spray or wind!
But now and then, as once to thee,
The Master turns and looks at me!
And now to thee I turn, my Lord!
Help me to fear nor fire nor sword;
Let not the cross itself appall!
Know I not thee, the Lord of all?
Let reeling brain nor fainting heart
Wipe out the sureness that thou art.
Oh, deeper, thou, than doubt can go,
Make my poor life ring out, 'I know!'
And so, when thou shalt please to say,
'Come to my side,' some stormy way,
My feet, attuning to thy will
Shall, heaved and tossed, walk toward thee still;
No leaden heart shall sink me where
Prudence is crowned with cold despair;
But I shall reach and clasp thy hand,
And on the sea forget the land!

I can give you no idea of the inimitable way in which he read this, but it made us feel as if we ourselves were having this very talk with Peter and were hearing his reproofs. Then he went on for an hour of loving homely talk about the love of Christ and faith in Him, that seemed as if it almost might be the old father in Warlock Castle pouring out his heart, as he sat with George Fox on his knee. If you have never read it, be sure to get *Warlock of Glen Warlock*. You will see in that father a perfect picture of what George Macdonald is. Can you imagine how I enjoyed this fulfilling of one of my fondest dreams? The dear old man and I got very close, and I have the warmest invitation to visit them at Bordighera where they live. I hope I may do it some day.

Circular letter, 32 Broadlands, Romsey

Hannah Whitall Smith died in 1911 at her son Logan's home in Iffley, near Oxford University. She entered the next stage of her development as she called it. She had always had an intense longing for God and heaven, but she never shunned her responsibilities in this world—a world that had brought her a major trial for every unusual triumph she had enjoyed. Her book *The Christian's Secret of a Happy Life* was, for many years, the most-read devotional book in the world. She became a noted preacher and lecturer as well as a leader in the temperance, women's suffrage, and other social causes both in America and in England.

The other side of life's coin told a different story. She lost three of her six children in the prime of their childhood or youth. Robert's manic depressive nature always hung like a cloud over all their hopes and dreams. His spiritual apostasy and eventual agnosticism, after his fall from grace in England, did little to keep the children from following the same loss of faith. Encouraged by the liberal thought pervading the universities they attended, they too lost the faith of their mother and their childhood. Mary finally deserted her first husband and her two children to live in Italy with Bernard Berenson, the noted art historian. Hannah had to rear the young children, Ray and Karin. Alys became the first wife of Bertrand Russell and was soon swept into his agnosticism. Logan became a professor of English literature at Oxford University and a moderately famous author. He never married and went mad towards the end of his life, having inherited the same genes as his father.

Through all of this Hannah maintained her faith in God and his love for her and for everyone. She had learned "the secret" long ago and her faith remained unshaken. God was omnipotent; God was love; and that was enough! She had committed herself to him unreservedly and "regardless" many years before. It had included her sorest disappointments as well as her greatest accomplishments. It was all in his hands, and he would do what was best for her. Who dare say that he did not?